Jane Paech grew up on a farm in South Australia,
where her lifelong love of food was born. Living
in New York further ignited her passion for both
food and travel, and when an opportunity to live in
Paris arose, she turned from a career in nursing to
travel writing, unable to resist documenting all the
wonderful sights, smells and tastes she discovered.
Her work has been featured in various publications,
including *Australian Gourmet Traveller* and *Qantas
The Australian Way* inflight magazine.

A Family in Paris won the Australian category for
Food Literature at the prestigious Gourmand World
Cookbook Awards in 2012. Her second book,
Delicious Days in Paris, is also published by Lantern.
Jane blogs at knifeandforkintheroad.com

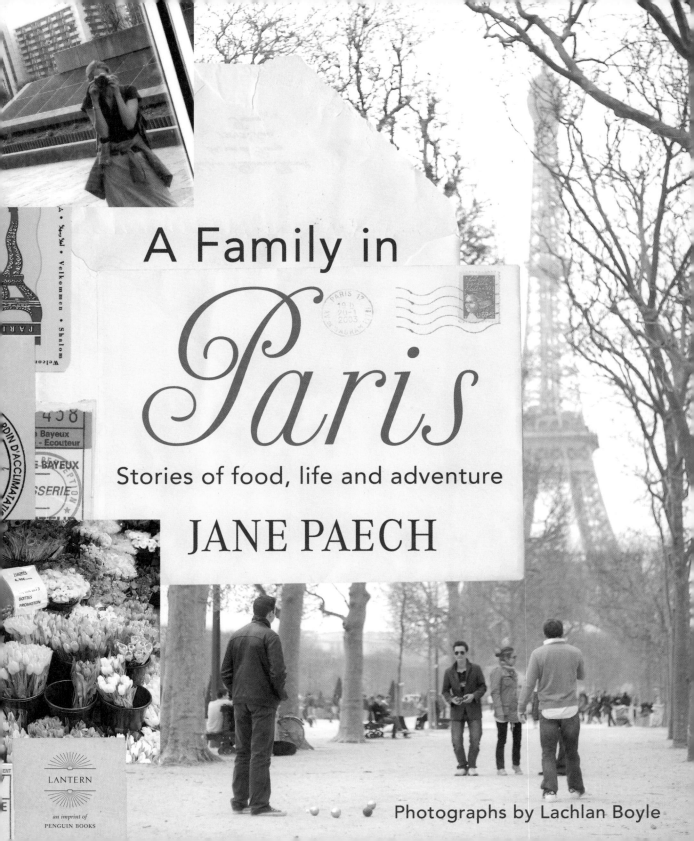

A Family in
Paris

Stories of food, life and adventure

JANE PAECH

LANTERN

an imprint of
PENGUIN BOOKS

Photographs by Lachlan Boyle

For Livi,
Who we will
always hold
in our hearts

Prologue:

Bonjour, Paris

Spring blooms outside Au Nom de la Rose florist

WE SLIP OUT of our hotel and onto the cobbled streets, marvelling at store windows, the beauty of the buildings, the art that seeps from every pore of Paris. Outside a corner florist shop, a riot of the palest pink peonies sit in shiny white buckets, revelling in puddles of sunlight. Spring has arrived and the florist is giving away bags full of rose petals with every bouquet.

I have to pinch myself. We are in Paris, in the springtime, and two glorious years stretch before us.

Only a few weeks ago, my husband, Tim, who is employed by a multinational wine and spirits company, came home from work and asked, 'How would you like to live in Paris for a couple of years?'

'Paris?' Picture-postcard images leapt into my head: fashion, art, style, romance, the capital of food. Fascinated with French culture and mad about food, I wondered if this was too good to be true.

'When do we go?' I replied swiftly, the decision made in a flash.

We have lived overseas before (a three-and-a-half year stint in Manhattan) so we know that, as heart-wrenching as goodbyes always are, two years will fly by. We prime ourselves for a wonderful extended holiday.

Beneath a blue sky, our daughters, Georgie and Annabelle, aged eight and four, skip across Pont Marie to Île St-Louis. No matter how many tourists are wandering about, the islands have a way of whispering, 'Hey, you're in Paris.' On rue des Deux-Ponts, the smell of chocolate wafts from the door of l'Île Flottante, a tiny, old world *chocolatier* and gift shop that also sells beguiling French accessories for the doll's house. The girls are enchanted. They choose a selection of tarts on a miniature tray and a miniscule croissant with a pot of jam, along with a (real) bag of delicate sugared violets to munch as we stroll down rue St-Louis-en-l'Île. The main thoroughfare on this ancient island, it's crammed with crooked shops, art galleries and ambience. Down an alleyway buskers dressed in peasant clothes are singing songs of Paris. Their backdrop? The Seine. We pass hand-painted Venetian masks, a cosy *crêperie*, farmhouse cheeses and rows of Provençal olive oil that glisten like bottled sun.

Mountains of paperwork surround an expatriate move to France and due to complicated visa restrictions, as 'the trailing spouse' I am ineligible for a work permit. With communication playing a vital role in the provision of healthcare, jobs for non-French-speaking registered nurses are somewhat restricted anyhow. But, as always, when one door shuts, another opens. A perfect opportunity has arisen to pursue my dream of becoming a food and travel writer; perhaps I can send articles back to Australia. I visualise spending my days writing furiously,

A river boat gliding down La Seine

eating in bijou bistros, and hanging out in the cafés and bookshops of the Left Bank with my new friend Julie. Struck by the unlikely odds of two families relocating from Adelaide to Paris at the same time with daughters the same ages, our mutual removal company has thoughtfully put us in touch.

We cross the Pont St-Louis and watch the river boats glide past the monuments of Paris. In the distance is the sound of a trombone playing. A crowd has gathered on the bridge to watch the jugglers and street performers, and Tim, in a jovial mood, is roped in to help. Just beyond the bridge looms Notre-Dame, the renowned Gothic cathedral. The girls frolic ahead in the sunshine and laugh at the gargoyles: one with a hat, one with big ears, one with its tongue out. The queue to climb the bell tower is long; now that we live in the City of Light (I pinch myself again), we can leave that for another time. Plenty of carefree days and months stretch before us. Filled with joy, I feel so blessed to be here. I steal softly inside the dark cathedral with its splendid rose windows, and light a candle for our new life.

⚜

When girls pick the petals of a daisy in France, the rhyme goes like this:

Je t'aime . . .
un peu,
beaucoup,
passionnément,
à la folie,
pas du tout.

(I love you . . . a bit, a lot, passionately, madly, not at all.)

Let's face it, there's considerably more room for a good outcome here than gambling with 'he loves me, he loves me not'. You also get to call the shots.

Paris,

je t'aime . . .

Street corner, The Marais

Beauty at every turn: an ornate apartment door

L'Appartement 1

It's time to start hunting for an apartment. The four of us spend a sunny May morning being driven around in a zippy little Peugeot by our stylish relocation consultant. Véronique is a seasoned Parisian driver who, incredibly, seems oblivious to the honking horns and pedestrians around her.

'If you stopped for a pedestrian at every crossing,' she says with a wave of the hand, 'you would never get anywhere in Paris.'

I make a mental note for the next time I step out the door.

As we fly down the boulevards, Véronique gives us a quick rundown on the city and its layout.

'The city of Paris has around 2.2 million inhabitants and is divided into 20 *arrondissements* (boroughs), each containing several *quartiers* (neighbourhoods). They run clockwise in a spiral shape, like the shell of *un escargot*, starting in the centre with the 1st and finishing out in the 20th,' she says with another wave of her bejewelled hand. 'These *arrondissements* all sit inside *le périphérique* (ring-road); greater Paris has close to 12 million inhabitants.'

Many people, she explains, dream about living in the old medieval and artistic heart of Paris close to the river: the Latin Quarter in the 5th, St-Germain-des-Prés in the 6th, and the Marais in the 3rd and 4th with its Jewish community and village atmosphere. However, these areas are also expensive and very busy. Véronique continues her haphazard review and I rifle for my pen and attempt to jot down a few notes as we rush over cobblestoned streets:

- ✤ The 7th is old money.
- ✤ The 16th (not quite as elite as the 7th) and 17th are upmarket residential with large apartments and wide avenues.
- ✤ The 1st is the heart of classical Paris with luxurious real estate; the 2nd is crammed with businesses and banks.
- ✤ Ethnically diverse, the 10th boasts the up-and-coming Canal St-Martin area with apartments along the water; the 9th is home to l'Opéra Garnier and a warren of nineteenth-century covered passageways, but is devoid of green space.
- ✤ The 11th: Bastille, rue Oberkampf and rue Roquette are lively areas full of cafés and bars, popular with young artists, designers and *les bobos* (bourgeois-bohemians). Some parts of the 11th and 12th are quite affordable.

- The 13th is *un quartier chinois*, home to Paris's largest Chinatown and mostly occupied by Chinese, Cambodian and Vietnamese immigrants. There's also a second, more recent Chinatown at Belleville in the 20th, a multicultural *arrondissement* where Chinese mix with Jews, Arabs and Africans.
- The top of the 14th is quite residential and includes part of the legendary Montparnasse area and the 15th is a large, mostly residential *arrondissement* popular with families.
- Excluding Montmartre, the northeast (18th and 19th) has a strong North African influence and exotic food stores and markets, but some areas can be unsafe.

My hand is aching as the little Peugeot screeches to a halt.

We park and climb the stairs to a modern apartment overlooking boulevard Haussmann, a noisy, major thoroughfare in the grandiose 8th. While pockets are residential, the 8th is home to many corporate headquarters and major shopping boulevards, and the French presidential residence, the Elysée Palace. It lacks a neighbourhood feel. The kitchen is tiny. We cross it off the list.

Besides, living in Paris conjures up visions of romantic nineteenth-century buildings with French windows opening onto quaint wrought-iron *balcons*. No modern flat for me.

Many old apartment buildings in Paris are Haussmannian in style. Baron Haussmann, Napoleon III's Interior Minister, was hired to flatten half of Paris and modernise the city. Medieval alleyways were sliced through and wide avenues, long, straight boulevards, open spaces and splendid buildings were created. Built between 1850 and 1920, a classic Haussmannian is six or seven stories high with the second and fifth floors boasting full-length balconies bordered by ornate wrought-iron railings. Both the second and third floors were built for the wealthy, with extra-high ceilings and larger windows. The second floor, however, was considered *l'étage noble* (the finest floor), far enough away from the street noise but without too many stairs to climb. The ground floor was designed for shops, and shopkeepers lived on the first, while the tiny *chambres de bonnes* (maids' rooms) were up in the attic. Despite strong criticism at the time, Haussmann established the foundation of modern Paris.

The demolition forced the poor out of the city to settle on the outskirts, and even now the thought of giving up a postcode starting with 75 and moving to *la banlieue* (suburbs beyond *le périphérique*) makes some born-and-bred Parisians

quake in their Christian Louboutin boots. While *la banlieue* is now home to many middle-class communities, it still has its fair share of struggling working-class suburbs to the north and east of the capital, particularly in the department of Seine-St-Denis. Largely occupied by North African and Arab immigrants and plagued with unemployment, these neighbourhoods represent the most challenging aspects of contemporary Parisian society, defined by rundown *cités* (housing projects) and high levels of poverty, violence and drug abuse.

In stark contrast, the platinum-rimmed inner west has an abundance of affluent, leafy suburbs such as St-Cloud, St-Germain-en-Laye, Versailles and Le Vésinet. Many of these areas were originally beautiful towns and they have maintained their charm along with their *châteaux*, churches and forests.

We stop for coffee and flaky *pains au chocolat* before looking through more apartments in and around the residential 17th, close to the school we have chosen for the girls. As we sip our *café crèmes*, Véronique explains that kitchens in Paris are notoriously small with minimal storage space, making everyday life much easier if you have neighbourhood shops close by and a fresh produce market around the corner. She also warns that when you rent an unfurnished apartment, you really do start with a blank canvas. No curtains, light-fittings or anything that can be unscrewed or disbanded. This often includes whitegoods, cupboards and bench tops. Tenants design and fit their own kitchen and take it with them again when they leave.

'In some apartments,' says Véronique, 'you even have to provide your own toilet.' There's just an empty space with a gaping hole awaiting the throne. How peculiar! There is so much to digest, to learn, to consider.

La Bise

In France, there are certain rules of etiquette. Gallantry and formal politeness are proof of good breeding and *savoir vivre* (good manners). Even in the workplace, the French greet each other with a handshake or a kiss. *La bise* (the kiss on the cheek) is one custom that is commonly practised between family, friends, colleagues and schoolchildren alike. The question is whether to kiss twice or three times or four. The total number of kisses depends on the region, person and circumstance but, generally, in Paris two kisses suffice unless you are very close to the kissee, or you are family. Women should offer their right cheek first.

'For mixed exchanges, the woman should always be allowed to choose either handshaking or kissing . . . The man should always keep his options open and be ready to extend his hand or deliver the requested kisses. In order to prevent lipstick smearing, the woman should not actually kiss the man's cheek, but merely offer her cheek to be kissed lightly – although energetic kissing by women is no cause for social ostracism.'

The Junior Service League of Paris, *At Home in Paris: Your Guide to Living in the French Capital*

Parisian buskers fill the air with jazz

L'Appartement 2

Advice from Tim's work colleagues on renting a flat:

- Light, light, light – the all-important commodity in Paris. Make sure it really is light and it doesn't just feel that way because the walls have been freshly painted, it is empty and the agent has taken you there at just the right time when sunshine is flooding through the French windows, ensuring you fall madly in love with it.
- The higher the floor, the lighter your flat will be.
- Steer clear of the ground and top floors. The former is noisy with foot and road traffic and is generally the domain of *le gardien* (concierge). Easy accessibility means it is targeted by burglars. So is the top floor – from the roof.
- There are generally two or more flats on each floor. The back flats are often quieter and smaller while the front flats are larger, face the street and are more sought after. Aim for a balcony so you have some contact with the outside world and can watch the streetscape below. (It will also help you determine the weather in the morning and choose what to wear.)
- Most lifts in Paris are works of art with decorative wrought-iron cages. While tiny and impractical, they are still a godsend after a trip to the supermarket.
- Make sure the apartment is going to be painted throughout and the parquet floors polished before you move in. (Most apartments are painted stark white and have identical carpet on the stairwell, providing a continual sense of *déjà vu*.)
- Check out *la cave* (cellar). Lined up in the basement, they are used to store wine, bikes, etc. Some are flash with concrete floors and temperature control. Others are damp with dirt floors.
- *La chambre de bonne* is a feature of most old apartment buildings, accessed by a separate service stairwell that passes by all the kitchen doors. Find out if yours is available to you. They are handy for storage and the continual flow of guests, or an *au pair* if you have one.

Annabelle at home

Le Pickpocket

The first rule of *le métro* is to avoid making direct eye contact with anyone you don't know. The second rule is to avoid smiling at anyone you don't know. These rules also apply on the streets of Paris. Locals will think you are intellectually challenged, ridiculing or flirting (which is fine if that's your intention). The third rule is to keep your conversations private. In addition to rowdy exchanges being extremely impolite in a crowded space, loud foreigners put themselves at high risk of being pickpocketed.

Other tell-tale signs of a foreigner are sneakers, shorts and a great big map. No self-assured Parisian woman of a certain age would be seen dead in shorts. They are for the beach. *Mon Dieu!* While in Paris, dress up. Not only will you look and feel like a million dollars, you will be treated with more respect in boutiques and restaurants, and on the street. You will also receive more attention – and may even be the recipient of a smile, or 'the look'. Buy a discreet little book of maps with one *arrondissement* per page. Blend in like a local and you will no longer be the target of *le pickpocket*.

'The amount of curious staring you generate on the street is directly proportional to the degree to which you've got it wrong.'

Alicia Drake, author of *A Shopper's Guide to Paris Fashion*

The legendary La Coupole brasserie on boulevard du Montparnasse

L'Appartement 3

It is love at first sight: a *très joli* Haussmannian with three bedrooms, two newly tiled bathrooms and a long hallway wide enough to fit a piano. The walls are freshly painted, the ceilings and cornices adorned with fat plaster cherubs, flying birds and garlands of flowers. Large, antique mirrors with ornate white frames are fixed above three marble fireplaces and the parquet floors gleam. Down the hall, *les chambres* (bedrooms) look out onto an inner courtyard planted with shrubs and flowers – and straight into other people's lives. French windows on six levels are thrown open to the courtyard, which resounds with the sounds of summer and domesticity.

After three months of living in a hotel (*sans* laundry), we have finally found our apartment. Our new neighbourhood of Passy is right across the Seine from the Eiffel Tower and packed with BCBG types: *bon chic, bon genre* (chic and well-bred), not to mention well-heeled.

Drawbacks:

* Our apartment is in the genteel 16th (*le seizième*), which is *un peu calme* (a bit quiet) and quite a distance from the school.
* It is on the first floor at the back of the building with no balcony, just baby balconettes.
* *La cave* is lined with dirt.
* We don't have access to *la chambre de bonne*.
* There are two baths – but no shower.
* The kitchen isn't big enough to swing a chihuahua in and is stark naked, except for a single white porcelain sink, a second-rate stove and a lone cupboard.

Justified by: it has character.
C'est la vie.

Julie calls, humiliated.
She has just dialled the number for information, and *they* hung up on *her* because they couldn't understand her French. I ask you, is it ethical for a helpline to hang up on a client?

L'Appartement 4

I punch in our code and push on the heavy black door adorned with a wreath of wrought-iron roses. Finally the morning has arrived to move into our building. Madame Gardienne, who lives on the ground floor with a scruffy black poodle who pushes his nose around the lacy curtain and barks at everyone who passes, greets us in the foyer, a large tiled area with enormous arched mirrors. As well as saying *bonjour* a billion times a day, our *gardienne* looks after the building, delivers mail to the door and wheels *les poubelles* (rubbish bins) out to the street. She also mops a lot.

Even though our apartment is on the first floor, Madame Gardienne insists the four of us squeeze into the ancient lift with her, along with her poodle. The inside doors snap shut for take-off. We hold our breath and ever so slowly rattle up one floor in the wire cage. Georgie points to a sign inside the lift that reads ATTENTION: 3 PERSONNES. Madame shrugs her shoulders.

Boxes and delivery men are already lined up outside our enormous wooden doors. Madame turns the key with a '*Voilà! Entrez s'il vous plaît (SVP)*' and we file in, only to be confronted by an overpowering odour. How could this be in our newly renovated flat? We quickly throw open the French windows. The poodle takes charge like a truffle dog on the hunt, sniffing from room to room, followed by Madame and a stream of delivery men. The smell lures the poodle to the kitchen cupboard. We look at each other to see who will open it.

Madame motions for everyone to stand back. Tentatively, she opens the cupboard door and peeks in.

'*Ooh là là, c'est un fromage,*' she says laughing, picking up a wooden box. And not just any old cheese but a very ripe Livarot, a washed rind cow's milk cheese from Normandy renowned for its assertive aroma. Accompanying the Livarot are the dregs of *un vin de jour* (cheap bottle of red) and a length of rock-hard baguette – the remains of a workman's lunch.

Passy

Passy is the kind of neighbourhood where the dogs are as immaculately dressed as their owner's children, pearls are still *de rigueur* and bourgeois families have lived at the same address for generations. Friends have known each other since birth and air-kiss twice on each cheek, and the baker greets a regular customer with 'A baguette not too well done as usual, Madame?'

While some locals lament in hushed tones that the area is changing (*les nouveaux riches* are moving in, along with a younger international and diplomatic community), Passy remains a very French enclave of Paris that will never fall from grace. This residential quarter is dripping with understated elegance and visiting it is like slipping into town through a secret back door. There are few flashy café terraces and no major monuments. Immediately you are privy to a behind-the-scenes Paris that rarely rates more than a mention in guidebooks.

Fringed with forest on the western edge of the city, the thin golden ribbon of the 16th has always been a retreat for the wealthy. But Passy is unique in maintaining an intimate village feel, even though the Eiffel Tower, the river cruises and the sunny cafés of Trocadéro are just a ten-minute walk away.

Passy's small merchant street is **rue de l'Annonciation**. Late on a Sunday morning as the church bells toll at the nearby Notre-Dame de Grâce de Passy and locals are busy filling their baskets with *tartes aux fruits rouges*, rustic loaves, bunches of field flowers and wild salad greens, you could very well be in a French country village.

Ficelle "Passy" ↓ 0,80€

Passy passion 1€40 250gr Prix au kg : 5,65

Tradition 1€40 250 gr Prix au kg : 5,65

Quignonnette 250 gr Au kg 5€60 1€40

BAGUETTE DE CEREALE 1€50 250 gr PRIX AU KG : 6€00

BAGUETTE DE CAMPAGNE 1€50 250 gr PRIX AU KG : 6€00

PAIN 400g 1,20

GROS DE CA 2€ 250 gr PR

PETIT CAMPAGNE LEVAIN 1€80 250 gr PRIX AU KG: 7€20

GRAND CAMPAGNE LEVAIN 2€40 400 gr PRIX AU KG: 6€00

Bread and *pâtisseries* at Desgranges bakery, Passy

The centre of life in the quarter is rue de Passy, a long street crammed with boutiques. It comes alive around noon, when all the stores are finally open, the schoolchildren are running home for lunch and the queue for a 'baguette Passy passion', a popular artisanal bread at **Desgranges**, snakes out of the door.

A shopping spree is best left to the afternoon. For the *seizième* look, direct your poodle towards **Franck et Fils**, the small, classic department store at the top of the street with unmistakable yellow awnings and a fabulous millinery department. A little further down, enter through a poky doorway and climb the stairs to **l'Entrepôt**, a vast loft-like space overflowing with linen, *l'art de la table*, and decoration for the home. For fine-dining, head to **l'Astrance**, a three-starred restaurant located just steps from the Seine. Here, phenomenally talented young chef Pascal Barbot replaces the ubiquitous cream and butter with locally sourced, fresh ingredients to create inventive dishes that burst with flavour. Choose the number of courses you desire and await the surprise. The only hitch is securing a table: in 2010 it was rated number 16 in the San Pellegrino World's 50 Best Restaurants list. Reserve well ahead.

Rue de l'Annonciation
merchant street
Metro: Passy/La Muette
Tue–Sat 9 a.m.–1 p.m.
then 4 p.m.–7 p.m.;
Sun 9 a.m.–1 p.m.

Desgranges
6, rue de Passy, 75016
Tel: 01 42 88 35 82
www.maison-desgranges.com

Franck et Fils
80, rue de Passy, 75016
Tel: 01 44 14 38 00
www.francketfils.fr

L'Astrance
4, rue de Beethoven, 75016
Tel: 01 40 50 84 40

L'Entrepôt
50, rue de Passy, 75016
Tel: 01 45 25 64 17
www.lentrepot.com

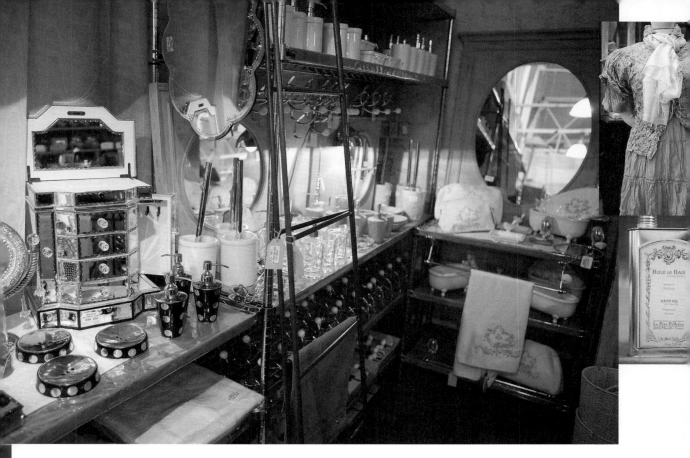

IKEA 1

7 JULY 'And what's this you want – an American-sized refrigerator?'

'We are entitled to a large fridge,' says Tim. 'You do not have a family, Madame.'

Madame HR, from the Human Resource department of Tim's company, has our destiny in her hands. As we have arrived for our two-year sojourn with little more than our beds, dining table and clothes, she is responsible for 'helping' us with the loan to furnish our flat.

'And an exhaust fan above the stove? I don't know anyone with one of those.'

'Yes, Madame, we want to take the cooking smells out of our tiny little kitchen, which, by the way, still has no cupboards or benches.'

'But you do have a stove. These things take time, Tim.'

15 JULY Visit French electronic giant, Darty. Pick out Madame HR-approved whitegoods and appliances in under thirty minutes; eeny, meeny, miny, moe. Purchases include *un aspirateur*, which, despite sounding like a sterile surgical instrument, is a vacuum cleaner. Also a dependable European washing machine with (I am soon to discover) a cycle time of two hours ten minutes.

25 AUGUST 9 A.M. Yes! Approval from Madame HR to purchase rest of household items. Just as well. Mickey and Big Bird beanbags are beginning to resemble breasts of very old woman. Also, the girls start school in two weeks. Hire car for day and zoom out to IKEA to order houseful of furniture with our trusty pocket dictionary.

12.30 P.M. Lunch on Swedish meatballs in IKEA cafeteria with two little bottles of Burgundy. How civilised!

5.15 P.M *Finalement*, after fighting extraordinary crowds, we have chosen and ordered everything on list, including doll's-house-sized table and stools for kitchen. Everything is to be delivered except for the desk, which we opt to shove in car to assemble at home. An abode for the computer at last!

5.30 P.M. Get to checkout.

'I am sorry,' says the checkout operator, eyes already on the next customer, 'but your card is declined. Next please.'

'*C'est impossible*,' cries Tim indignantly. Customers in queue tell us to get out of the way if there is a problem. A Franglais screaming match erupts. We didn't spend the whole day here to go home with nothing!

Manager arrives. 'I'm just going to call someone to see if we can do something about this. *Asseyez-vous, SVP*,' he says, motioning for us to sit down. Not sure if he means for half a minute or half an hour . . . or who he is calling. Soon find out he means half an hour. Girls amuse themselves playing dogs in handbags.

6.15 P.M. Girls tired, hungry and bored. Now pretending they own Swedish restaurant and are serving smoked salmon with mustard and dill. Manager returns and, with a feeble shrug of the shoulders, says he can't do anything about it. Tim demands to call bank.

6.45 P.M. Girls have invented entire Swedish smorgasbord. Tim still on hold to bank. Twenty-six minutes, but who's counting? I remember the rental car has to be back by 7 p.m. or we pay another day's rent. Tim eventually gets connected to *un homme* who sounds like a recording.

'Why can't you give me approval?'

'Please take it up with your customer service officer, Monsieur.'

'Then could you put me through to customer service, please?'

'*Non*,' says Monsieur Monotone, 'they are not available on Saturdays.'

'Well, I really need approval NOW,' says Tim. 'Can you do something about it?'

'*Non*,' he says.

'*C'est ridicule!* I can't get to my own money. I am going to close this account,' Tim says fuming.

'Please take it up with your customer service officer,' he parrots. '*Au revoir.*'

7 P.M. Pay IKEA for thirty-six-minute call (local calls charged by units of time) of which only five minutes were speaking time. Pay cash for desk and leave everything else. Girls have tired of their smorgasbord and are now whizzing about in a trolley. Crash into a family's cart. Split boxes splattered across floor. I hide behind seat.

7.15 P.M. Eventually fit extremely rebellious box containing desk into matchbox-sized car. Illegally put Annabelle on knee and drive home.

8.15 P.M. No food; too tired to step out door. Also too weary to risk possibility of another altercation . . . with anyone. Fusion food for dinner: Vegemite on stale toasted baguette. Tim starts to put desk together and discovers huge gash on desktop. It has to go back.

3 A.M. Friends call from Australia – got the time wrong.

'Can't imagine what a wonderful time you must be having. All those fabulous restaurants and museums right on your doorstep!'

Paris,
je t'aime . . .
pas du tout

Ritz and glitz: the Hôtel Ritz as night falls

1774

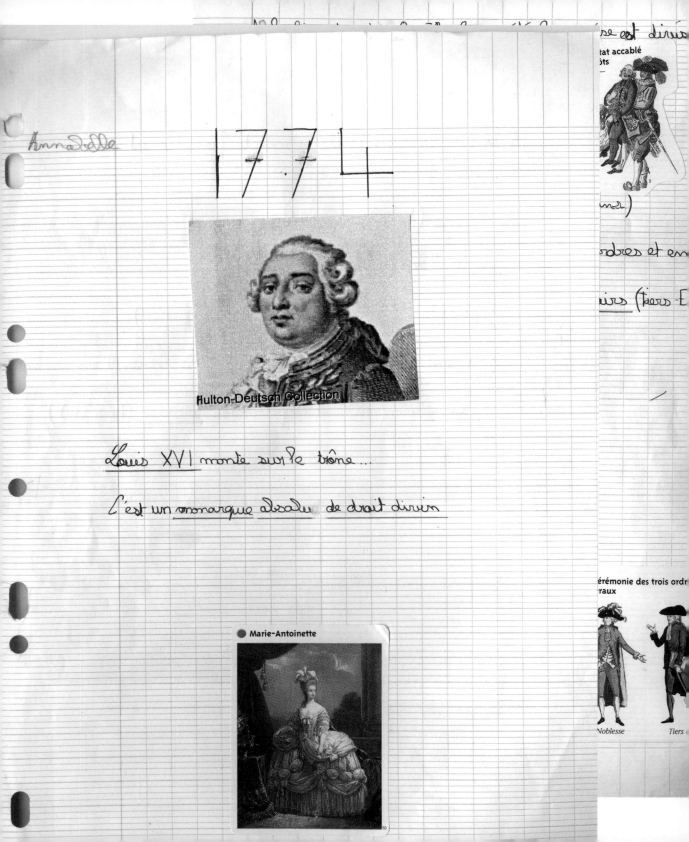

Hulton-Deutsch Collection

Louis XVI monte sur le trône...

C'est un <u>monarque</u> <u>absolu</u> de droit divin

état accablé ôts

(md.)

odres et en

irs (Tiers-É

érémonie des trois ordr
raux

Marie-Antoinette

Noblesse   Tiers

L'École

She buckles up her sandals and slaps on her broad-brimmed hat. We walk through the school grounds, past the playground and under the shady gums to her bright, airy classroom. Already she is familiar with her teacher, who greets her warmly.

It is Georgie's first day of primary school: an Australian school with swimming carnivals, sausage sizzles and everything else that we as Aussies imagine when we think of school.

But three years on, our vision of a typical education is to be severely challenged. It is now Annabelle's turn to experience her first day of school.

She buttons up her Mary Janes and puts her crisp navy smock with white trim over her clothes. We ride *le métro* and walk through the elegant Parc Monceau, arriving at a set of heavy black doors. She has never met her teacher or seen her school, a respected bilingual *école* in the centre of Paris. Her French language skills are limited to colours, numbers and basic greetings. (Mine are limited to Champagne and *petits fours*.) I wait with the other mothers, all slender and beautifully dressed, until the doors open. Then, to my surprise, I am told to leave. The inner sanctum of the school is strictly forbidden to parents. I kiss Annabelle goodbye and hope for the best.

After much investigation, our decision to send the girls to a bilingual school was twofold. Firstly, we were concerned about them losing their English at an all-French school. Secondly, we couldn't see the point of living in Paris and enrolling the girls in an international school. For older children already entrenched in other education systems, an English-speaking school is unquestionably the best option, but with the girls at an adaptable young age where they still soak up information like a sponge, we want them to get the most out of their two-year stay.

Bilingual schools in France attract many foreign families who want their children to preserve their English as they learn French. They also draw French families eager for their children to learn or maintain English. The girls' school offers a full French curriculum plus five lessons of English per week, with students divided into groups according to their level of *anglais*. Annabelle has been slotted into the English Mother Tongue group, which comprises around 30 per cent of students in her year-level. The group consists mainly of Anglophone expatriates, with a sprinkling of Parisian children from families who have lived abroad or have one English-speaking parent. Most children in the other groups are Parisian.

The French system commences with *la maternelle* (kindergarten) at three, followed by *l'école élémentaire* (primary school) at six. From this age, the school years work backwards, starting with ııème (grade ı).

Having just turned five, Annabelle is thrown straight into *la grande section*, the third and final year of kindergarten. From ııème, however, new pupils must commence with a year of *adaptation*, an immersion process that aims to provide a gentle transition to the French system.

Très Cochonne

Georgie has just finished her first day of *adaptation* at a building in the next street. With a large amount of inner-city real estate impossible to secure in one location, campuses are spread out.

Waiting for her on the footpath I meet David, a Chinese Canadian single father whose daughter Elaine is also in *adaptation*. Then there's Iris from the Black Forest who has a daughter, Sarah. They've recently relocated from the US. I also meet a fellow Australian, Sharon, with a son, Sam, in Georgie's class.

As Georgie and I walk towards Courcelles metro station, I learn there are children in her class from all over the world: Korea, Portugal, South Africa, Turkey, Hungary, the United Kingdom . . .

Delving further, it seems she doesn't remember exactly *what* she learnt today, but she certainly remembers having the first page of her new exercise book ripped out.

'Why?' I ask. She opens her book.

'Because my writing is *très cochonne* (sloppy),' she mumbles self-consciously. No wonder! She's had to change from South Australian link script to French cursive overnight *and* write with a fountain pen. I see that, being left-handed, she has left a smudge across every page.

'Did anyone else get their page ripped out?' I ask, concerned. She counts on her fingers.

'Yes, seventeen of us,' she replies.

Annabelle, Sarah and Georgie ready for school

Julie calls, panic-stricken.

She had lost her way deep in the labyrinth of the Charles de Gaulle-Étoile metro station and stopped a well-dressed Frenchman to ask for directions. While he was patiently explaining the best way for Julie to get to her desired destination, his briefcase was stolen, wrenched right out of his hand. With gangs of gypsy children well known for operating pickpocket rings in the major metro stations, Julie was immediately suspected of being a gypsy woman acting as a decoy. As she was frozen with fear, it didn't look good.

'You know the bureaucracy here . . . how long it takes to acquire documents. Well, when I was questioned by police, I realised I had nothing in my possession to prove I actually reside here. All I had in my bag were a few euros and a tourist visa.

'Then they turned to Madeline, suspecting she was a gypsy child, especially as she didn't speak French. "If you live in Paris, Madame, why is your daughter not at school?" one of them asked. "We will have to report you to the authorities."

'They refused to believe she was waiting for a place to become available at the International School of Paris. Eventually, they let me go as they couldn't prove anything but they were still very suspicious. I was followed on the metro to the 16th by four armed police, all the way to our door!'

'Well, *la vie parisienne* is certainly not dull,' I reply.

'You can say that again,' says Julie, with a sigh.

L'École . . . encore

Annabelle *sans* teeth
in her school smock

Outside the heavy black doors on her third morning, Annabelle clings to me like a koala to a tree. Exhausted from two taxing days of *la grande section*, she has decided she's had enough of school in a foreign language. Two teachers prise her, kicking and screaming, from me and take her inside. I watch on helplessly. Even though her *maîtresse* (teacher) can speak English, she is forbidden to speak to Annabelle *en anglais*. This means there is no way to pacify her.

I watch tentatively as Annabelle emerges through the heavy black doors at 4.30 p.m. talking to two sweet little girls: Olivia, an English girl who began school here a few months ago, and Claire, from the US, who has also just started. It's interesting to note that even at a young age, when you find yourself in an unfamiliar environment you identify elements of society you recognise, and are naturally drawn to the familiar.

Bloom

Now that school's in, I have time to begin acquainting myself with the city and French culture. I attend *Bloom Where You're Planted*, an annual orientation program for English-speaking newcomers to Paris, sponsored by the Women of the American Church of Paris (WOAC). The two-day program covers practical information and tips on cultural adjustment and includes a number of guest speakers, the most entertaining being a savvy English Francophile who runs a seminar on how to pass for a Parisian – and how to shop for clothes in exclusive Parisian boutiques.

Les Règles:

* Don't be nice. Leave your smile at home. French women take clothes as seriously as if they were betting on a horse race or playing the stock market. Look like you mean business. This includes dressing up to go shopping.
* Say goodbye to sneakers.
* Only buy classic, good-quality, well-cut clothes that will last the distance. 'American women like to look like big children,' says the speaker. 'Fun is not a good adjective when it comes to choosing a wardrobe. You must have *bon goût* (good taste).'
* Wear what suits you and makes you feel good; clothes that work to *mettre en valeur* (this means clothes that highlight your best feature, preferably an erogenous zone). That is what style and chic is about. It's not about wearing an item just because it is the 'must have' of the season.
* Accessories are all important. Buy good-quality handbags. Scarves, especially, can change an outfit. A good collection of scarves means you don't actually need to have many clothes, just a few classic pieces that look altogether different depending on the scarf you are wearing. Many Parisian women see Hermès scarves as an investment and own up to twenty.

'If the assistant declares that you have American-sized breasts,' the speaker continues, 'this is not intended as a compliment.' Anything big in Paris is referred to as American (like an American-sized fridge). Parisian women are generally small-boned with small breasts and 'American-sized bras' are few and far between. Sometimes, lingerie boutiques keep a few out the back, but you will rarely find them displayed.

N.B. A bra in French is *un soutien-gorge*, which translates to 'support for the throat'.

So, this is what you do. You walk in and say *Bonjour, Madame*. (This is a must. You are invading their territory and are lucky to be in their boutique so you had better suck up by saying *bonjour* first.) Don't look at any clothes. Don't touch any clothes. Name your price and make them work. They will come up with a couple of outfits in your price range. Here comes the catch. You are most definitely expected to parade your new look out of the security of the fitting room and onto the shop floor for all the sales assistants to see.

The key here is to NEVER apologise for anything. Get some attitude. Never say, 'I can't get this done up' or 'My thighs look big in this' and mope around trying to make up excuses for your body. It is not your fault; it is the clothes' fault. Instead say, 'Look at the cut of these pants – they are atrocious' or 'What a dreadful mistake this fabric is – it sits so badly.'

A French acquaintance finds it very amusing that Anglo-Saxons are forever making up excuses and saying sorry. 'It is island thinking,' she says. 'Small-mindedness. And you say thank you for anything and everything too! If you called up your dentist with a dreadful toothache but he couldn't fit you in, I bet you would say, "Thanks, bye". Why would you thank someone who can't accommodate your needs? *Très bizarre!*'

www.woac.net/bloom

'Fashion fades, style is eternal.'

Yves Saint Laurent

IKEA 2

7 OCTOBER Yes! We have royal permission from Madame HR to buy and install the kitchen, more than three months after moving in. Armed with basic French and even more basic kitchen vocabulary – *tiroir* (drawer); *placard* (cupboard); *banc* (bench) – we hire a car and drive out to IKEA again. After seeing our kitchen plan, the assistant, who speaks a little English, asks whether we'd like the three old doors underneath the existing sink replaced to match the new ones. 'Good idea,' we reply.

'What height are the old doors, 50 or 75 cm?'

Tim and I look at each other and shrug our shoulders. '*Aucune idée.*' (No idea.)

'Let's toss a coin,' Tim says. 'If it's heads we'll order 75 cm. We're not going all the way home and coming all the way back just to tell them that. And you know what will happen if we try to call . . .'

Using the phone when your French is fractured is asking for trouble. The message always seems to get scrambled along the way, lost in translation. Understanding a new language is even more difficult when you don't have the cues of body language and can't see lips move. You hang up never quite knowing whether you have actually made that appointment, or whether you have ordered something you don't really want. For more difficult dialogue, I practise first, and am often so shocked when I have been perfectly understood that I forget to listen to the reply, or the receiver thinks I speak excellent French and launches into a long, fast monologue and I am very soon lost. *Répétez, SVP* (Repeat, please) becomes a very handy phrase. For important information it is best to communicate face to face.

It's heads up so three 75 cm cupboard doors it is. We finish ordering and cross our fingers, hoping that we'll be blessed with a sparkling white kitchen in a week's time. Zoom home and measure doors under sink – 50 cm. *Zut!*

L'École . . . encore

Georgie is distraught after school. To complete her homework last night she had to draw a circle and, not having her compass, used a glass. She determined the centre with a ruler and pencil; close enough to perfect, or so she thought.

'You did not have your compass at home last night, did you Georgina?' said her *maîtresse* sternly, looking at her circle.

'*Non*,' she whispered.

'Then this dot can not be the true centre,' her *maîtresse* yelled, ripping it out.

Eyes smarting, Georgie couldn't think of how to tell her in French what she had done, so she said nothing.

Her *maîtresse* turned to her again.

'And your writing is getting worse and worse, Georgina!'

Le Vigny

After a disheartening day, the need for conversation in one's mother tongue with others facing similar challenges becomes a necessity. To lift my spirits I drop into Le Vigny, a café that has become a beacon for foreign mothers at the school; a place to comfort and console, to share addresses and survival knowledge, and to laugh and cry at the highs and lows of daily Parisian life. Brought together by culture shock, feelings of powerlessness and the need to express concerns, we exchange stories and support each other when pages are ripped from our children's books, when low grades are held up and named in class, and when the heavy black doors are once more slammed in our faces.

Through the café door comes a constantly changing blur of interesting women, with a solid core group who organise lunches, museum trips and various outings. Today, over my morning *café crème*, I meet Ann-Françoise, a French Canadian artist; a woman studying fine and decorative art at Christie's auction house; and an American pharmacist whose husband has recently passed away . . . their dream had been to take the children to Paris to live and she is bravely following it through alone. Regulars Teresa, Karen and Pam, three warm and friendly Englishwomen, sip their coffees and recount their latest misadventures. Susan – the café's immaculately groomed matriarch – is there, as always. Having lived in Paris for many years, she offers constant guidance.

Le Vigny
88, blvd de Courcelles, 75017
Tel: 01 47 63 09 56

Monsieur Précision

I am ushered into a white amphitheatre equipped with lecture chairs. An assistant flits around in the final throes of preparation. A translator awaits. Tiers of serious students wearing white coats sit facing a huge bench with a tilted overhead mirror, pens poised. For a moment, I think I have mistakenly entered a hospital auditorium and am about to have the fundamentals of orthopaedic surgery thrust upon me. On further inspection, I see a space-age cook-top and groups of ingredients. I have entered a demonstration room at Le Cordon Bleu cooking school and apart from the 'white coats' there are only four amateurs present: Sharon, Iris, Karen and myself, all feeling like mutant mushrooms in a bag of prized truffles. We hadn't realised the daily demonstrations are part of the regular program followed by the diploma and certificate students.

Today's session is pastry. We have come to watch the creation of a perfect *quiche Lorraine, une quiche aux champignons sauvages* (wild mushroom quiche) and two seasonal *tartes aux fruits*. The session begins with the savoury tarts. *Le grand chef* cuts and weighs with a surgeon's precision and swiftly sifts the flour, twice. He rolls the pastry north to south, east to west. He sautés the melange of mushrooms separately so the juices don't mix and advises us not to lose sleep over *les trompettes de la mort*, the dubious trumpet-of-death mushrooms.

'Only one in a thousand is bad,' he reassures us.

It is while *le grand chef* is executing his *pâté sucrée* (sweet pie pastry) that the extent of his precision is revealed.

An ardent student asks, 'What size eggs do you use, *Grand Chef*?'

'50 gram eggs,' he replies. 'They must be 50 grams.'

Then another zealous student asks, 'Is that with or without the shell, *Grand Chef*?'

The next five minutes are spent discussing and visualising the disastrous effects of a 55 gram shell-less egg on a sweet pastry case. The flow of the animated discussion is considerably stemmed, however, by the English translator who dutifully butts in each time a new person speaks. The final word? If your eggs (with shell) are heavier than 50 grams, the water content added to your pastry must be reduced accordingly and precisely. Next case, please.

Le grand chef prepares the filling for the fruit tarts.

'Can you use canned fruits in the tarts?' asks a student.

'It all depends,' he says smiling, 'on who is coming to dinner.'

He whisks the almond cream vigorously and advises that it must be the same consistency as Nivea face cream. I watch the students write Nivea on their shopping lists.

In just under three hours Monsieur Précision has miraculously stitched up four quiches and four fruit tarts. The pastries are whipped out of ovens and placed decoratively on a table to be greeted by a round of applause and flashing photographs. Operation Tart is complete. The room fills with the tantalising smell of fresh baking as the assistant starts to cut the tarts into tiny helpings and place them on tiny plates. Time is running out. It is nearing school pick-up time. We push our way through the white coats, grab four little plates each, and run for the metro. After all, a student's palate must be developed.

IKEA 3

24 OCTOBER Bribe children with promise of new English books to get them into hire car then nip out to IKEA to change order for cupboard doors. Soon we are speeding back to Paris, new shorter doors in tow (decided on pick-up rather than delivery to prevent further mix-up). Arrive home after another scintillating afternoon in the City of Romance and strip away cardboard to reveal three spanking-new doors – in brown.

'No, it can't be!' cries Tim, his head in his hands.

To cheer ourselves up, we treat ourselves to dinner from our trusty local *traiteur* (caterer), **Lenôtre**, just down the steep steps of rue des Eaux and a short walk along the Seine. French pastry king Gaston Lenôtre opened his first shop in the 1950s before expanding into catering, and the emporium currently organises around 6,500 events a year, from weddings and cocktail parties to gala dinners. Like all the premier *traiteurs* in Paris, his stores are known for their wide variety of quality French food to take away. We decide on *un terrine de lapin l'ancienne*, which translates to 'ancient rabbit terrine' (at this point I don't care how ancient), a tall leek tart, and some salad. We swing by our local *cave* for a bottle of dry Alsatian Riesling to pair with the tart, pick up a fresh baguette for the terrine and close the door on Paris.

N.B. *L'ancienne* actually means the dish is made in an old-fashioned way.

www.lenotre.fr

31 OCTOBER Try to convince children to go on lovely Sunday drive to IKEA. Georgie on knees begging not to go. Tim makes expedition alone. Of course the door debacle is all our fault but Tim eventually persuades staff to change them. Rips hole in top of box to make sure they are white. *Voilà!*

Monsieur Panache

The procedures of Monsieur Précision are followed, one wet autumn afternoon, by the colourful adventures of Monsieur Panache. The two prove to be as different in style as the art of Ingres and Gauguin, for Monsieur Panache is no by-the-book chef. Like Gauguin, Monsieur Panache is not afraid to colour boldly, or to break the mould. He works on instinct: smelling, touching and tasting. In three flamboyant acts, he entertains us with *une grande performance* – largely without intermission, much to the dismay of the open-mouthed translator.

Dishes appear to be created simultaneously and with exquisite timing, despite his opening-line advice that 'One should always prepare dessert first, then main course and, lastly, entrée.' Today's menu consists of *une salade de chèvre chaud* (warm goat's cheese salad) followed by *jambonettes de volaille et son jus au madère, pommes caramelisées* (boned, stuffed chicken legs in a wine sauce with caramelised apples) and *une mousse au chocolat à l'orange*.

Pots bubble and wobble. Spoons fly around the bench. He tastes theatrically, adding a dash of this and a sprinkle of that until everything is 'right'. The air is thick with passion and wonderful aromas. He bones the chicken in a flash.

'Keep the wishbones to use for slingshots,' he says.

Slowly, he stirs the melting chocolate in the bain-marie. 'Rule number one,' he says, licking a chocolaty finger, 'is never dip your finger in the chocolate.'

He checks the wine sauce simmering in a saucepan, lithely turns the apples sautéing in butter and sugar, and strains the oranges to make syrup. He adds a dash of bright red *sirop* (non-alcoholic cordial) and stirs.

'Red is very appetising,' he says, with a twinkle in his eye. 'Like lipstick on a woman. Something well presented is half-eaten already.'

Then Monsieur Panache lifts from a bowl what looks like a piece of white netting. It is, in fact, a length of *crépine* (caul), the large, enveloping membranes from pork intestines used to encase sausages, or, in this case, chicken legs.

'My grandmother used to hang a net like this in front of her head,' he proclaims, holding it up to his face. 'Perhaps I can do a deal with Yves St Laurent?'

Le Cordon Bleu has earned an international reputation built on the excellence of its culinary education, with schools around the world offering a bounty of courses. At the original Paris school, courses range from Le Grand Diplôme, an intensive, progressive nine-month program, to vineyard visits, workshops and demonstrations of French cuisine for the enthusiastic amateur.

Le Cordon Bleu
8, rue Léon-Delhomme, 75015
Tel: 01 53 68 22 50
www.cordonbleu.edu

Non!

Georgie is refusing to do her weekend homework. If she doesn't do her homework she will get told off, and if she does her homework she will get told off.

Julie calls, windblown.

She tells me how she spent yesterday flying down the freeway on the back of a truck, holding on for dear life to a load of new mattresses and a pile of IKEA boxes. Her geo-physicist husband, Mark, was at the wheel – and had just discovered a passion for Formula One truck racing. His company, in typical French style, was still procrastinating (sorry, 'negotiating') about all sorts of things to do with his contract/furniture/reimbursement, so rather than sleep on the floor of their new apartment for the next few months, he decided to take matters into his own hands. He rented a truck (despite having no truck licence) to deliver the furniture, picking Julie up outside their apartment with a grin from ear to ear and a 'Jump in, love'.

'The real test, though,' says Julie, 'came when we tried to get everything up to the sixth floor. French lifts, as you know, are totally impractical. Do you know how difficult it is to get a floppy queen-sized mattress up six flights of stairs? It's like climbing Mount Everest carrying a large drunken cow!'

'And then,' she says wearily, 'I turned every carton sent from Australia upside-down (the boxes arrived a couple of days ago via the scenic route), and NO bed linen. Goodness knows where it is! We were so tired we hardly noticed we were sleeping between tablecloths with our heads on tea towels.'

'Well, glad you're getting settled, Julie,' I say, as I plate up dinner on the kitchen floor once again.

I hear Mark hammering away in the background, no doubt miraculously transforming identical white IKEA planks into cupboards and bookshelves.

Le Goûter

I am delighted to have met Françoise, a beautifully dressed Frenchwoman who lives across the road. 'Come for tea and a little *goûter* after school,' she says.

We sit in her perfectly wonderful *salon* with bouquets of fresh flowers on the tables, and soft cream carpet. We sip tea and pick at pastries while the girls eat *pains au chocolat* in a playroom down the hall with her daughter Capucine. Typically consisting of some form of bread, chocolate and a drink, the traditional five o'clock *goûter* (snack) staves off children's hunger until a late family dinner.

Françoise tells me she has lived in Paris for twenty years.

'Paris is a very hard city to live in,' she says. 'There is no service. Everything takes so long. The bureaucracy is startling. But there are lots of wonderful things too.'

IKEA 4

9 NOVEMBER Smelly IKEA man arrives to fit kitchen. He spends all day banging away installing cupboards, drawers and benchtops. I dream about preparing dinner in a real Parisian kitchen. He rips open box containing *placards* to go under sink to reveal three white doors of correct height – with glass centres.

'*Pas très bien,*' he says, shaking his head. I don't know whether to be thankful they are wrong, AGAIN, so that smelly man will leave NOW, or to throw doors from window followed by piercing scream.

Close door on smelly man who says he will come back to install doors when they are changed.

12 NOVEMBER Tim arrives home from trip. Eventually drum up courage to tell him about doors. He pours himself into a chair.

'That's it. I am defeated.'

28 NOVEMBER With the memory of cupboard-door debacle fading *un peu*, we make another trip to IKEA amid pre-Christmas hysteria, and are swept along the festive aisles with the masses. I manage to snatch the last tall white candle. The French are crazy about candles, especially at Noël.

Change cupboard doors. Physically strip packaging off for thorough assessment, like examining critically ill hospital admission. They are white, all over, the correct size and style (and in good health).

Zoom home and put doors next to maid's entrance (not that we have maid) along with bag full of IKEA knobs and hinges until smelly man returns.

Non! Non!

It is the third time in a row that I've had to leave Georgie alone while I take Annabelle to school. She is refusing to go and I cannot physically drag her. She is too heavy.

La Catastrophe

Disaster has struck. Our giant glass jar of Vegemite is a screaming black mess on the kitchen tiles. We all stand around it, debilitated, as though a beloved pet has been run over.

La Maîtresse

As we dine at **La Matta**, a busy little local with authentic Italian pizzas and a warm Italian welcome, Annabelle tells me that a little boy in her class had to read out loud today, but he couldn't quite get the words out.

'*La maîtresse* told him he was *très stupide*,' she says casually, sawing through her pizza.

'That's not very nice,' I reply, shocked.

'*C'est normale*,' she shrugs.

La Matta
23, rue de l'Annonciation, 75016
Tel: 01 40 50 04 66

Beautifully penned cursive, by Annabelle

Annabelle
Paech

a a
i
i
u
u — u — u — u —
e — e — e — e —
e — e — e — e —
o — o — o — o
o — o — o — o

co
coca
m — m — m — m
m — m — m — m

Annabelle

pupitre

plumiers
tion

MÉTHODE D'ÉCRITURE DROITE
Modèles à reproduire sur le cahier N°5
Majuscules et minuscules

Aa. Bb. Cc. Dd. Ee. Ff. Gg. Hh.
Ii. Kk. Ll. Mm. Nn. Oo.
Vv. Ww.
es romains
L. C. D. M.
5. 6. 7. 8. 9. 0.
e bien I.
ute vertu.

DATE: Le 10 Novembre 2

passé — Passé Passé
présent Présent Présen
f futur — Futur Futur
annabelle Annabelle
Annabelle Paech

La Décision

Georgie tried to escape from school today. She got as far as the metro steps and was dragged back by a teacher who had luckily (or unluckily) seen her pelt through the front door.

I spend a sleepless night pacing the hallway searching for an answer. Paris was not supposed to be like this! After seven months, the days are not getting any easier. Am I going to spend the next precious seventeen months struggling with a new calamity every day, in a foreign language?

I Google the American School of Paris. It is an exclusive school located at St-Cloud with large grounds and an American curriculum, but I can't get past the fees: annual tuition is 21 000€ (34 000 AUD) for primary school students, plus a one-time fee of 8 000€ (13 000 AUD) in the first year.

I Google the British School of Paris. The junior school is situated out in the Impressionist village of Bougival in a gorgeous setting. It offers a fine British education with a daily French language class. But what's the point? We may as well be at home. I am also put off by Julie's experience. 'As soon as they found out we were from the colonies, they didn't want to know us,' she said.

I Google the International School of Paris. It is the only English-speaking school within the city of Paris and the only school in France to offer all three International Baccalauréat programs. The student body comprises sixty-four nationalities. I know Julie is happy with the school (enhanced by the fact that she sees Gerard Depardieu at drop-off). I look up the fees. An entry fee of 6 000€ is required and an annual tuition of 17 000€ for kindergarten to grade 5. Forget it! While many companies and embassies pay the fees for *any* school chosen by their expatriate employees, we unfortunately do not have that option. I cross all three schools off the list. So where does that leave us?

Option A: Go home.

Option B: Tim to commute from the UK.

Option C: Tough it out.

Option A: I don't give up that easily.

Option B: The company would never approve relocation; it seems rather extravagant, especially as we're only here for another year or so.

I step out onto *la balconette* grappling with Option C. The air is cool and the sun is rising over the rooftops. I stay there for a long time, my arms resting on the wrought-iron railing as the shutters across the courtyard flick open, one by one.

A new day is dawning in this beautiful city.

We'll give it one more shot. French kids survive; it's just a matter of getting through the shock of transition and perhaps finding the girls a pleasant diversion, a physical outlet. We can take Georgie to WH Smith every weekend for a new English book to escape into and, although sporting options are limited compared to Australia, she can always continue with dance classes. My thoughts are disturbed by Madame Gardienne filling her mop bucket in the courtyard below. I hear footsteps and flushing on the floors above and below me – it's time to try and wake Georgie up for school.

Yes, dance may just be the answer.

Salle Pleyel

I stop by Le Vigny after a draining drop-off and ask if anyone knows of a good ballet school. Everyone shakes their head. The mothers here today either have boys who go to martial arts and trek out of town for soccer, or girls who attend art or music classes.

'Try Salle Pleyel down the road on rue du Faubourg-St-Honoré,' says Ann-Françoise, as Serge the waiter delivers our coffees. 'It has a very good reputation.' I check it out on the way home and find a beautiful old concert hall where

Stravinsky directed *Agon* in 1957. The performing arts centre houses a stream of concerts by the Orchestra of Paris and many visiting orchestras. Hidden behind sets of soundproof double-doors over the six floors are also a number of music and dance schools. I take a stab and enrol the girls.

www.sallepleyel.fr

The Trailing Spouse

It may sound glamorous, but the life of a trailing spouse can be difficult and lonely, especially when there's a new language and culture to learn. Many women (who make up the majority of trailing spouses) have not only given up their own careers to help their partner climb the slippery corporate ladder, but often their entire emotional support systems. The notion of having family and close friends to call on in times of need is suddenly thrown out the French window, and even when they eventually start to settle into the new country, countless expat wives find that their husbands have a common trait. They travel – a lot.

Many women never seem to know where their elusive partner is (or was) at any particular moment in time:

'Umm yes, well, I think he's going to Brussels today or tomorrow, or he might have already gone.'

'He's in London at the moment. No, I'm not quite sure where he's staying.'

'He'll be back Tuesday night . . . I think.'

The way you know your husband is going somewhere is the clean white shirt on the bed:

'Are you off somewhere?'

'Oh, did I forget to tell you? I'm going to Geneva. Just overnight. Be back by ten tomorrow evening.'

'Where are you staying?'

'Not sure. You can catch me on my mobile if you need me. Bye, gotta fly,' he says, zipping up his suit bag and throwing it over his shoulder.

It seems that the life of a trailing spouse is perpetually in one of three states:

A) Partner away, somewhere.

B) Partner home, jetlagged and snoring on couch.

C) Clean white shirt on bed.

Tips for Trailing Dogs
(as opposed to Trailing Spouses)

* Only some taxis take dogs. No one, man or dog, is allowed to sit in the front passenger seat of a taxi in Paris. Something to keep in mind if you own a large dog or second child.

* On Air France, dogs weighing less than 5 kg may ride in the cabin as long as they are in an enclosed, vented bag.

* If you have a small dog in a handbag or backpack, you can take it on the metro, bus or suburban train. Large dogs are not allowed (in theory). Small dogs really do get special treatment. They are permitted in hairdressers and beauty salons, boutiques, restaurants and libraries. They can also ride on country trains for a nominal fee, while large dogs must buy a half-price second-class ticket.

* Many hotels in Paris do not accept dogs – can you imagine? – while others accept *chiens gentils* (nice dogs) only. The Hôtel Ritz has a special 'Ritzy Luxury Pet Package for small travelling dogs', so guests and their canine companions can enjoy a luxury stay together. According to the Ritz's website, the package includes 'luxurious accommodation for pet and owner, and VIP-welcome amenity for the pet consisting of ritzy bowl, ritzy rug, bottle of aromatised mineral water, candy doggy bag, ritzy medal engraved with pet's name, street walk with certified canine professional, and menus and spa treatment for the owner and dog in supplement, upon request'.

Julie calls, crestfallen.

She explains how she had stopped for afternoon tea to quench her growing addiction to strawberry tartlets. Not seeing any on the menu, she had asked the waiter.

'*Bonjour Monsieur, est-ce que vous êtes une tarte aux fraises?*'

'No, Madame,' he replied in perfect English, tweaking his bow tie, 'I am not a strawberry tart. I am a waiter and I would be very pleased if you addressed me as one.' Not concentrating, she had got the verbs *avoir* and *être* jumbled and had asked the waiter if he WAS a strawberry tart, instead of if he HAD a strawberry tart.

'Well, you won't make that mistake again,' I say, trying not to laugh.

IKEA 5

1 DECEMBER Smelly man here to put doors on. *Zut alors!* IKEA bag containing matching knobs and hinges must have been thrown out with other rubbish bags that pass through maid's entrance. Race down back stairs to *les poubelles* in courtyard but bins are empty. Feel sick. Tell smelly man we will fix doors ourselves. He throws his arms up in the air, gives me the big Gallic shrug and slams door behind him. Can't bring myself to tell Tim about doorknobs: might precipitate a heart attack. Will sneak out to IKEA on the train (hour and a half each way) and buy more.

10 DECEMBER *Dieu merci!* Exhausted after six months of combat, *la cuisine* is complete and I cook our first meal in a gleaming white Parisian kitchen.

Georgie, Olivia and Annabelle

Le Cours de Danse

Georgie is having her first dance class in the studio next door as I put Annabelle and Olivia's hair in buns. Neither has spoken much about their debut class last week, but I notice they're not particularly keen to go this afternoon. As I wave goodbye through the door, Annabelle starts to cry.

'You can stay for ten minutes if you like,' says the *instructrice*, a rare privilege that I jump at. I watch as all thirty little girls are pushed and shoved into place while *arrêtez!* (stop!) is screamed around them. More boot camp than ballet class. Annabelle and Olivia stand quaking in their new pink slippers. Is this how it is at school? They look at me wistfully as I quietly tiptoe out. I slip down the stairs and onto the street where I find Georgie, who has already made a run for it. I give her a hug and wipe her tears. She is emotionally spent. I am emotionally spent. Time to start looking for a new ballet school.

To cheer everyone up, I suggest we go to **Ladurée** for hot chocolate. Georgie's eyes light up. It's already twilight, the time the French call *entre chien et loup* (literally, between dog and wolf), and few things bring such pure pleasure on a gloomy winter afternoon in Paris as a cup of intoxicating, wickedly thick *chocolat chaud à l'ancienne*. When it comes to hot chocolate, the French prefer it the old-fashioned way, dark and bittersweet. It's classically rich in taste with very little sugar.

We watch with delight as the silky, molten *chocolat noir* is poured from silver jugs into pretty cups. Connoisseur Georgie rates it the best in the city. My heart leaps to see her happy. Now all we need is our plate of *mini-macarons* in a rainbow of flavours . . .

Filled with society doyennes, businessmen with immaculate mistresses, and Kelly bags, this chocolate box on rue Royale remains *the* address to have tea. It opened as a bakery in 1862, before Ernest Ladurée's wife, Jeanne Souchard, had the brilliant idea of combining café and pastry shop, creating one of the first true tea salons in town. Plump cherubs bake bread on the ceiling against a blazing sun. Old friends gossip *tête-à-tête* and eat fruit tartlets with a knife and fork. Divine *millefeuilles* and golden *financiers* are whisked out the door in perfect pale green boxes. Oozing with style, it's the place to go to taste the best gooey *macarons* in town and rub shoulders with the regular clientele, many of whom are taking a break from the exhausting task of shopping in the nearby luxury boutiques. Ladurée whips up over 12,000 *macarons* a day between its Paris stores and creates a new flavour each season to add to the perennial classics that include lemon, raspberry, chocolate and *caramel au beurre salé*. To be sure of a seat downstairs (the only ones that count), it's best to come outside of prime time (4 p.m.–5.30 p.m.).

Ladurée
16, rue Royale, 75008
Tel: 01 42 60 21 79
www.laduree.fr

La Sucette

Ten days before Christmas and *tout le monde* (everyone) is here. Boulevard Haussmann, home to Paris's grand department stores, is wrapped in Christmas madness and tied with tasteful bows. The sound of carollers fills the air and chestnuts roast over hot tin drums on the footpath. Store windows are alive with animated displays of flying dolls, serpents and swaying dragons. There's a kitchen with dolls busily stirring and pouring *chocolat*, a tea party, and *une pâtisserie* with Noël logs in the making.

Galeries Lafayette, the famous Parisian department store, sparkles under its splendid cupola. Thousands of tiny orange lights cascade from its art nouveau arches and chandeliers twirl and twinkle from the enormous Christmas tree in the centre of the store. If only you could blink away the crowds, it would be everything you imagine an enchanting Noël in Paris to be.

On the ground floor, Hermès scarves are softly wrapped in tissue paper and placed in crisp orange boxes. Everywhere is the wafting of fragrance, as one would

expect from the largest perfumery in the world. A glittering *Étoile* section has been installed on the third floor with fragile baubles and cherubs to deck the hall. Along with your Fragonard candle, you can pick up a box of Belgian chocolate cigars or sweet treats from Fauchon presented in a pyramid of pale pink tins.

It's up on the fifth floor among toys and screaming toddlers that I stand at a counter ten-deep with customers to buy a triplet doll dressed in *une robe de Noël*. *Les Triplés*, by Nicole Lambert, is Georgie's favourite French comic strip about the antics of a set of adorable, naughty triplets (whose mother is gorgeous and glamorous at all times, albeit a tad flustered). Wildly popular, it has flourished into an emporium.

I fight a tide of women armed with sleeping *Corolle* dolls and triplets in boxes. Finally my doll is placed in a plastic bag and I am directed to one of the myriad counters installed for pre-Christmas gift-wrapping; they're also ten-deep with customers. Given the Parisian sense of style, I'm sure it will be worth the wait.

I watch as an earnest young man is given *une sucette* (lollipop) to wrap. He diligently assesses various boxes for size, slowly, one by one, before ditching the lot and deciding on exquisite gift paper adorned with French Christmas text. This alone takes five minutes. I begin to fidget and glance at my watch. The queue seems transfixed.

Ever so carefully he wraps *la sucette* and positions the tape. Ever so meticulously he ties the ribbon. And ever so artistically he curls it.

Solemnly he positions a red sticker adorned with a prancing black reindeer on his creation and holds it at arm's length to evaluate his work. It flashes through my mind that this perfect presentation will probably be ripped apart in a flash by an excited child not in the least interested in anything but the contents. The ribbon is fussed with, rearranged. The gift is complete. It has taken almost ten minutes but the result is a masterpiece. Proudly he holds it up for his audience to be greeted by a round of approving nods and *bravos*.

It is times like these I have to remind myself to relax and enjoy the occasion. How often is wrapping a lollipop elevated to an art form?

Galeries Lafayette
40, blvd Haussmann, 75009
Tel: 01 42 82 34 56
www.galerieslafayette.com

The *doyenne* of department stores, Galeries Lafayette.

Galeries Lafayette on boulevard Haussmann, home to Paris's *grands magasins*

Le Pain d'Épice

What's unique and remarkable about Paris is that so many elements of life are raised to an art form. If the French do something, they do it properly and perfectly, with enormous attention to aesthetics. Style is infused into every intricate detail, even down to the eye-pleasing, patterned air vents on the outside of buildings.

How could you not be captivated?

Walking the streets is like witnessing a continuous slideshow of beautiful things; snapshots of art. I pause to stare at whimsical hats, dreamy lingerie and tiny, artisan perfumeries whose scent drifts from open doors. Our noses are forever pressed against store windows, drooling over delicious handmade chocolate creations and multicoloured *tartes aux fruits*. French *art de vivre*, that intriguing mix of art and life, is always inexplicably present.

To window shop in French is to *faire du lèche-vitrines* (lick the windows). Never knowing what surprise you will find in the next store window fills every outing with pleasure.

Passing a chic boutique showered with tiny white lights mid-December, my eye is drawn to a forest of Christmas trees made from *pain d'épice* (gingerbread). They are dangling and twirling in the window, their trunks ceremoniously tied with red ribbon. Perfect, I think, for a ready-made Christmas activity: a bowl of icing, a packet of sprinkles and *voilà!*

'Look girls,' I say excitedly, pointing to the trees. 'Shall we buy some to decorate?' Annabelle is fixated on tugging my coat. I point to the candy canes and *bonbons* (lollies) and, getting carried away now, suggest we buy some of those too. The girls begin to giggle as I prattle on.

'But Mummy,' says Annabelle, pointing to the very bottom of the window, 'LOOK!' I look down, getting a child's (and dog's) eye view of bones tied with tartan ribbon and jewel-encrusted collars. Dog biscuit anyone?

L'Alphabet

Annabelle is busily practising French sounds accompanied by sign language – on *le métro,* in the bath, at the table. In what other country in the world would the sound and sign for the letter 'P' be likened to a cork popping from a bottle of Champagne?

A Spoon, SVP

I am feverishly devouring words on cereal boxes, milk containers, shampoo bottles and metro billboards in an effort to function at a basic linguistic level. Labels are stuck on objects all over the apartment; there are lists of French vocabulary in the bathroom and the lounge, on the kitchen wall. The girls' rooms are covered with conjugations. After each harrowing school day, I help Annabelle and Georgie with their homework as best I can – the splattered, dilapidated dictionary now a permanent fixture on the sink as I cook dinner. Having arrived in France with no French, I feel I am learning at an incredible pace, yet in reality the enormous catalogue of new words that reside in my head is of no use.

Vocabulary without the verbs and grammar is like being served a beautiful *crème brûlée* without a spoon. There is nothing you can do until the spoon arrives.

Julie calls, jaded.
She tells me how this morning she rang a restaurant to check on opening hours and the call had gone straight through to the answering machine. 'I had to call SEVEN TIMES to catch the whole message and write it down,' she despairs. 'It was SO fast!'

Pamplemousse Rose

It is a long and lovely winter evening, commencing with half a *pamplemousse rose* (pink grapefruit) topped with succulent prawns in a creamy dressing, and ending, late into the night, with a tangy lemon tart. We have been invited to our first dinner party in a French home. Finishing our *digestifs*, we farewell our new friends.

'Nice to meet you both,' we say with a smile, shaking the hands of the amicable French couple who were seated beside us. 'Perhaps we can get together again sometime.'

'That's very kind,' says the wife, ever so graciously, 'but we have enough friends, thank you.'

Le Bureau

Just as it generally takes a long time to be welcomed into a Parisian home, acceptance by colleagues in the workplace is also tediously slow. Olivia's mother, Jan, who works for a large multinational company, was surprised to learn one Friday that a colleague with whom she had been working closely was about to go on a week's annual leave.

'Are you going on vacation?' she asked.

'Well, actually I'm going on my honeymoon,' he replied.

'How can you work with someone for hours every day and keep that quiet?' she asked later in a shocked voice. 'Nobody knew that he was engaged or about to be married the next day and that's the way he wanted it. He left work with no collective present, no party, not even a good-luck drink!'

Private lives rarely spill over into working lives.

When Tim first started his job, he used to ask his colleagues as an ice-breaker on Monday mornings, 'So what did you do on the weekend?'

The standard reply was, 'We stayed in Paris.' Realising he was stepping into private territory, he stopped asking. In his colleagues' defence, why should they divulge details of their personal life? In Australia, by contrast, you can hear someone's entire life story in the office tearoom or standing at the supermarket checkout.

When I relay Jan's episode to Françoise, she warns, 'The French like to be individual and private, and certainly don't mix a lot with work people.'

Roving Gourmet on the Right Bank

South of the River Seine, *le Rive Gauche* (Left Bank) tempts with its laid-back cafés, bookshops and bohemian spirit, but for more formal glamour, *le Rive Droite* (Right Bank) wins hands down. At its heart are the gold-plated 1st and luxury-laden 8th *arrondissements*. The 1st, dominated by the Louvre Palace, is a patchwork of elegant squares and breathtaking gardens. The 8th centres on the Champs-Élysées and the Triangle d'Or neighbourhood of avenue Montaigne, rue François 1er and avenue George V. Here, horse chestnut trees line broad avenues, designer dogs sulk on fashion-house floors and haute couture rules.

The food is as stylish as the surroundings. Fashionable restaurants in sleek modern settings, celebrated gourmet stores and faithful old favourites result in a delicious melange of trend and tradition.

For an elegant introduction to the Right Bank, take a stroll via the Tuileries Gardens to **Café Marly** on the stone balcony of the Louvre Palace's Cour Napoléon. It has an uninterrupted view of architect I. M. Pei's glass pyramid. Come for a pastry and a pot of Mariage Frères tea delivered by dashing black-jacketed waiters, or while away the late afternoon sampling soft, creamy rounds of Rocamadour cheese washed down with a glass of Lalande de Pomerol. Late in the evening, when the pyramid glows golden, the terrace is jammed with the media and fashion pack.

Café Marly is the creation of restaurateur brothers Jean-Louis and Gilbert Costes, the pair behind many hip establishments in Paris including Le Georges restaurant atop the Centre Pompidou and the luxury Hôtel Costes on nearby rue St-Honoré. On occasion, it must be said, these gorgeous, fashion-driven settings outshine the food.

By contrast, the gardens of the Palais Royal nearby provide the setting for **Le Grand Véfour**, one of the city's oldest and most beautiful Michelin-starred restaurants where contemporary haute cuisine collides with 1850s decor. It is here that Napoléon courted Josephine. Inspirational chef Guy Martin presents dishes that are lively and bold, with an accent on truffles. Specialties include *foie gras* ravioli in a creamy truffled sauce, and rich and flavourful oxtail with puréed potatoes and truffles (shepherd's pie taken to new heights). The signature dessert is a surprising *crème brûlée* made with artichokes, garnished with sweet vegetables and served with almond sorbet.

Exit through the back of the gardens for a less formal meal. Just past the Paris Bourse (stock exchange), **Aux Lyonnais** has been serving up hearty fare from the Lyon region since 1890. Super-chef Alain Ducasse and Thierry de la Brosse (owner of esteemed Parisian bistro, L'Ami Louis) have taken over, restoring the deep red façade to its original charm and re-creating the interior with bevelled mirrors, a tiled floral wall frieze and zinc bar, all of which gives the feel of an authentic *bouchon Lyonnais*. Specials change regularly and include *quenelle à la Lyonnaise, sauce nantua* (a crayfish-dumpling recipe dating from 1892), traditional *charcuterie* served on a wooden board and a lighter rendition of classic *sabodet*, an earthy sausage dish made from pork.

Walk off lunch by winding your way west to the exclusive Place Vendôme. Its edges form a glittering necklace of jewellery shops, with the **Hôtel Ritz** its crowning glory. Nothing captures the Right Bank like the Ritz. Sink into a plush

velvet banquette in the rococo dining room of the luxurious two-star Michelin restaurant, l'Espadon, where chef Michel Roth delivers one of Paris's best dining experiences. By day, the pretty garden courtyard is filled with the perfume of flowers. By night, it flickers with candlelight. A superb wine list offers a choice of more than 1000 exceptional wines.

If dinner is out of the question, there's always a half-day demonstration class at the Ritz Escoffier School of gastronomy, afternoon tea in the Jardin Vendôme or a cocktail in the Hemingway Bar.

A stone's throw away, Chanel drifts down rue Royale and limousines jam Place de la Madeleine, the location of the majestic Madeleine church as well as two of the most revered gourmet stores in France. On one side of the square is **Fauchon**, dressed in pink; directly opposite is **Hédiard**, striking in red and black. Long-time rivals, they are equally glamorous and decadent. On special holidays, traffic grinds to a standstill on the square, with horns honking and cars double-parked as platters of salmon and pyramids of *macarons* disappear into waiting cars.

Fauchon began as a lowly fruit cart on Place de la Madeleine in 1886 and today reigns as Paris's grandest food emporium, stretching over half a block. Its specialist counters offer one-stop luxury shopping and fabulous gifts for gourmands. There is a *fromagerie*, *pâtisserie*, *boulangerie* and *traiteur* along with a staggering range of beautifully boxed delicacies and an exhaustive selection of premium French wines. Pick up a single, exquisitely packaged chocolate or black truffle, or a jar of honey collected from the rooftop of the Opéra Garnier. The privileged bees gather nectar and pollen from flower-filled window boxes and clipped city parks.

Hédiard is smaller but perhaps snobbier. A doorman ushers you in past baskets bursting with exotic fruits, perfect baby vegetables and bags of aromatic spices. A pioneer in importing mysterious produce from faraway lands, Ferdinand Hédiard set up on the square in 1854, and introduced the banana and pineapple to France. There are jewel-hued jams and dozens of rare teas and coffees, as well as a choice cellar.

Both Fauchon and Hédiard offer lavish party dishes, allowing the time-pressed society matron or executive to throw an effortless yet impressive dinner – as long as she remembers to dispose of the telltale boxes.

Dotted around the square are more treats for the gourmand. If you're feeling extravagant, indulge in some fresh black truffles from the Périgord region at **La Maison de la Truffe** for a mere 2490€/kilo. Equally appealing is a jar of Béluga caviar from **Caviar Kaspia**, or some pistachio and orange mustard from **Maille**, the most famous mustard house in France, founded in 1747. The Maille boutique

Fauchon, the grandest food emporium in Paris

Irresistible treats for
the gourmand at Hediard

stocks an exclusive collection, including fresh *moutarde* on tap, pumped into earthenware crocks. Giftbox sets and hand-painted replicas of antique mustard pots are also available.

Stocked up on gourmet goodies, it's time to head around the corner to rue du Faubourg-St-Honoré, home to Hermès, Dior and many more of the world's top designers of fashion and luxury goods. The couture houses of Triangle d'Or will still be there tomorrow . . .

Aux Lyonnais
32, rue St-Marc, 75002
Tel: 01 42 96 65 04
www.auxlyonnais.com

Café Marly
93, rue de Rivoli,
Cour Napoléon du Louvre, 75001
Tel: 01 49 26 06 60

Caviar Kaspia
17, Place de la Madeleine, 75008
Tel: 01 42 65 66 21
www.kaspia.fr.

Fauchon
24–26, Place de la Madeleine, 75008
Tel: 01 70 39 38 00
www.fauchon.com.

Hédiard
21, Place de la Madeleine, 75008
Tel: 01 43 12 88 88
www.hediard.fr.

Hôtel Ritz
15, Place Vendôme, 75001
Tel: 01 43 16 30 30
www.ritzparis.com.

La Maison de la Truffe
19, Place de la Madeleine, 75008
Tel: 01 42 65 53 22
www.maison-de-la-truffe.com

Le Grand Véfour
17, rue de Beaujolais, 75001
Tel: 01 42 96 56 27
www.grand-vefour.com

Maille
6, Place de la Madeleine, 75008
Tel: 01 40 15 06 00
www.maille.com.

When asked by a social-climbing Paris hostess how he liked his truffles, the celebrated twentieth-century food writer Curnonsky replied, 'In great quantity, Madame. In great quantity.'

L'Académie Américaine de Danse de Paris

The music starts. I watch Annabelle and Olivia exercise at *la barre* before skipping to the centre of the floor in their white leotards. They take their places.

'First position, *plié, grand plié*,' instructs Brooke, gently but firmly, as she floats around the dance studio shifting feet and repositioning arms. The class continues with lots of encouragement: '*C'est bien* Olivia, well done Annabelle, *bravo* girls.' Dare I say it, but I think the girls are having 'fun'. I relax to the music and sink back into my chair, happy that we have found not only a great new ballet school, but a steam vent.

L'Académie Américaine de Danse de Paris was recently founded by Brooke Desnoës, an energetic American with blonde curls, a warm smile, kind blue eyes and a soft Southern accent. Originally from Alabama, she danced professionally with the Scottish–American Ballet under the direction of Alexander Bennett before coming to France. As the first American classical dance school established in Europe, the Academy offers Paris a fresh, new teaching philosophy. Most importantly for us, the students are enveloped in a caring, nurturing environment with no yelling and no pushing around. Nevertheless, there is still discipline and respect, and students are required to put in the effort. Every class is bilingual in approach, although, of course, many ballet terms are *en français*. Today is open day for parents. A French couple and Olivia's father, Steve, join me to watch our girls dance. Between classes we all visit a tea salon down the street. Halfway through her chocolate éclair Georgie says, 'Oh, I forgot! Brooke told us not to eat anything too heavy before ballet, especially today.' She looks alarmed for a moment, and then with a '*Ce n'est pas grave*' (It is not serious), takes another bite.

The back wall is lined with large, red tins of tea. The adults choose a tea each

L' Académie Américaine
de Danse de Paris

Presents
The
Nutcracker
A children's ballet performed
by children for children

December 18, 1999
4:00 pm

6, rue Albert de
Lapparent
75007 Paris

For Ticket
Information
Call
01.56.08.14.26

Ticket Order Form

Name : _____

Address : _____

Tel. : _____   email : _____

_____ Child Ticket(s) 40 F each   _____ Adult Ticket(s) 60 F each

_____ Total Ticket(s) Ordered   _____ Total Amount Enclosed
Return with Check made payable to **Friends of AADP** and a self addressed
stamped envelope to :
L'Académie Américaine de Danse de Paris

Georgie à la barre

and presently, four steaming pots arrive at the table. The conversation soon turns from tea to alcohol. Steve and I explain that in the UK and Australia campaigning against drink-driving is extremely prominent and the general population is very aware of the dangers. Roads are patrolled and graphic advertising material shows the devastating consequences of drink-driving.

The Frenchwoman looks surprised.

'That will never come in France,' she says confidently. 'French people see it as their right to drink and drive. It would take away their independence, their freedom of choice.' This attitude seems to prevail about a lot of rules, especially on the road. Come to think of it, I've never seen a breathalyser unit on the streets.

As we pour another cup of tea, her husband announces that he thinks smoking in France has declined drastically over the past few years. To me, it looks like everybody smokes. *Non fumeur* sections are treated as a joke; people exhale into your food in restaurants, and onto your freshly washed hair at the hairdressers. Steve and I agree we have never seen any highly visible anti-smoking campaigns or billboards.

'They would not work in France; it would be a waste of time and money,' says the Frenchwoman.

This lack of pro-active campaigning and public health education seems to stem back to a stance of 'nobody has the right to tell us what to do' and 'the rest of the world is so puritanical'. Smoking is a Frenchman's right, like a baguette every day and parking on the pavement.

N.B. Smoking is now banned in cafés, bars and restaurants.

Les Toilettes

Nothing in Paris is easy. Even a trip to *les toilettes* can be complicated. Most toilets don't appear to have been renovated this century (or last) so it's wise to pray that you will be awarded a spotless one as you descend to the dungeon of an establishment, often down steep spiral stairs. Occasionally, you will come across an old-fashioned Turkish squat, which for females with handbag, winter coat, no coat hook and a wet floor can be especially challenging. If you're also wearing jeans, the task becomes a near impossible feat. This situation becomes even more dire if the light doesn't work or is on a timer switch, so that suddenly you are plunged into darkness.

If you are granted a modern toilet, beware: there may still be pitfalls. The toilet may be modern but the door and lock may well be old. During a weekend trip to Brittany, after banging on a jammed beach-café toilet door for fifteen minutes (family didn't notice I was missing) and yelling *attention* at the top of my lungs, I was finally rescued by a flashy Frenchman with a flashy Swiss army knife – and made a relieved entrance to an applauding crowd. Later I learnt that shouting *attention* does not mean 'give me attention, please', but 'watch out, be careful'. So what was this woman doing yelling 'watch out, be careful' from inside the toilet cubicle?

Lesson 1: If the lock looks dodgy don't lock the door, but as many doors must be in the locked position to make the light turn on, you may find yourself in darkness. If you happen to be in a more modern toilet it may be unisex, so do not be alarmed if a man walks into your dark cubicle through your unlocked door.

Lesson 2: Don't go anywhere without your pocketknife (or pocket dictionary).

N.B. Help is *au secours*.

If you're desperate to go, you may have to take your chances in one of the space-age, rocket-ship toilets to be found on street corners. Surrounded by ancient apartment buildings and beauty in every direction, *les sanisettes* stand out like beacons, the sun catching itself in horror on their shiny aluminium doors. You put a coin in the slot and the curved door mysteriously slides open. You step inside wondering if you are about to meet Dr Who and the door slowly slides shut behind you. You emerge with a sigh of relief back to the outside world. But a word of warning – the units have an automatic cleaning cycle that operates when the cubicle is presumed empty. A woman dying for a pee but having no coins slipped in after another patron, or so the story goes. With the door fastened shut, she was snuffed out by the fumes.

If you're now thinking that toilets supervised by attendants may be the safest option, think again.

Crunching through Parc Monceau to catch the metro home after school one afternoon, Annabelle tells me she is bursting to go. We make a quick detour to the eighteenth-century tollhouse on the edge of the park, which houses *les toilettes*. Dashing in, we are stopped by a crabby attendant who informs us we must buy *un jeton* (token). I whip out my purse, place a couple of coins on the counter and receive the token. I push it into the slot in the door and it drops down with a clang. I push on the door. It doesn't budge.

'*Excusez-moi, Madame*,' I say urgently, and reluctantly she slides off her chair. She glares at the door, she glares at me, and she accuses me of stealing her *jeton*.

Just why I would want to steal her *jeton* when I have a cross-legged child in tow is beyond me. I plead with her to open the door. Instead, she offers me a mouthful of colourful expletives before grabbing my purse and inspecting every corner of it in search of the stolen *jeton*. She doesn't find it.

I refuse to pay again, on principle. She refuses, with folded arms, to let Annabelle in. As far as I can see, there is only one thing to do. I pick Annabelle up, run out of the tollhouse and jump the fence onto the manicured, FORBIDDEN lawn of Parc Monceau. Coat up, pants down, deed done! We escape down the metro steps as we hear the whistle-wielding *police du parc* starting to close in on us – just before we are arrested for trespassing, urinating in a public place and indecent exposure.

The eighteenth-century tollhouse housing *les toilettes* at Parc Monceau

Julie calls, baffled.

She explains that her favourite coat was ready to be picked up from the dry-cleaners, but that she had lost her ticket. So on Thursday, she popped into the drycleaners after practising in French, 'I want to pick up my coat which was due for collection today, but unfortunately I have mislaid my ticket'.

'Well then, there is nothing we can do,' Monsieur glared with a shrug of the shoulders, turning to the next customer. Bewildered, Julie went home and turned her purse inside-out and her apartment upside-down but there was still no sign of the ticket. Undeterred, she decided to study French words that had anything to do with coats and their styles, materials and colours.

On Friday, Julie braced herself and returned to the drycleaners. She described her coat in elaborate detail only to be told, 'But, Madame, your coat was due to be picked up yesterday. Why didn't you pick your coat up?'

'Because I couldn't find my ticket,' she said.

'Well then, now we can't find your coat and it's your fault because you didn't pick it up on the right day.' Restraining herself from jumping over the counter to whack Monsieur Le Drycleaner, Julie went home and studied French words that had anything to do with higher authorities, police, exposure and legal action.

On Saturday, she put on her battle gear and strode into the drycleaners. Her practised rant fell flat on Monsieur Le Drycleaner, who shrugged his shoulders and kept serving.

After one more attempt and a lot of newly acquired French phrases later (including a couple of words not in the standard dictionary), she gave up.

'In Paris, one is always reminded of being a foreigner. If you park your car wrong, it is not the fact that it's on the sidewalk that matters, but the fact that you speak with an accent.'

Roman Polanski

Les Résultats

Last day of school before spring holidays. Annabelle's report is sparse in words and rather blunt in places: *créatif – non; sens des responsabilités – non; fait preuve d'imagination – non* (creative – no; sense of responsibility – no; proof of imagination – no).

Les Amis

'What's the point of learning French if you can't practise it with the French?' a Dutch friend laments over coffee at Le Vigny. 'Even though I am in the middle of Paris,' she moans, 'I feel very much on the outer of French life and society. Unless you marry into a French family, you are never going to be fully accepted.' Everyone nods in agreement.

For new arrivals, this insular culture – coupled with poor French language skills – can make life particularly challenging and exasperating. There are some elements of society simply impossible to penetrate, closed to foreigners, out of bounds. Even expats who have lived in Paris for years don't necessarily feel fully integrated. It takes a while to comprehend that fluency doesn't give you an automatic entrée into Parisian society.

A surprising outcome of living in Paris, largely in reaction to French ways, is that we have formed friendships with families from an array of countries, widening our knowledge of many other cultures. David, for example, has introduced us to Chinatown at Belleville and we often join him and Elaine for lunch at his favourite restaurant, **Le Président**. Iris has passed on her delicious recipes for the traditional German Christmas cookies that take over her kitchen in December.

Most of our friends have lived outside of France and are more open-minded and accepting of other cultures and ways of life. A number of couples consist of one French and one expat partner; the downside of this is that the French partner usually speaks excellent English, which results in most conversations reverting to *anglais* – making it even harder to practise your French with the French.

Serge takes more orders. The banter turns to the looming *grandes vacances*, the almost obligatory summer holiday that coincides with the end of the school year and the closing of many shops and offices.

'I have never met so many people who have never left their own country,' says Jan, 'especially in Europe.' She tells us that she asked her boss where he was going over the summer. He replied, 'To the south of France as we always do.'

'I asked him if he'd travelled much outside of France and he looked at me as if I were mad and said, "No, and why would I need to? We have the best of everything right here: the best food, the best wine, the best mountains, the best beaches, the best countryside, the best culture and the best city in the world."'

We all gasp, shocked, but come to think of it, some Australians also believe they live in the best country in the world!

Le Président
120, rue du Faubourg-du-Temple, 75011
Tel: 01 47 00 17 18

Le Concert

We wait outside the heavy black doors until they are opened by *la directrice* (principal) and climb the stairs to Annabelle's classroom with the other *grande section* parents. It is Annabelle's end-of-year class concert (yes, we have survived one school year) and while Tim and I are looking forward to the entertainment, we are also excited about seeing her classroom for the first time. On this sticky June day, we squeeze into the tiny room and wait eagerly for the show to begin.

First up, we watch each five-year-old in their navy smock jump up and over the seat of a chair to great applause. Next, we are entertained by observing all twenty-seven students jump over a rope held 2 inches off the ground. The French parents beam at their athletic prowess. Unbeknown to us, Annabelle had her little finger stepped on by the class bully just as the concert began and refused to participate in either activity. We thought she was quietly rebelling.

⚜

Afterwards, we go straight to a parents' meeting for the *adaptation* students entering the straight French system in September. Georgie will be entering 8ème, corresponding to our grade 4. She will be expected to keep up with native speakers and learn new concepts at the French academic standard expected for her age. Memory and the need to learn things by heart are stressed time and again.

'Anything asked of your child that entails learning by heart must be taken very seriously,' says *la directrice*. 'There is no time to learn things by heart at school, like verb conjugation; it must be done at home.' This makes sense, but I shudder at the extra homework.

'Come September, French must come first. They must read from French books every night. Watch only French television.' (When are they going to have time for that!) 'To an extent,' she says, 'they have all been somewhat privileged in the cocoon of *adaptation*. Now they will be treated like the French.' She smiles.

'Over the summer vacation it is vitally important that your child reads and speaks French every single day. Otherwise it will be forgotten and they will be desperate when they return and are thrown into a straight French class. But do not expect too much of your child. 4/10 for a test in creative writing is very good against children who have been writing in French all their lives.' (Just devastating for the self-esteem.)

Then there is the issue of whether to start a third language or not. (Forget it!)

Annabelle, of course, was thrown straight into the French system, but at her age has been lucky enough to have learnt through play. The curriculum is set with exacting precision and, while she is learning to read, she has not as yet been introduced to writing or had any formal homework. That will start this September in 11ème, and will include reciting a lot of French poetry.

Skipping about Town: Paris for Children

The puppeteer swoops into our metro carriage just as the doors clap shut. He flaps open his black sheet. Quickly he ties it between two poles at the front and disappears. Georgie and Annabelle look up in expectation, along with all of the children in the carriage, some swivelling in their seats for a better view. Loud music starts and a puppet begins dancing wildly above the sheet. The train rounds the long corner to Kléber metro station, straightens up and stops. So does the puppet and the music. In a flash, the sheet is down, coins jangle into the puppeteer's hat and he runs into the next carriage.

The Corinthian colonnade, Parc Monceau

For children, wide-eyed and full of wonder, the simple pleasures of Paris and chance encounters with ordinary Parisian life are often more memorable than methodically ticking off monuments. The girls are just as happy patting the dogs that go by and watching French games in *le parc*.

Paris is full of children who live in apartments without gardens, so the city's green spaces are an integral part of daily life, offering places to play and patches of tranquillity. There are plenty of neighbourhood parks, varying in size and style from grand formal gardens to tiny pockets of peace in the most unlikely of places. For the visitor, they provide a looking glass into French culture and the personality of the neighbourhood. At dusk, the park police blow their whistles, a signal that gates will be locked for the night – a practice that keeps all city parks clean and safe.

Walk through the gilded gates of **Parc Monceau** and bump into classic, old-fashioned Paris where smartly dressed couples promenade arm in arm. The park is graced with six statues of great French writers and musicians, which are fun to find, as well as waterfalls and a moss-covered Corinthian colonnade that runs around the edge of a lily pond. Schoolchildren play along the central path after lunch, each year-level designated to stay and play between consecutive lampposts (the public playground is forbidden). Watch for the popular game *Un, Deux, Trois, Soleil* (One, Two, Three, Sun).

In contrast, the futuristic **Parc André Citroën**, built on the site of the old Citroën automobile factory in the 15th, is all glass and clean lines. There are gigantic greenhouses, concrete bridges and trickling canals, as well as a huge map of Paris to scamper over. A tethered hot-air balloon provides a fun way to view the city. The real drawcard, though, is the fountain installation. On hot summer days when there is little relief from the heat, parents bring children to run and squeal through the tiled square punctuated with hundreds of holes that squirt fountains of water unpredictably at random heights and pressure into the air. The girls have spent many afternoons here in their bathers, running amok and balancing balls on the jets.

Children who really need to run wild will enjoy the sprawling **Bois de Boulogne** – 865 hectares of forest on the western edge of the city. Crisscrossed with muddy bridle paths, and walking and cycle tracks, it is to Parisians what Central Park is to New Yorkers. Formerly a royal forest and hunting ground, it's now full of families seeking the country life on *le weekend*. Bikes and horses can be rented, as can the rowboats on the lake. The **Jardin d'Acclimatation**, an old-world children's fairground, is also tucked away in Le Bois.

One of our favourite little picnic spots is conveniently situated around the corner from chic Left Bank department store Le Bon Marché (and its fabulous food hall, La Grande Épicerie). Dating to 1633, the **Jardin Catherine Labouré** was originally the *potager* (kitchen garden) of a convent, and later bestowed on the public by the nuns. Surrounded by tall stone walls and entered through a discreet gate, this delightful secret garden has a quiet, provincial charm. Sometimes we slip here between ballet classes to read and relax on the sunlight-dappled grass. There are fruit trees and flowers, a shady grapevine-covered walkway and, in keeping with history, a community *potager* where garden-deprived children of the neighbourhood can monitor the magical growth of green beans, tomatoes, basil and artichokes.

Another secret family spot is **Allée des Cygnes** (Path of the Swans), a lane that runs the length of Île des Cygnes, a small, manmade island in the middle of the Seine. Located southwest of the Eiffel Tower, it is not an area tourists have any reason to visit, leaving its serenity mostly to those who live nearby. At the far end is a small-scale replica of the Statue of Liberty. Canopied by spreading horse chestnut trees, a walk down the central path is like escaping to the country. Birds circle above fishermen who sit peacefully dangling their legs and their lines. Dogs scamper past and couples relax on the benches, watching the grey Seine sweep by and listening to the soft drone of the river barges. It's about as far away as one can get from the city without leaving it. Whenever school is getting her down, Île des Cygnes is the one place Georgie wants to go – it's the only spot nearby safe enough to ride her bike. During the warmer months, an alternative way to see the river is to take a ramble along the Right Bank quay on a Sunday, when the roads east of the Tuileries Gardens are closed to motorised traffic. Bikes and scooters sail past a roving trail of dogs, skipping ropes and strollers.

In winter we sometimes head to Hôtel de Ville for a skate, when the large square transforms into a shiny white ice-rink. Around its rim, chestnuts roast, crêpes cook and an antique carousel twirls. Paris has more than two dozen carousels. Many were carved in the Belle Époque and have delighted generations of children ever since. Take a spin on the Venetian merry-go-round at the foot of Sacré-Cœur, or whiz around on the endangered-species carousel in the Jardin des Plantes. Georgie likes to ride the wistful, long-extinct dodo while Annabelle prefers the bright green Tyrannosaurus Rex. But perhaps because it's just down the road, their firm favourite is the vintage double-decker at Place de Varsovie, with its prancing wooden horses, swings and carriages.

Eating *en famille* is extremely important to the French and dining out is another way to be quickly immersed into local culture. Most cafés and brasseries

offer *un menu enfant* for under twelves, a good-value children's menu consisting of a main course, drink and dessert. To look like a local kid, tuck into *steak haché* (high-quality hamburger patty), *poulet frites* (chicken and chips) or *un croque monsieur* (fancy toasted ham and cheese sandwich). Chocolate mousse and *la coupe Parisienne* (three scoops of ice-cream) remain all-time favourite desserts.

To take home some French style, rue Vavin in the 6th near the Luxembourg Gardens offers a range of children's and babies' fashion as well as shoe stores and a children's hairdresser. **Petit Bateau** is the place preppy Parisians go for cotton basics, and for more affordable fashion with lots of colour, French style and detail, you can't beat the chain store **Du Pareil Au Même (DPAM).** This is the store that mothers dream of. The stock changes so frequently that I don't think I have ever stepped out the door empty-handed. There is always something new and wonderful. **Monoprix** is also an inexpensive option for children's clothing and gifts with French flair. If you're after the BCBG look, slip down to **Bonpoint**, where *les mamans* come in droves to snatch up a new-season party dress or two, flying out the door with sugar-pink bags.

Art is an integral part of French society, and galleries and museums are frequented by people of all ages. For the sanity of the whole family, it's best to expose children in measured doses. Often, mini-museums are more manageable and enjoyable. If you're brave enough to tackle the **Musée du Louvre**, turn the outing into a treasure hunt. Focus on one section and allow small children to choose five postcards of paintings before letting them loose to find the real thing.

The **Centre Pompidou** with its colourful external pipes is a great way to introduce children to modern art. Jugglers and performers clutter the sweeping Place Georges Pompidou and around the corner at Place Igor Stravinsky is the city's first contemporary fountain. The **Cité des Sciences et de l'Industrie**, featuring hands-on design and technology activities, is eternally popular with local kids, as is the **Musée des Arts et Métiers,** the historic science museum. Set in a medieval abbey, it boasts a collection of thousands of machines, drawings and models, including the Lumière brothers' cinematograph.

Finally, the most spectacular view of the City of Light will always be from the top of the Eiffel Tower. Zoom up as darkness falls. Queues are generally shorter and lifts run late into the night. High above the orange chimney pots, children love identifying each landmark. As Paris slowly lights up, rest assured that you have shown your children not just the glitter of the Eiffel Tower but also the treasure that lies beneath.

Le Jardin d'Acclimatation
PLEIN TARIF

PARKS/GARDENS

Allée des Cygnes
Île des Cygnes, 75015/75016
Metro: Bir-Hakeim/Passy

Bois de Boulogne
Metro: Porte Maillot/
Porte Dauphine/Les Sablons/
Porte d'Auteuil
(Bikes available for hire across
from main entrance of **Jardin
d'Acclimatation**. Metro:
Les Sablons/Porte Maillot)

Jardin Catherine Labouré
29, rue de Babylone, 75007
Metro: Sèvres-Babylone

Parc André Citroën
Metro: Javel-André Citroën/
Balard

Parc Monceau
Metro: Monceau/Courcelles

BOUTIQUES

www.bonpoint.com
www.dpam.fr
www.monoprix.fr
www.petit-bateau.fr

GALLERIES/MUSEUMS

Centre Pompidou
Place Georges Pompidou, 75004
Tel: 01 44 78 12 33
www.centrepompidou.fr

**Cité des Sciences
et de l'Industrie**
30, ave Corentin-Cariou, 75019
Tel: 01 40 05 70 00
www.cite-sciences.fr

Musée des Arts et Métiers
60, rue Réaumur, 75003
Tel: 01 53 01 82 00
www.arts-et-metiers.net

Musée du Louvre
99, rue de Rivoli, 75001
Tel: 01 40 20 50 50
www.louvre.fr

Berthillon

It's only a hop, skip and jump from Notre-Dame cathedral over to the enchanting Île St-Louis for a taste of Paris's favourite ice-cream. There is nothing better than standing on the Pont St-Louis watching the boats ply by while licking a Berthillon sorbet. The famous artisanal *glaces* are sold in many cafés on the island and around the city but the original store is at 29–31, rue St-Louis-en-l'Île where, during warmer months, a neverending queue chooses from seventy or more rotating *parfums* (flavours).

We are working our way through the luxurious list. So far, favourites include cinnamon, blood orange, strawberry of the woods, gingerbread and blackcurrant. Made from natural ingredients, the sorbets are so intense that the fruit seems to ripen and explode in your mouth. Purists may prefer the incredibly creamy vanilla speckled with real vanilla bean. One hot day we saw three snow-white little dogs taking turns to lick a vanilla cone outside the store. *Chocolat* would be *une cat-a-strophe*!

N.B. The primary store is operated by descendants of Monsieur Berthillon who faithfully abide to French tradition, shutting their doors peak summer.

Julie calls, bewildered.

With everyone in holiday mode and the summer evenings still long, Mark had finally got around to calling up his long-lost French relatives and invited them for a casual dinner. He thought something relaxed and friendly would be appropriate, having never met them before.

'Let's eat early,' he said, 'then take the kids over to the Champ de Mars to play while it's still light.'

'*Quelle bonne idée*,' they said, and arrived late afternoon. Being a tad nervous about what to serve, Julie had decided on a lovely, light tangle of primavera pasta loaded with bright, fresh vegetables, and a big green salad. A plate of ripe seasonal cheeses from the market with some crusty baguette to start, some Australian white wine, and *voilà*! Perhaps they could stop for ice-cream on their way home from the park.

'Well,' Julie says, with a sigh, 'nobody touched the cheese because, *bien sûr*, the French only eat cheese *after* main course, even in the home of Australians. You know, if I went to a Japanese home in Australia, I would respect their customs. Why should I have to follow the French way if I am not familiar with it? It was like the cheese had a magnetic field around it.'

I giggle and ask, 'Did they like the pasta?'

'They loved the pasta,' says Julie, 'but I was a bit puzzled when they called it a salad.

'Anyway, we went for a walk but on the way home they kept stopping at restaurants and looking at menus.'

'Yeah, I'm guilty of that too; can't help myself.'

'Yes, but wait for it. One of Mark's aunts then cried out, "Oh, this one looks lovely!" "*Oui, très bon*," replied one of the cousins and before we knew it, they all bolted in and asked for a table,' said Julie. 'We followed, a little confused. Then – you won't believe it – they ordered an entire dinner! So we ordered a couple of courses too and forced them down. The kids just looked at us like, what's going on?

'So *my* dinner was just a little appetiser,' she moans.

'Next time they come to dinner, Julie, you might have to do the whole proper French thing,' I say.

'I know,' she heaves another sigh, 'with the right number of courses and everything in the correct order. But you know what I still don't understand?'

'What?' I ask.

'How they are ALL SO THIN?'

Le 14 Juillet

Just as we are mourning the fact that we're without a good, high vantage point to enjoy the fireworks on the Champ de Mars in comfort, Tim and I receive a welcome invitation to a Bastille Day dinner at the Australian ambassador's residence in the Australian Embassy.

Commonly known as *le quatorze juillet*, Bastille Day is the French national holiday that commemorates the storming of the Bastille prison on 14 July 1789. It marks the beginning of the French Revolution and symbolises the new republic with its ideals of *liberté, égalité, fraternité*. Festivities are held in the morning on the Champs-Élysées with military parades and *tricolore* flags. A quirk of tradition sees fire stations open their doors to the public for live demonstrations and dancing (*Bals des pompiers*), and in the evening the skies light up with fireworks.

We start with *apéritifs* in the salon of the ambassador's seventh-floor residence, the full-length windows providing a panoramic view of the city. Outside, the vast terrace reaches out to kiss the Champ de Mars, the Eiffel Tower so close it feels like it's hurtling towards us. As night falls, it gradually becomes gold-plated before our eyes.

We are seated for a late dinner on the terrace with a bunch of rather snooty *septième* types. Conversation is trite; the fireworks are yet to begin. My glass is topped up and without thinking I raise it and say, 'Happy Bastille Day.'

The table falls even more silent, followed by sniggering.

The Frenchman across the table looks at me intently before saying, 'No, Madame, it was not a happy day.'

Let the fireworks begin.

L'Arc de Triomphe

One of Paris's landmark monuments, the Arc de Triomphe was built by Napoléon as a tribute to those who fought for France and to commemorate the victories of his armies. At 50 metres high, 45 metres wide and 22 metres deep, it is the world's largest triumphal arch, and is decorated with intricate battle scenes and sculptures. It is also known as *l'Étoile* (The Star), as twelve major avenues radiate from the monument. Underneath is one of the city's major metro stations, Charles de Gaulle–Étoile. Visitors can climb the 284 steps to the top of the Arc for a panoramic view of Paris, but we find it far more thrilling to peer straight down for a bird's-eye view of the traffic below. The accompanying acoustics add to the pandemonium.

How to drive around the Arc like a Parisian:

* Zip your windows up.
* Turn your radio up.
* Put one hand on the wheel and the other on the horn.
* Look straight ahead and keep your nerve.
* Put your foot to the floor and zoom into the roundabout (vehicles already on the Arc must give way to incoming traffic).
* Ignore all horns and screeches, if you can hear them.
* Shout and swear and make rude gestures with your fingers if anyone gets in your way. Even elegant Parisian women do this. *Bah oui!* (Well yes!) It is called survival . . .
* When it's nearly time to exit, nudge towards the outside of the roundabout. Then put your foot to the floor and drive straight out, otherwise, *zut alors*, you risk getting stuck in a whirlpool!

Le Renard

We stop to let a gaggle of geese waddle across the road. Stone farmhouses and barns with black slate roofs sit peacefully behind thickets of trees. There are makeshift signs for *foie gras fermier*, fields of maize and crumpled sunflowers. Meandering through the sunlit back roads of the Périgord, we finally shake off the pace of Paris, passing green hills, quietly flowing streams and sleepy villages.

We are on our way to the seaside resort of Biarritz in the Pyrénées for our *grandes vacances*. Close to the Spanish border, it is an excellent location in which to explore both southwest France and the mountainous Basque country. A former playground of the rich and famous, it now exudes a faded, old-world charm. Striped canvas tents still line the sandy Grande Plage and although they haven't been compulsory for 'changing' since the 1930s, they have become an interesting landmark.

Most of the Pays Basque is in Spain with just 10 per cent lying in France. The region's oldest inhabitants, the Basque people, have kept a strong identity and hold their own language, culture and folklore dear, with music festivals, bullfights, circuses and games of *pelota*. Bayonne, the capital of the French Pays Basque, is known for its superb ham, while restaurants in the popular coastal resort towns serve up the local specialty of *chipirones* (baby squid), cooked in their own ink.

Once we have explored Biarritz, we take a trip to the summit of La Rhune. The little wooden train rattles its way up the steep mountain and through the clouds, past goats and ponies and lone whitewashed houses. We see the odd hiker with a *makila*, a traditional, handcrafted Basque shepherd's staff. At the summit, it is desolate. A line on the ground marks the border of France and Spain; standing on the top of the world the girls plant a foot in each country.

North of Biarritz is Landes, a heavily forested region of France bordered by the crashing Atlantic Ocean that attracts a large influx of holidaymakers in summer. Although officially outside the Basque region, it is still imbued with an intriguing mix of French and Spanish influences. This mix is what makes the entire coast so enticing – and the produce markets a food lover's dream.

At the vibrant Vieux-Boucau-les-Bains market we find vendors cooking up enormous pans of paella and *poulet Basque* and selling seafood in little boats. Strings of garlic and pimento chilli hang from awnings. A vendor wearing a beret deftly carves up a leg of Bayonne ham. Behind him, rows of guinea fowl, rabbits and ducklings sizzle and spit on the rôtisserie, dripping fat onto the potatoes roasting below. There are bowls of spicy olives, Armagnac and local wines to sample along with slivers of *gâteau Basque* in cherry and apricot flavours. This traditional cake is so revered that a museum has been set up in the hilltop town of Sare in its honour. Further on there are jars of *confit de canard*, Brebis (sheep's milk cheese from the Pyrénées), and cheese made from the milk of sheep dogs! Yet despite these wonderful new culinary sensations, it is a simple dinner at Le Renard, a farmhouse restaurant not far from Soustons, that becomes our sweetest memory, reinforcing that the best culinary adventures are often made of more than food . . .

We drive through the gate and up the lane towards the half-timbered farmhouse. As we approach, a man in his seventies comes out to greet us, dressed in brown corduroy trousers, a white shirt and bow tie. He motions for us to park next to the front door, before saluting us and opening all four car doors.

'*Bonsoir*,' he says with a smile, 'welcome to Le Renard.' He introduces himself as Lucky Luke. Then he introduces us to his black dog, Batman.

'*Il est bête*,' (He is stupid) he whispers, out of earshot of the dog. Next, he introduces his white cat, Robin, who is *intelligent*.

He takes us inside, past his wife in curlers and his daughter and son-in-law who are watching TV, before inviting us to sit down in the dining room: 'Please sit wherever you like.' We appear to have the place to ourselves. The room is warm and rustic with chintz curtains, pictures of dogs around the walls and softly glowing lamps. We sit down and Lucky Luke lights the candle.

'Do you have a regional wine you can recommend?' Tim asks.

'No, but I have something you will prefer,' says Lucky Luke. He excuses himself with a *j'arrive* and dashes over to the cellar of his 99-year-old mother, who lives across the way.

He's soon back with a bottle of flinty Chablis Chausseron.

'She still calls me *mon petit*,' (my little one) he says with a chuckle, 'even though I am seventy-five.' He explains that his grandmother lived to over 100. 'It's the slow and easy life down here,' he says, 'and, of course, all the duck fat.'

'What's on the menu for dinner?' I ask.

'The leftovers from lunch,' he says with smiling eyes, handing us *la carte*.

His daughter brings out a generous wedge of homemade pâté, some cornichons and crusty baguette to whet our appetites. We peruse the menu and Tim and I both decide on smoked Bayonne ham with thick slices of home-grown tomato drizzled with oil, followed by *magret de canard et pommes sautées* (breast of duck with sautéed potatoes).

'For you, girls,' says Lucky Luke, 'how about we cook up a little bit of veal with some crispy potatoes?'

'*Merci, Monsieur*,' they say. Then he asks the girls if they would like to see his new chestnut foal. 'I can also introduce you to our three horses – and a donkey who thinks he is a racehorse,' he says. He pours us a glass of wine and the girls run off with Lucky Luke, Batman and Robin while we sit back and enjoy this wonderfully warm and welcoming place.

We all finish our main course and order a serve of rustic pear tart in a puddle of *crème anglaise* and *un gâteau au chocolat,* as light as mousse. The desserts are all made by Lucky Luke's daughter.

'Would you like some ice-cream?' he asks the girls, who are patting Robin curled up in the windowsill.

'*Merci, Monsieur,*' they chime. He returns with two ice-cream bowls, each containing a ball of lemon, pistachio and chocolate *glace.*

After coffee, Lucky Luke delivers glasses of Armagnac, *gratuit* (on the house). He pours himself a glass of red, pulls up a chair for a chat and loosens his bow tie. He speaks no English but, thankfully, once you are out of Paris the pace of the language slows significantly and it's easier to identify where one word stops and another begins; we understand a good part of the conversation. He tells us that the wooded farm has been in his wife's family since 1790, or maybe longer but that's as far back as records go.

'In high summer the tourists come,' he says, 'but the locals come out here when it's cold and eat by the roaring fire. Sunday lunch is always busy.' He talks about French wine and the treasures in his mother's cellar, while Tim and I finish our *digestifs.*

The girls say *au revoir* to all the animals and give them a final pat as we say goodbye to Lucky Luke, who by now feels like an old friend. What a kind and generous man! Who says duck fat isn't good for the heart?

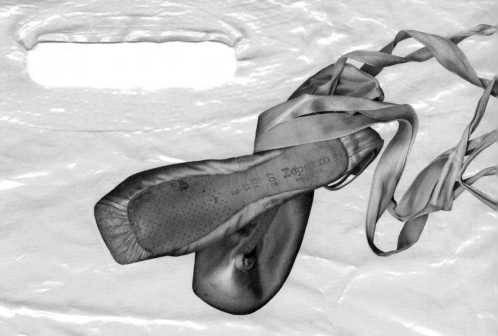

La Danse c'est...

Tepetto

PARIS

La Rentrée

It's the beginning of September. On the metro Parisians wearing dark-coloured jackets and pants sit perspiring through their tans, wiping brows and fanning themselves. Summer holidays are officially over, and the success of *les grandes vacances* is directly proportional to the degree to which one's skin is *bronzé*. Cashmere sweaters are once again thrown stylishly over shoulders, strappy sandals are banished to *la cave* and even the odd scarf is back, elegantly tied around tandooried necks. It seems that everyone has succumbed to warmer, more serious clothes in an attempt to psych themselves back to work and into the winter that already leers over September's suntanned shoulders.

La rentrée (the return) is once more upon us, and Paris pulls into full gear. It is a time of considerable cultural significance in France, when academic, social, political and commercial activity begin again in earnest.

Thoughts turn to preparation for school, a project in itself. The educational bookshops are brimming with hot, frustrated parents as they attempt to tick off everything on their children's punishing and exhausting school lists. In the space of a week we have collected 106 items. Included on the list for Annabelle: a wooden apprentice fountain pen with ink cartridges and blotting paper, *une règle NON FANTAISIE* (plain rulers please – no fun allowed), and *une ardoise*, which means 'slate' in French. As slate has now gone high-tech, we are handed a little plastic whiteboard.

With the school supplies taken care of, we join the queue of mothers and daughters spilling out of **Repetto**, the renowned ballet shoe and clothing store near l'Opéra Garnier. On Brigitte Bardot's request, Rose Repetto made the first ballet flats for the street in 1956, creating the classic Cendrillon Ballerina. Inside, boxes of exquisite pale pink slippers are sprawled across the floor, as budding ballerinas do their *relevé* on tippy toes and walk gingerly *en pointe* about the room.

With just a snatch of days left before school, we endeavour to embrace the last clutches of summer. The girls unleash some energy on the vast chequerboard of black-and-white stone columns in the gardens of the Palais Royal. Colette scribbled away in her flat overlooking these gardens. Jean Cocteau lived above La Muscade tearoom, where we guzzle down freshly squeezed *citron pressé* on the terrace. We hop on the punt over to Chalet des Îles in the Bois de Boulogne (the only means of access to this restaurant on a tiny island in the middle of the lake) for ice-cream.

On our last Saturday, we visit **Vaux-le-Vicomte**, a fairytale *château* southeast of Paris created by Nicolas Foquet, France's young Minister of Finance from 1653–1661. One of the superlative feats of seventeenth-century French architecture, it was the inspiration for Versailles. Candlelight evenings are held during the warmer months.

On our last Sunday, with Annabelle's little friends Claire and Olivia in tow, we watch clinking games of *pétanque* under the shady lime trees at the Jardin du Luxembourg. Lithe old men in white vests and worn sandals gather in groups and sit smoking fat cigars as they contemplate their next *boule*. One is not to be fooled by their casual appearance, for the game is taken seriously.

We strain to watch as the shooter crouches low. Aiming directly at the jack, he carefully brings his arm forward and up; the ball swoops high in the air before landing with a thud. He stays in this position, crouched like a wide-eyed wax figure until his fortune is revealed. The safe ball. The next player, 'the smasher', is much more exciting to watch. It's all or nothing. The crowd lulls, waiting for the crisp, sharp clank of a fast ball as it cleanly knocks out the nearest to the jack, winning the game. The risk-taker puffs out his chest as he walks away. He is patted on the back and handed a congratulatory glass of pastis. Ripping a piece of bread from his baguette with a flourish, he prepares for his next game – and we head home to prepare for *école*.

Repetto
22, rue de la Paix, 75002
Tel : 01 44 71 83 02
www.repetto.com

Vaux-le-Vicomte
Maincy, 77950
Tel: 01 64 14 41 90
http://www.vaux-le-vicomte.com
www.operaenpleinair.com

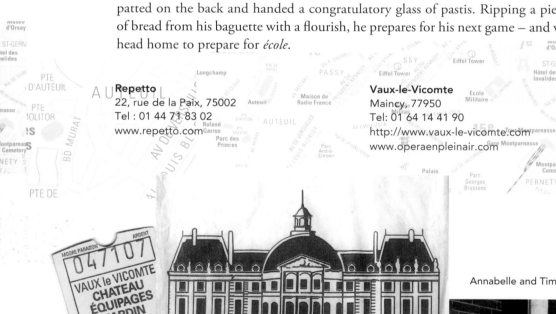

Annabelle and Tim: Sunday lunch

Insider Dining Tips

Whether it's biting into a *millefeuille* from a sweet-smelling *pâtisserie* or tucking into *cassoulet* at a candlelit bistro, Paris is about indulging your palate. In a city where culinary culture runs deep and gastronomic traditions are strong, dining at a Parisian table takes you straight to its heart. Although dynamic chefs are dishing up excellent contemporary fare, French cuisine remains tenaciously tied to its roots. Most visiting foreigners yearn for classic French dishes coupled with that elusive dollop of authentic Parisian ambience, changing a dining experience into a memory that lingers long after the last dreamy spoonful of chocolate soufflé. Add a handful of insider tips and your gourmet adventure will take on yet another dimension.

Most importantly, except for a quick café lunch or *menu express*, a French meal is expected to be leisurely. Sit back, keep conversations low and enjoy. Notre-Dame will still be there when you finish. Wherever you choose to dine, however, there are unspoken rules that apply. The city is full of old-fashioned codes of etiquette. To transgress these is seen as rude and that's where misunderstandings often begin. French waiters are professionals and take their job seriously. Waiting on tables, especially in more formal establishments, is regarded as a respected, life-long vocation, not a way to get through university. Be polite, earn a waiter's respect by asking his opinion, and get out of tourist Paris. The key to an authentic dining experience is to explore smaller streets and quieter quarters. Generally, the food is of superior quality and value, the staff are friendlier, and the clientele local.

As obvious as it sounds, always say *bonjour* when you enter a café, and wait to be seated at mealtimes. Many travellers don't, which starts them off on the wrong foot. With order-and-pay-at-the-counter-style cafés so prevalent in Australia, it's refreshing to sit and be waited on, even for coffee.

Obtaining the bill is not always easy. Never try to attract attention by calling *garçon*. Indicate from a distance by gesturing a signature or ask for *l'addition SVP*. For a waiter to hand you an unsolicited bill is regarded as very bad service. It is not for the waiter to judge when you are finished: you may want something more, a *digestif* perhaps, or simply wish to linger. You are expected to ask. (This can be mistaken for slow service.) Finally, always say *merci, au revoir* as you leave.

Le Café

Before you even think about sight-seeing, take a seat on a sunny café terrace and watch the world go by. It's the best way to feel instantly integrated into the city. Paris has a long-standing café society and today life still revolves around *le café*, which effectively becomes a backyard in summer and a lounge room in winter. Relax and sit for as long as you like; you won't overstay your welcome.

Coffee is mostly drunk short, black and strong. Ask for *un petit noir*, *un express* or simply *un café* – they are all the same. Throwing back a shot at *le zinc* (bar) will cost you half as much as a shot on the terrace. For those who can't take their shot without milk, try the very Parisian *noisette* – a short black with a dash of milk or small jug on the side. Milky *café crèmes* are rarely drunk by the French after midday and are deemed bad for digestion after a substantial meal. Leave them for the morning with a croissant. Save the cappuccinos for Italy. They are mostly below par. (*Crèmes* can also be hit or miss.) Leave a 10–20 cent tip each. If you can't leave a proper tip, it's best to leave nothing. There was once an angry waiter who ran after a tourist because she left a lousy tip. He gave it back, telling her she needed it more than he did.

Many cafés scribble their *plat du jour* (daily special) on a blackboard outside for all to see; reading these is a sure-fire way to whet the appetite while wandering the streets. Depending on the season, you might find anything from duck in green pepper sauce to a fresh Lyonnais salad tossed in creamy dressing. Alternatively, tuck into a café classic such as *steak frites*, or a fluffy omelette. The French like their meat served quite bloody, and generally order their steaks *saignant* or *à point*. This loosely equates with Australian blue/rare and medium–rare.

Most Parisians order *une carafe d'eau* (carafe of tap water) or a bottle of mineral water with their café lunch along with *un pichet* (pitcher or jug) of wine. A basket of sliced baguette is given with every meal. Bread rests on the tablecloth, not on your plate.

Le Bistro

Don't go home without dining at a classic little bistro serving honest, hearty fare. It's the perfect opportunity to indulge in simple, soul-satisfying French cooking. Many are small, family-run affairs full of charm, warmth and traditional home-style dishes. You might find cream of watercress soup, followed by crispy roast chicken with a golden potato gratin, or a richly sauced *daube provençale* delivered to your table in a cast-iron pot. Finish with a dessert that could have been lovingly made in a French farmhouse kitchen – a puckery apricot tart perhaps, or *crème caramel*.

Reserve a table for 8.30 or 9.00 p.m. to dine with the local crowd. This also gives you plenty of time beforehand to sit and relax on the terrace with *un kir*. A popular French cocktail made with a measure of *crème de cassis* topped up with white wine, *un kir* can also be made with blackberry or peach liqueur. If you prefer bubbles order *un kir royale*, made with Champagne.

To avoid confusion, it's helpful to know that the full bill of fare is called *la carte*, whereas *le menu* refers to a set number of courses with a small choice of daily specials, all for a fixed price. Choosing *le menu du jour* is an excellent, value-for-money way to eat if you want more than one course. It is the option locals often select.

La Brasserie

For another authentic slice of Paris, don't miss an entertaining dinner at a large, lively brasserie, complete with racing waiters in long starched aprons and plush burgundy banquettes. Dating from the sixteenth century, brasseries (literally translated as 'breweries') were originally owned by Alsatians who brewed their own beer and cooked up mountains of steaming *choucroute* (sauerkraut and assorted sausages) for a hungry crowd. Full of life and colour, they were often found near railway stations and became popular all over France, seducing patrons with their noisy charm. Dining rooms were large, extravagant affairs with endless banquettes and an endless buzz. Over time, the true definition of brasserie has been slowly diluted, and now simple corner cafés serving food falsely claim to be brasseries.

There are, however, a number of timeless venues that live on, although the best of them are known as much for their fanciful art nouveau and art deco interiors and boisterous atmosphere as for their monumental seafood platters. If you're craving a dozen freshly shucked oysters, great people-watching and a mythical ambience, you can't go wrong. Many provide all-day dining, and don't take reservations in the evening. Arrive just before 8 p.m. to avoid a long wait for a table.

Haute Cuisine

To dine in classical grandeur at a top Paris table is one of the ultimate experiences for epicureans, where sublime food is served beneath crystal chandeliers and impeccable waiters attend to your every whim. However, dinner can be prohibitively expensive. The trick is to reserve for lunch and order *le menu prix-fixe*. For a fraction of the cost of dinner, let yourself be carried away by the pomp and ceremony, safe in the knowledge that you are receiving an unforgettable, value-for-money dining experience – providing of course you don't splurge on a vintage Bordeaux!

Often in haute cuisine restaurants, a few tables are set aside for an international clientele and the remainder are reserved for French patrons. Ask your hotel concierge to reserve. A French speaker will not only have a better chance of securing a good table, but any table at all. While some haute cuisine restaurants require dinner reservations weeks (even months) ahead, a long lunch does not usually pose the same problem.

Before you go, brush up on French etiquette. In more formal situations, the person inviting will always enter a restaurant first. Generally, women are seated on the banquette against the wall, looking out onto the restaurant. Men get to focus on their partner (and the wall).

Haute cuisine always starts with *un apéritif* (*une coupe de Champagne*, perhaps) and *une amuse bouche*, a complimentary bite-sized hors d'oeuvre to excite the taste buds and 'amuse' the mouth, offering a glimpse of what is to come. This is followed by entrée, main course, cheese, dessert, coffee and digestive.

A formal meal offers the perfect opportunity to indulge in a lavish cheese course of exceptional quality; a must at least once during your visit to France. For many, it's the highlight of the French meal. When selecting from a large *chariot de fromages* (cheese cart), it is considered polite to choose four, maybe five, cheeses. (Six is really pushing it.) For smaller cheese selections the general rule is: if there are four cheeses, choose three, and if there are five cheeses, pick four – but never choose them all. Mix selections and regions, and try cheeses that vary in texture. Cut and eat your cheese with a knife and fork, followed by a bite of bread.

Late afternoon, when you finally emerge from your feast, you'll need a long promenade. Head for the Seine and take a leisurely stroll along its banks, past the *bouquinistes* (book stalls) and artists, and over the bridges of Paris. What better way to finish a most memorable meal?

Le Vigny . . . encore

'Her behaviour is just not acceptable – even in France,' proclaims an American woman in Le Vigny who describes her daughter's teacher as 'brutal'. After just two weeks back at school, mothers who have children entering the straight French section after *adaptation* are shocked and bewildered all over again. Teachers are showing absolutely no compassion towards children unable to grasp new work or react as speedily as their French counterparts. Uncompromising and remorseless, they do not acknowledge that our children may take longer to do their homework.

'*Adaptation* is a piece of cake compared to the French section,' recalls Karen as she sips her coffee, an old hand who has been in Paris for three or four years now.

All of last Saturday was taken up trying to help Georgie with her homework: long-winded French poems to be recited *parfaitement, par cœur* (perfectly, by heart); dates and events in French history, *parfaitement, par cœur*; the conjugation of four or five verbs, *parfaitement, par cœur*; and corrections and rewrites of last week's errors. No doubt homework time will decrease as her written French improves, but she will always be competing with native French speakers. Homework is set on Friday evenings for the week ahead, so this Saturday vigil, however daunting, will considerably lighten the weeknight load.

It is interesting to note that many American and Australian parents are stunned by the amount of homework our children are dished up as they enter the straight French system and by the way children are treated generally in schools in France. The English seem to have mixed opinions, depending on whether they themselves attended a strict boarding school, while some Asian parents think school here is a picnic.

To the French, of course, it is all taken for granted.

Les Bandes Dessinées

I have just muddled through my first *bande dessinée* or BD (comic book) in French, an entertaining and innovative way to improve essential French language skills, and guess what?

- Guns don't go bang, they go *pan*.
- If you hurt yourself you say *aïe*, not ouch.
- The sound of an ambulance siren is *pin-pon, pin-pon*.
- A crowing rooster does not say cock-a-doodle-do but *co-co-rico*.

Comic books have a huge following in France and are not restricted to children. **Fnac** is the place to go, a popular chain of stores packed with classic French comic strips along with the latest DVDs and music, books, French language aids, hi-fi and camera equipment. My favourite is the store at 26, avenue des Ternes in the 17th, a pleasant stroll from the Arc de Triomphe and a stone's throw from the Poncelet produce market. I could spend all day wading through its five fascinating floors.

On weekdays, when it's quieter, you will find otherwise serious adults propped against walls in their suits, sniggering away in their lunch-hour. On weekend afternoons, especially in inclement weather, Fnac is crammed with aficionados of all ages sitting on the floor engrossed in their favourite strip. While Georgie loves *Les Triplés* and *Lili*, Annabelle prefers *Tom Tom et Nana*. And then there's *Tintin* and *Lucky Luke*, the world's greatest cowboy who travels around delivering justice with his faithful companion, The Jolly Jumper, the smartest horse in the world. Lucky Luke can outshoot his shadow and lasso a whirlwind.

Astérix et Obélix is one of the most popular strips, revolving around the exploits of a village of ancient Gauls resisting Roman occupation. Several of the Franco–Belgian books have been adapted into films starring Gerard Depardieu. There is even a park themed around the series, **Parc Astérix**, providing a refreshing alternative to Disneyland Paris.

www.fnac.com
www.parcasterix.fr

La Recette

With the family settled into Parisian life and the new school year (to a degree), I finally get around to acquiring a French teacher *pour moi*. The company has approved a few hours of tuition. Through the girls at Le Vigny, I am delighted to find Margueritte, a chic Parisian in her fifties who is not only a great teacher but a *bon vivant* and gourmet. She comes to the apartment once a week for a two-hour lesson, often pulling a pungent cheese from her handbag for me to taste, or asking whether she can store her pâté in my fridge (I inevitably sample it first). Without fail, the subject turns to food.

Today, Margueritte gives me her recipe for *lapin-chasseur*, a rustic rabbit dish cooked with *champignons de Paris*, bacon and herbs in a rich tomato sauce.

'You simply must cook rabbit in September and October,' she urges, 'and *ma recette* (my recipe) is excellent because it keeps very well.' So it should – it calls for Cognac, Armagnac and 750 ml of white wine! A distinctive characteristic of basic French cuisine, Margueritte explains, is the addition of cream and wine to dishes.

'That is our secret,' she says discreetly, 'along with lots of butter, *bien sûr*. Whenever a recipe calls for water, replace it with wine and always add cream before serving.'

She also shares her recipe for *la poule au pot*, a dish that dates back to the time of Henri IV in the early 1600s. The 'Good King' decreased taxes and, in one of the first social policies, ensured that every needy family was given the ingredients to prepare boiled chicken and vegetables every Sunday. The chicken was filled with seasoned bread stuffing and the one-pot meal slowly simmered in the fireplace. The broth was served as a soup to start the meal, followed by the chicken and vegetables as a main course.

Les Devoirs

Georgie is beside herself after receiving -20/20 for her *dictée* (dictation) from a story by Colette. Her page is covered in ugly red pen. This means she has made 40 grammatical and accent errors – easily done in a new language. *La dictée* is to be corrected tonight on top of her regular homework (*les devoirs*), which includes learning a difficult poem *par cœur* in the future tense.

'It's not even funny and it doesn't even rhyme,' she says. 'It's just about Napoléon getting fat.' Crucial to memorise, I'm sure.

She sits in the kitchen and starts correcting her *dictée* while I start preparing dinner. The French/English dictionary, along with *La Bescherelle: La Conjugation Pour Tous* (a dictionary of 12,000 conjugated verbs) and *La Bescherelle: La Grammaire Pour Tous* (a dictionary of grammar in twenty-seven chapters) are ready on the table. I foresee a long evening ahead.

Meanwhile, Annabelle is lazing on the couch watching Mr Ed the talking horse dubbed into French, practising her *séries de mots* on her slate. These daily lists of vocabulary are to be learnt perfectly, by heart and in the correct order – even though the words have no connection to one other. And then you have to remember the accents . . .

I unwrap a log of goat's cheese for dinner and, fascinated, I read out the serving suggestion. Georgie giggles. It suggests *pommes de terre en robe de chambre au chèvre chaud* – potatoes in a warm dressing-gown of goat's cheese.

Lasagne au Crabe

This evening, we look forward to a sublime creation courtesy of Georgie. Today marks her first cooking class at Les Petits Cordons Bleus and *une lasagne au crabe* is on the menu, along with a tossed green salad. The yearlong certificate course gives wannabe chefs over eight the opportunity to create a masterpiece every Wednesday afternoon under the guidance of *un grand chef*.

But despite an impressive entrance onto the dining table, the lasagne is hardly touched. After a graphic description of the grisly preparation process, everyone loses their appetite; Georgie herself has decided to starve in protest. She informs us that she received her very own bucketful of crawling crabs to club, and the primitive weapon of death – a wooden rolling-pin.

Waiters at Café Marly, the Louvre Palace

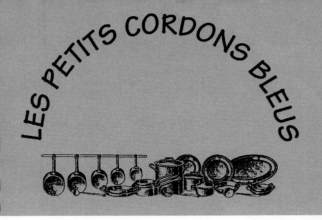

LES PETITS CORDONS BLEUS

LE CORDON BLEU
L'Art Culinaire
PARIS • LONDON • TOKYO

Georgina Paech

a suivi le Cours de Démonstration

et les Cours de Pratique

des *Petits Cordons Bleus*

de l'Ecole Le Cordon Bleu

du 18 avril au 28 juin 2000

ANDRÉ J COINTREAU, PRÉSIDENT   LA DIRECTION

LE CORDON BLEU, 8 RUE LÉON DELHOMME, 75015 PARIS, FRANCE. TEL: 33/1 53 68 22 50 FAX: 33/1 48 56 03 96

Fax 01/3 940 01 49   Fax 44 01/1 955 76 21   Fax 61/2 9809 5546

USA
Numéro vert aux USA et au Canada : 1 - 800 - 457 CHEF
Le Cordon Bleu's Corporate Office
404 Airport Executive Park Nanuet N.Y 10954 USA

Georgie's culinary creations

Le Ramonage

On a blustery afternoon in late October, I open the door to a sooty Dickensian character surrounded by a cloud of black dust and a collection of dirty brushes and brooms. Across his pocket in smudged, grey letters is embroidered the word *Ramonage*.

'*Bonjour, Madame*,' he rasps. 'Would you like your chimneys swept?'

I had been thinking how nice it would be to enjoy a fire in the dining room this winter. The central heating has just come on (the cut-off date for all heating to be turned on in Paris buildings is 15 October) but it just isn't the same as a crackling fire.

'How much to sweep two chimneys, Monsieur?'

'110 euros, Madame.'

'110 euros!' Well, he may look Dickensian but he certainly doesn't charge Dickensian prices.

'*Non merci*, maybe another time,' I answer, attempting to close the door.

'But it is *obligatoire*, Madame, if you have a chimney. Everyone has to have their chimneys swept, *tout le monde*,' he starts to shout, waving his murky hands in the general direction of the rest of Paris, '*tout le monde*, everybody!'

I try to close the door again and am starting to get a trifle scared when he sticks his broom in the door and says in a voice full of vengeance, 'If you light a fire without cleaning your chimneys, Madame, and one catches alight, you will be responsible for all damage caused to your neighbours if you cannot produce *un certificat de ramonage*.' It crosses my mind that the certificate could well be burnt to cinders. And then, with the whites of his eye shining through his sooty face, he whispers in his raspy voice, 'So, Madame – would you like your chimneys swept?'

La Leçon d'Art

Having an art lesson for the first time since arriving in France (they're scheduled once a month this year), creative little Georgie had to restrain herself from bounding up the school stairs this morning. (This is forbidden for good reason: the school owns three floors, which happen to be sandwiched between residential apartments. Would you like to live under a school?)

Her enthusiasm ended as the lesson began. Madame spent most of the time spouting dates and regurgitating information about the Renaissance –

no different to any other lesson really. Finally, the students were given a palette of black, white and grey paint, plus one bright colour each. Then they all proceeded to draw an identical picture.

Halfway through the painting process, Madame peeked over Georgie's shoulder, shook her head and said, '*Pas bien, Georgina, pas bien. Commence encore!*' Her painting was 'not good' and she was asked to start again because she had been unable to restrain herself from mixing the colours.

The next morning, Sharon and I walk to **Angelina** for morning tea. Across the street from the Tuileries Gardens, this grand tea parlour dating to 1903 is ensconced in a faded setting of Versailles-style mirrors and vast landscape murals. Once frequented by Audrey Hepburn, Gertrude Stein and Coco Chanel, Angelina's marble-topped tables and black leather chairs are now decorated with furs, the fashion set between shows and – like all Parisian institutions – plenty of tourists. We watch curt waitresses in frilly aprons serve tea and tarts from silver trays. *Une grande dame* shares her cake with her *petit chien*. Jugs of *l'Africain* arrive to muffled gasps of surprise. Made with tablets of melted chocolate and served with lashings of Chantilly cream, the richest hot chocolate in the city is not for the faint-hearted.

It is while we devour our *monts blancs* (sweet creations of meringue, Chantilly and chestnut cream) that I mention Georgie's disastrous art lesson to Sharon. She informs me that her four-year-old daughter, Jemima, who attends a French *maternelle*, was once reprimanded for colouring the sky red instead of blue – giving me new appreciation of just how much colour is a part of our Australian lives.

Angelina
226, rue du Rivoli, 75001
Tel: 01 42 60 82 00

Joyeux Anniversaire

We learnt our lesson when, to celebrate Annabelle's birthday, we invited fifteen spirited six-year-olds to our apartment for a fancy-dress party. Just after the half-time mark we had exhausted our ambitious list of games. Batman and Peter Pan were dive-bombing from the top of the couch and the fairies were sulking in the bedroom. The Lone Ranger was sliding through green puddles of *diabolo menthe* (lemonade with peppermint cordial) on the parquet floor as confused children tugged on our clothes asking, 'When is the magician arriving and where is the clown?' How we longed that long afternoon for a bit of magic ourselves – perhaps the materialisation of a fairy godmother or, even better, a backyard. Next year, like the Parisians, we will call in the professionals.

The success of a Parisian child's birthday party hinges on the entertainment. For children who have been fed a structured and steady diet of highly orchestrated activities since birth, *un spectacle* is not only expected but obligatory. Throw them an egg and spoon and they are likely to whip up an omelette. They have come to be amused. With such importance being placed on *le spectacle*, the party table plays second fiddle and usually consists of a simple *goûter* – a slice of cake and a drink.

Annabelle once attended a party in a sumptuous nineteenth-century apartment overlooking Parc Monceau. A maid dressed in black and tied in a frilly white pinny opened the door with an '*Entrez-vous, Madame*'. I stopped to check whether I was in the right century. She ushered us into an airy salon filled with helium balloons and streamers where a princess in a beautiful blue dress blew bubbles. The birthday girl's mother wafted around her magnificent baroque-style apartment taking coats and presents as the frilly maid poured coffee and offered pastries to parents. In a faraway room, a clown and a musician amused the guests before they all tucked into cake and *grenadine à l'eau* (pomegranate cordial).

Pam's daughter Rosie attended a party where the lucky guests were asked to present themselves at two o'clock to a prestigious beauty salon, whereupon they were each assigned a plush chair. By pick-up time, each little girl had been transformed – hair styled, nails painted, make-up applied – and given a bowl of *bonbons* to plunge their newly manicured hands into when the going got tough. A professional photo shoot to finish ensured they would all remember their stylish outing.

Perhaps the children's birthday party to 'take the cake', however, was one attended by Sharon's daughter Jemima. The occasion: a fifth birthday.

The venue: Hôtel le Bristol. Now the Bristol is not your average, run-of-the-mill establishment, but rather a hotel that drips with refinement and class.

It was a modest affair. Just thirty of the guest of honour's closest friends joined her around three circular tables in a private *salon* adorned with eighteenth-century furniture and Gobelins tapestries. The afternoon started with *le spectacle*. First, a miracle-performing magician followed by two dancing girls dressed in the traditional costumes of Southern France. Next, a full-blown marionette show with fluorescent puppets. At the end of the marionette show, a beautiful box studded with sequins was summoned. The guests were asked to count to three, and *voilà*, a perfectly clipped Yorkshire terrier jumped out to a round of *bravos* and was paraded around the stage by a sprightly, no doubt slightly put-out puppet.

The show was followed by *jus d'orange* and *chocolat froid* poured from silver pitchers into delicate crystal glasses. Then, as the lights dimmed, a flickering cake was carried to the table. The guests' eyes bulged with delight as the dreamy three-tiered creation of sponge, strawberries and swirling cream was cut into sumptuous slabs.

That evening, as Jemima was tucked into bed she whispered, 'Mummy, I know I said that I wanted my fifth birthday at *Le McDo* but you did say I could have it anywhere. Could I have it at the Bristol, please?'

By the time Parisian girls are plunging into puberty, however, they have been clowned out. Early one Saturday evening we pick up a euphoric Georgie from her first '*boum* party'. Her friend Victoire has just turned ten and to celebrate double figures has invited twenty girls to her lavish apartment on boulevard de Courcelles to dance to the latest French pop. A starting time of two o'clock is given but, as is often the case, no pick-up time. We arrive at seven o'clock to find a room brimming with girls sipping Champomy (fake Champagne complete with gold foil and cork) and puffing away on paper-wrapped chocolate cigarettes – a taste of things to come.

Le Garçon

Annabelle has made a new friend. Every Wednesday after ballet we go to a particular café for hot chocolate. The establishment in itself is nothing special, just an archetypal Parisian café that's worn around the edges and warm and inviting on a chilly afternoon. What *is* special, in Annabelle's eyes, is the charming, jovial waiter who works there. The thing is, he speaks ever so fast and I'm lost soon after he opens his mouth, although I'm sure he thinks I understand every word he says. I try to persuade Annabelle to go somewhere else, terrified that at any moment I'll be exposed for deluding *un garçon*, but it is no use. She is smitten.

He delivers our *chocolats chauds* and leaves to serve another table. I quickly ask Annabelle what he was talking about.

'Mummy, didn't you get that either? He said that I am very beautiful and when we are the same height he will marry me,' she says nonchalantly.

'Oh,' I say.

Soon he's back. He watches Annabelle writing her name in elegant cursive on the top of her homework with her apprentice fountain pen, and prattles away again, slipping an extra square of smooth dark chocolate onto her saucer. He laughs. Annabelle laughs. He looks at me and I laugh. I wait until he has gone again to ask Annabelle what he had said. She rolls her eyes, thoroughly disgusted that she has such a stupid mother.

He had said, as quick as a flash, 'Your name is Annabelle? What a beautiful name. My name is Jean-Jacques. Now don't you forget that, will you, because I do sometimes and you will have to remind me.'

'Oh,' I say again.

If only people had French subtitles when they spoke I would understand everything! I had no idea that I was such a visual learner, with my level of reading and writing already surpassing my level of spoken French. Annabelle, in contrast, seems to have a natural ear for languages – and youth on her side. While I need to *see* words written down or have visual cues to understand and remember them, Annabelle simply needs to hear them.

Immersed in the French language every day at school, our children's oral language skills soon overtake ours at such an alarming rate that they cringe every time we open our mouths. And let's face it, despite trailing spouses being fully responsible for the smooth day-to-day functioning of the family and all the communication that entails, we are just not naturally exposed to the language in the same way as our partners and children. Even in an ideal world, one in which we had the time, money and discipline to devote to the French language every day, we would still be lagging behind. This is not helped by the reality that, except to help with homework, the girls do not want to speak French to anyone at home. It is unnatural. They want downtime – in English. Consequently, with devastating swiftness, we are reduced to embarrassing 'parents' who are preferably seen and not heard.

It happens to us all.

Buskers, Sacré-Coeur

Our American neighbour, Greg, is a trailing spouse who relocated with his family a year ago from Singapore, 'where there are lots of rules,' he says, 'but, unlike Paris, everybody follows them.'

Anyway, he was on the bus with his girls the other day when they missed their stop.

In a panic he shouted out at the top of his voice, '*Arête, arête!*'

His daughter Rachel looked devastatingly embarrassed.

'Dad, you just yelled out "Fishbone, fishbone!"' she said, as the bus cruised on. What he had meant to say was *arrêtez* (stop), but his poor pronunciation completely changed the meaning of the word.

Les Saisons

'It's summer now in Australia, right?' questions Françoise as we walk along rue Raynouard on a cold afternoon in December.

'Yes, it is,' I reply.

'So winter's in July?'

'Yes, it is.'

'So do you celebrate Christmas in July then?'

Le Calendrier

Pinned to the communal board in the foyer of our building (usually the reserve of impending gas and water readings and advance thanks for gracefully accepting the noise of Saturday's *soirée*) is a note from our local *facteur* (postman). He advises that he will be knocking on our doors between seven and eight o'clock tomorrow evening, at which point we will all be given the unique opportunity of purchasing a delightful calendar from La Poste for next year.

The following morning, Margueritte kindly translates this for me.

'*Cést évident!*' she cries. 'The postman is collecting his Christmas tips. Don't give him more than 10 euros.'

At seven-thirty the doorbell rings and the postman cheerfully presents his collection of calendars, dutifully explaining the attributes of each: 'All come complete with the corresponding saint's day for every day of the year.'

We nod approvingly.

'Even *les grandes routes de l'Île de France* are covered and information on how to correctly post your letters and parcels,' he continues. Now that would be handy. We nod again in an appropriately amazed fashion and decide to quickly buy one to save ourselves from further scintillating revelations.

'Good choice,' he says, pleased with himself. Tim holds out a 10 euro note and now it's the postman's turn to look appropriately amazed.

'Thank you, you are very kind. *Bonne année*,' he says as he heads towards our neighbour's door, preparing to look suitably amazed once more.

With New Year just around the corner, *les papeteries* (stationers) are full of calendars. I flick through the pages of what appears to be a calendar for Parisian dog lovers. Predictably, there are beautiful photographs of pampered pooches, but far more interesting are the comments. In January, it advises, make *des bonnes resolutions*: do not let your dog get too fat! Do not hide Easter eggs in the garden in April. Don't terrorise your dog with firecrackers on Bastille Day. In August, if your dog bathes in the sea on your *grandes vacances*, rinse him gently afterwards in tepid water. Owners are warned not to neglect their dog during the preparations for *la rentrée*: the transition of the children going back to school must be soft. A visit to the dog salon for a bit of pampering and a brush will help. In November, spoil small dogs with a new-season coat. In December, guard against feeding your dog an excess of sweets, and put Christmas decorations out of reach in case your *toutou* (doggy) chokes on a bell.

Prelude to the Pavlova

'I feel like Australia doesn't really exist,' says Georgie after school. Today, her class learnt the flags of various countries from a book.

'Our flag wasn't there!' she says in disbelief. 'Then we went through a book of world celebrations and there was a special event mentioned for almost every country in the world, except Australia and New Zealand. We are so far away no one cares.' Once, when the class received a photocopied world map, Australia and New Zealand were inexplicably lopped off: banished from the world.

Nobody seemed to notice – apart from Georgie and Sam.

La Surprise

In the foyer of Le Cordon Bleu, Annabelle and I are greeted by eight excited little girls wearing aprons and carefully carrying salmon-coloured boxes. *Joyeux Noël* is embossed in gold on the top of each slender box, above two golden bells. Georgie beckons us to take a closer look. Inside is an exquisite *bûche chocolat-pistache* (chocolate pistachio log). The ganache is pierced with shards of fine, filmy chocolate and dusted with icing sugar. A sprig of holly sits nonchalantly on top.

Annabelle candidly informs me that Georgie is now a better cook than me.

Thank you, Annabelle.

Joyeux Noël

An early-evening trip to rue de l'Annonciation reveals that the festive season is truly upon us. The cobbled pedestrian lane is busy with shoppers preparing for *le réveillon*, the late-night feast following Midnight Mass on Christmas Eve. It is the culinary highlight of the year. Bundled in heavy coats and scarves, residents rattle their overflowing trolleys behind them as tiny lights twinkle down the length of the street. While every region of France has its own traditions (turkey with chestnuts in Burgundy, buckwheat pancakes with sour cream in Brittany and goose in Alsace), here in Paris, you can find anything you desire for Christmas.

La boucherie (butcher) is standing room only, filled with pointing customers and barking dogs, all looking skyward. Baby goats and half-plucked turkeys hang ceremoniously above our heads, along with the odd suckling pig. A row of fat, nude geese hang next to them, their long necks appearing to stretch down a little further each time I look up.

Everyone is buying *boudin blanc*, the plump, white sausage similar to our horseshoe-shaped white pudding that's filled with pork, veal or chicken. The tradition comes from the Middle Ages when worshippers warmed themselves on a milky porridge after Midnight Mass. Later, butchers encased this porridge in a membrane, bulking it up with minced meat. Originally eaten for Christmas in the Champagne region, this delicate sausage comes in many delicious flavours including morel, truffle and Chablis; it is often served as a starter with a French white wine or a glass of Champagne.

A long queue waits to present their invoices at a separate cashier's booth before taking their receipt back to the butcher to collect their meat. This is common practice in many fresh food stores in Paris and a sound tradition that ensures that staff handling food do not handle money. It does, however, double the purchase time. At the front of the butcher's shop is a row of sturdy hooks accompanied by a sign that reads, '*Parking pour nos amis chiens*' (For our dog friends). Their specific purpose is to provide a place to tie up your dog while buying meat – also a sound health practice. As usual, it is empty.

Further down the street, towers of *foie gras* in tall glass jars, *confit de canard* and freshly shucked oysters have taken over from the usual *saussion* vendor. Wisps of steam swirl from the hot crêpe stand. *Le fromagerie* is offering a carefully chosen selection of cheeses to complement Christmas dinner. Fresh pieces of Maroilles, Brie and Pont-l'Évêque are displayed on round wicker platters covered with a rush of twirled cellophane, tempting passers-by to squeeze them in between main course and dessert. Maroilles, a soft cow's milk cheese with a washed, orange-red rind, was first made in 962 by a monk in the village of Maroilles and became a favourite of several French kings.

Bulging hessian sacks are filled with fresh and dried fruit and nuts. Fleshy dried apricots huddle together like a thousand wizened ears listening to the chatter of the marketplace. Fresh dewy dates, the colour of tortoiseshell, cling like precious stones to their long wooden necklaces. The cafés are full of shoppers pausing for *un apéritif*, while at the chocolate shop, windows are awash with Santas in their sleighs and sombre priests. Lavish boxes of chocolate bells, snowmen and trees are stacked by diminishing size into towers and tied with ribbon.

Close by, rue de Passy resembles a winter forest. Whimsical white branches showered with tiny lights wind their way around doors and archways. *La pâtisserie* is bedecked with flowing garlands of pine punctuated with pine cones and red ribbons, and its windows are full of *bûches de Noël*. One popular story behind the creation of these traditional Christmas logs is that Napoléon ordered households in Paris to close off their chimneys during winter, based on the notion that draughts caused medical ailments. This prevented Parisians from using their fireplaces and also from engaging in the many activities involving the hearth in French Christmas tradition. An innovative chef came up with the idea of a cake decorated to resemble a real Yule log ready for the fire, inventing a symbolic replacement. The génoise sponge roll is covered with chocolate buttercream, dusted with icing sugar to resemble snow, decorated with meringue mushrooms and fresh raspberries, and stabbed with a perky *Joyeuses Fêtes* sign.

On avenue Paul-Doumer, the florist is alive with noise and colour as frenzied Parisians buy armfuls of flowers to decorate their *salons* and *tables*. Underneath the wide navy canopy, the corner sidewalk is bursting with winter bulbs: tulips in red and yellow and pots of dainty blue irises. A jolly man with a bell and a booming voice is calling out '*Sapins de Noël*' next to rows of freshly cut Christmas trees, lined up like dancers in hooped green skirts. There are tubs of bare branches painted silver and gold and pine cones on long wooden sticks. The star, however, is the grove of red poinsettias, symbols of Christmas and a favourite plant of the festive season, their bright red leaves adding cheer to both table and hearth. Inside, it is chaos as attendants behind the long counter wrap up bouquet after bouquet and pass them over heads.

'*Pour la maison ou un cadeau?*' (For the house or a gift?) they shout above the crowd. This determines whether your chosen bunch is wrapped in brown paper and tied with string or enveloped in clear cellophane, stapled tightly shut and adorned with a ribbon and an elegant label. Both look wonderful.

On our way home with a large, disobedient poinsettia and an unruly trolley, we meet Françoise walking her poodle. Looking rather flustered, she blurts out that she has just been picked up by the Pooper Police, landing a hefty fine because her dog had pooped too far out onto the road. Yes, this is an offence; the gutter is the correct place so it can be washed down into the sewers. But nothing can dampen my mood, not even *déjections canines*. Rounding the corner for home now, we pass the organ grinder, his sweet melody pervading the street and the apartments above. Windows open and coins flutter down, tinkling and twirling on the footpath.

Pavlova 1

On 11 January when Georgie's *maîtresse* said, 'It would be nice to do something for Australia Day,' I was astonished. 'Perhaps you can bring in something typically Australian to eat,' she suggested.

And so began the saga of the pavlova.

Although I had never actually attempted to make one before, I assumed it wouldn't be too difficult. Besides, I had a couple of weeks up my sleeve in case I needed any ingredients sent urgently from the forgotten world.

12 JANUARY Call Mum, pavlova-maker extraordinaire, to get recipe and tips.

Check ingredients. Can't find cornflour anywhere.

Stand in front of cream section in supermarket in search of whipping cream and freak out. Do I buy *crème entière*, *crème fluide*, *crème liquide*, *crème épaisse*, *crème demi-épaisse*, *crème fleurette* or fluffy *crème Chantilly* in horrid pressurised can? I have noticed that occasionally tarts are served with *crème fraîche*, but that won't do for pavlova. I ask the girls at Le Vigny who unanimously decide my safest bet for whipping cream as we know it is Marks & Spencer, the English department store three metro changes away. It is close to Tim's office, so the easiest solution is to get him to pop down there and buy cream in his lunch-hour on the 25th . . . if he's in Paris.

Call Mum to send over cornflour. (White powder through post from a sweet grandmother? Not suspicious at all.)

Les Foulards

We stand like a group of eager Girl Guides who are attempting to earn their badges for knot tying. In fact, we are a group of foreign women attending a scarf-tying workshop to learn how to perfect that elegant wrap and knotted scarf with French style. Something I can safely say I never envisaged myself doing.

'A scarf is the most versatile accessory there is,' begins the smartly dressed Frenchwoman at the front of the room. 'It adds flair, personality, detail and dimension to an otherwise anonymous outfit and gives French women that certain *je ne sais quoi*.'

We listen intently to her tips:

- When choosing scarves, pick two predominant colours used regularly in your wardrobe. These colours must work well with your hair and skin colourings as they will sit close to your face.
- Try to bring a lot of different looks into your wardrobe with diverse patterns, fabrics and styles.
- If you can buy only one scarf this season, choose *un carré* (a large silk square). It is the most versatile of scarves as it can be worn many different ways.
- For women who wear a lot of black and brown, a scarf can dramatically transform an outfit. In fact, the same suit can be worn for a few days in succession but with a different scarf every day. No one will ever know. (I guess it never gets to 40°C).
- Don't hang scarves up in the wardrobe (yeah, right) because you can't try them on quickly with an outfit. Keep them in a basket next to your mirror, or somewhere accessible.

'A wool scarf is *une écharpe*, a silk scarf is *un foulard* and a shawl is *un châle*,' she informs us, passing out scarves. Before we know it, she is demonstrating the basic folds, lithely tying *les foulards* around her neck, effortlessly flicking, tossing and twisting. I attempt to imitate but have suddenly become all fingers and thumbs. We look rather like a group of fumbling four-year-olds learning to tie our shoelaces.

The two most basic knots she demonstrates are the simple slip knot and the classic French knot or twist. (N.B. Tie right over left, then left over right.) She explains the versatile and popular French knot is used with any material that's not too bulky and can be worn with jackets, trenches or almost any top, jauntily off to one side. It can also accessorise a collared shirt but the knot must be centred.

'*Les foulards* live between the seasons – *demi-saison* – being dependable and giving flexibility in untrustworthy weather.

'If you have a jacket with nothing suitable to wear underneath,' she continues as we try to keep up, 'the flip knot will save the day. On an extra-large scarf, the cowl as well as the slip knot works especially well, worn low and flouncy.'

Perusing *la carte*

I am still back on the flip knot as she lauds the muffler, which is great with coats on a cold day. Finally there's the concertina oblong scarf that stays looking good all day long.

'If you want to wear a large rectangular scarf over your coat, simply wrap it around your shoulders tightly and flick it dramatically over one shoulder, with a little twist if you prefer,' she says, as I start on the muffler at a rate of knots...

Pavlova 2

23 JANUARY Cornflour arrives. Make practice pavlova with pathetic hand-held whisk, my KitchenAid being in storage in Australia along with many other handy gadgets. Takes forever. Whips up to size of a tartlet. Start to panic. Can see myself standing over bowl whisking white mixture for three days to make enough for class of hungry children. May have to splurge on a new mixer now that Tim's contract has been extended for another year or so and we won't be going home in a few months as planned. Such is our life in France. You never know what's around the corner.

Call Mum. 'You have to use eggs that are at least four or five days old or they won't whip up to any great volume, and they must be at room temperature,' she says. Okay, so where do I get old eggs from in Paris? I haven't got time to age them myself!

Scoot down to *la fromagerie*. '*Bonjour, Madame*. A dozen old eggs, please.' She looks at me kind of strangely and says slowly, '*D'accord.*' (Okay.)

Scoot home again with eggs hoping they are actually old and try again. Yes! Whites whip up; look wonderful. Near the end of cooking time I peek in to find a perfect pavlova. I whip it out of the oven and before my eyes it sinks like an air mattress you have pulled the pin on, except for stoic upright edges.

24 JANUARY Call Mum. 'You can't just whip it out of the oven. You have to turn the oven off and let it cool first. If you put warm meringue into cold air, it will crack and collapse.' Well, yes, so I discovered.

25 JANUARY Third attempt. Better, although centres still sunken. It will have to do. Call Tim to bring home lots of cream to fill craters.

Julie calls, exhausted.

'I've been running a guest house all week,' she says wearily. 'They just left for Rome this morning. Four friends of my parents. I kicked the children out of their beds and Mark and I surrendered ours too, because, you know, these people are my parents' age – you can't put them on the floor!'

The thing about relocating to Paris is that it's everyone's favourite destination. Australians have an enduring fascination with all things French and any Aussie who makes it to Europe will no doubt pass through the city. Eventually, you will hear from everyone in your address book (and a lot of people who aren't). The average occupancy rate for our rather unprofitable little B&B is around 30 per cent. Don't get me wrong: it's wonderful to see family and friends. You just have to learn where to draw the line.

'Anyway,' says Julie, 'yesterday morning I dropped the four of them off at the Louvre in the car because they were having trouble working out how to use *le métro*. I happened to mention that I hadn't been there myself yet. They couldn't believe it.

'"What, not been to the Louvre yet and you live in Paris?"

'"No," I answered awkwardly. What I felt like saying was, "No, because I'm too busy running a guest house, travel agency and taxi service." Must go! I have to deflate two airbeds, do a few loads of washing, clean and shop before I pick up the kids. We have a couple from Adelaide arriving in time for dinner.'

Pavlova 3

26 JANUARY Australia Day. Up early to decorate pavlovas. Turn fridge upside-down. Can't find cream. 'Where is the cream, Tim?' I yell into sleeping mound. He mumbles that it is still in briefcase from last night and turns over. My heart sinks. At this point any normal mother would say, 'That's it, I'll send Vegemite sandwiches.' No, think positively: the cream is most likely fine. It was cold last night, the windows were open. It passes the smell and taste test. Whip it up and slap it on. Pile on loads of fruit and *voilà*, ready to go!

Push family out door. Georgie carrying heavy satchel on back and holding plastic bag full of paper plates and serviettes, Annabelle carrying her bag and large, empty shoebox that she is required to take today (for unknown reasons), leaving Tim with briefcase and two pavlovas in large plastic containers, juggling one atop the other. 'I'll manage,' he says. 'No need for you to come.' I close the door behind them and heave a sigh of relief. Then it hits home that if cream really is off I will be responsible for a class of sick children, who will by tonight hate pavlova and Australians. Why is it that Australians like to be friends with everyone and call everyone their mate? From a French perspective this is very superficial.

Tim calls from work. Nightmare morning. Couldn't see where he was going on footpath because he was carrying pavlovas and stepped in the biggest, freshest dog *merde* he has ever seen. Nearly slid right over. A Frenchman, who was walking with him, said, 'It's okay, don't worry. It's on your left foot, which is considered good luck.' Yeah, right. Then there was a problem with the metro at Charles de Gaulle–Étoile. Platform heaving with people when train eventually sped into the station. Annabelle couldn't carry shoebox any longer. They squeezed in as the doors snapped shut, Tim juggling two pavlovas and shoebox above swerving heads, with briefcase sandwiched between his knees. Luckily it was so sardine-packed he didn't need to hold on. On top of that there were the commuters trying to peek and poke at the pavlovas and wanting to know all about them.

'Yes, but did the pavlovas survive?' I ask.

'Yes, they were delivered in one piece,' he says. 'Happy Australia Day!' Suddenly I feel a pang of homesickness as I imagine balmy backyard barbecues and fireworks in a hot evening sky.

P.S. Everyone loved the pavlovas and nobody got sick.

P.P.S. For whipping cream buy *crème fluide* or *crème fleurette*.

La Chandeleur

Arriving early today at Le Cordon Bleu, Georgie had time to slip into the adult demonstration class. Being 2 February, the Catholic holiday of Candlemas, it was only fitting that crêpes were on the menu. Known as *la Chandeleur* in France, the holiday commemorates the purification of the Virgin Mary and the presentation of baby Jesus, and is celebrated by feasting on crêpes for good luck. It is traditional to hold a coin in one hand while trying to flip a pancake into the air with the other.

The kind chef offered Georgie a crêpe with *beurre-sucre* (salted butter and sugar) before she went downstairs to see if any of her class had arrived. A chef's

Spring bulbs, Jardin du Luxembourg

assistant in the foyer was trying to dispose of another stack of crêpes, so Georgie had another.

Then she set to work with her class making *brochettes de moules panées à l'anglaise*. First they simmered the mussels in herbs and white wine until the mussels opened their mouths and smiled. Then they threaded them onto skewers, crumbed them and fried them in butter until golden. To accompany *les brochettes* each student filled six little pots with spinach, eggs and cream and baked them in a bain-marie. The next step was to boil fresh tomatoes and herbs down into a tomato sauce. Seeing a cupful of chopped tomatoes left over, Georgie thought they'd better not go to waste. How was she to know that the chef would come around with orange juice and crêpes for *goûter*?

By the time she waddled down the stairs after her lesson she looked as green as the spinach cups she was carrying, with enough good luck for the entire family.

Un Café Crème, SVP

I drop into Le Vigny in time to hear Ann (a South African friend with a son, Kaan, in Annabelle's class) tell the girls that her family had dined at a two-star Michelin on the weekend. Her Turkish husband had ordered a steak cooked *bien cuit* (well done), equating to Australian medium/well. The waiter had dutifully taken his order, containing his disapproval to a subtle roll of the eyes, but when, at the end of the meal, the husband requested a milky *café crème* (*quelle horreur!*) the waiter could restrain himself no longer.

'As quick as lightening,' Ann shrieks with laughter, 'the waiter asked, "*Avec un croissant, Monsieur?*"' (With a croissant, Monsieur?)

Mercredi

To fall in step with the rhythm of the French family, it's helpful to understand the routine of a typical week. In return for long and arduous school days (including Saturday morning) French children are given Wednesday off. Our school, however, exchanges a half day on Wednesday for all day Saturday off, which leaves the weekend free for homework.

Regardless of the school you attend, *mercredi* is the traditional day of play, when most extracurricular activities are squeezed into the busy schedule.

Pick up the weekly entertainment guide *Pariscope* from any news stand and you'll find countless children's activities on Wednesdays, from theatre and museum workshops to circuses. Cinema tickets are reduced, marionette shows run in the afternoon and parks brim with happy children.

On Wednesdays, I live on the metro, navigating sixteen or more trains and their labyrinth of connecting steps in order to shuffle the girls between school, home, Les Petits Cordon Bleus, ballet, piano and the obligatory birthday party. *Le métro* is a quick, safe and reliable way to get around – unless there is a strike. Deep underground there are sixteen train lines and over 320 stations. During peak hour, trains arrive every ninety seconds. The system is designed so that no point in Paris is more than 500 metres from a station.

On a *mercredi* in March, I pick up Annabelle and Georgie at noon and we walk towards Place des Ternes under a blue sky swirled with milky white clouds. It is good to be above ground. I have already done my morning metro workout, climbing eighteen flights of stairs. No wonder gyms are few and far between: the metro is a natural Stairmaster.

Sunshine thaws stony faces and floods footpaths in pools of light. After months of winter, we revel in our first lick of spring. Buckets upon buckets of daffodils sit jubilantly next to bright bouquets at the Place des Ternes flower market. There are pots of pansies, blue hydrangeas and fragile branches of prunus. Down the road at the Poncelet produce market, mountains of peas sleep snugly in their shells and the first plump strawberries have arrived from Spain, a glorious sight after the citrus quilts of winter. We grab three little salmon quiches and a brown bag of fragrant strawberries and eat them on the run.

The café on the corner has tumbled its tables onto *la terrasse* and diners jostle for a seat. They sip beer and enjoy the sun, picking at the first lofty salads. I catch snippets of conversations, which centre on spring vacations, sun and *plein air*. The cobwebs of the dreary Paris winter are brushed away before our eyes. It is a mere two weeks until the first official day of *la Saison* (the Season), which starts in earnest on 1 April and continues, unabated, until September. May is traditionally sprinkled with sunny long weekends, a prelude to *les grandes vacances*. *Gîtes* (holiday rentals) in popular areas of the countryside are already booked solid and those who are late with their summer planning miss out or opt for less desirable accommodation.

We head towards Ternes metro station. Store mannequins are dressed for spring and tailored blazers have made their debut on the streets, covered with large, elegant wraps. We fly down the metro steps and are swallowed by a tunnel.

The train that pulls into the platform is full of excited 'Wednesday' children clutching soccer balls, violin cases and birthday presents. Feet are slipped into long black riding boots and hair is swept into ballet buns. We stand, pinned precariously against a door until we tumble out at Charles de Gaulle–Étoile. All afternoon, we hop on and off trains and whiz around the city.

We surface each time from the long, dark tunnels to breathe in yet another part of the city, gathering a series of flashing frames that define Paris in spring:

- The quote on the whiteboard as we emerge from Vaugirard station
  '*Sans la musique, la vie serait une erreur.*' Nietszche
  ('Without music, life would be a mistake.')
- Daffodils for sale on metro station steps.
- New spring menus on blackboards.
- Dogs scurrying down the footpath, free of their winter coats.
- The quickly snatched coffee on rue de Sèvres, the café doors thrown open to catch the fresh spring air.
- The chamber orchestra playing in tuxedos at Montparnasse station.
- Petals sprinkled on the footpath outside Au Nom de la Rose, a chain of florists specialising in roses.
- The sudden March shower that turns the blue sky grey as quickly as washing out a paintbrush in water.

At seven o'clock, I drag myself up the last brutal flight of stairs to our door. Annabelle is still fresh as a daisy, wearing a party hat, a smile and a pretty blue necklace made from metro tickets. Georgie is proudly peeking at the freshly baked *pissaladière de sardines* she created at Le Cordon Bleu. The girls are happy, and dinner is ready. Suddenly Wednesdays all seem worthwhile.

'*Métro, boulot, dodo.*'

(Metro, work, sleep – the daily grind.)

La Chemise Blanche

A clean white shirt is on the bed. Tim is throwing a few things into his suit bag while talking on the phone. Georgie is sprawled out on the quilt struggling through *Les Petites Filles Modèles* by Comtesse de Ségur, a French author with whom she has become enamored (the central path in Parc Monceau is named after her).

'Where are you going, Daddy?' she asks, when he finishes his business call.

'To London,' he says, zipping up his bag.

'Oh, good,' she says. 'Do you mind bringing me back a sausage roll?'

Camembert ou Brie ma Cherie?

Last night I attended Annabelle's 11ème class meeting with Jocelyn (Claire's mother) and Jan. As far as I could follow, it proved a rather mundane affair until the subject of school lunches came up. Everyone sat up in their seat, their eyes brightened and it was on for one and all.

'Why do the children have to eat in their classroom?' asked one mother (the older children eat in *la cantine*).

'Why can't they talk at lunchtime? Lunch is important, it should be civilised!' cried a father passionately. 'Why can't the children face each other when they eat? You just have to turn a few chairs around.'

And so it went on. In fact, it was all news to me. I hadn't realised that Annabelle's four-course lunch (which cost around $AU18 a day) was just like any other lesson.

'They must be as silent as if it was a mathematics class, otherwise chaos would reign,' said *la maîtresse*, almost swooning at the thought. 'They must eat in their rows so they are not tempted to talk.'

It entered my mind that it must be like eating lunch on an Air France flight . . . business class.

A glance at this week's spring menu makes an Aussie meat pie look like a feeble snack, which brings me to another point. They don't – snack, that is. Sated after a big lunch, French kids don't have the need to nibble, except for that structured five o'clock *goûter* after school. An *escargot au chocolat* perhaps, or a whippet-thin tablet of chocolate slipped into *un pain au lait* (soft milk roll).

Monday's menu offers a choice of salads, followed by *navarin d'agneau* (classic lamb stew with baby spring vegetables), Camembert with crusty baguette, and a chocolate éclair filled with dense chocolate custard. Thursday beckons with *avocat vinaigrette* (avocado with dressing), *sauté de veau avec gratin dauphinois* (sautéed veal with a creamy potato gratin), yoghurt or Brie, and *un gateau Fête des Mères* (a cake for Mother's Day). Being a predominately Catholic country, fish is still served religiously on Friday. *Frites* are always served on Tuesday, usually with a rare *steak haché*, putting a morning bounce in the step of every pupil.

The lunch break is two hours long and children have the option of going home, where they are served up similar gastronomic delights. Surprisingly, despite the expanse of butter, cheese and cream and the sheer number of courses dished up, I have yet to see an obese Parisian child. This is known as the French Paradox for which there are various and continually changing explanations.

The challenging task of producing a gourmand starts at a young age. By the time a French child leaves school, they certainly know their onions, not to mention being well on the way to recognising and appreciating many of France's hundreds of cheeses. School lunches, as well as providing nourishment, reinforce what is taught at home, helping children form a discerning, sophisticated palate and a deep-seated belief that meal times are important and not to be rushed. Food and wine are inseparable in France. Small amounts of wine or Champagne are offered on special occasions from around the age of ten so that, slowly, children are able to form an appreciation and respect of alcohol, and develop healthy habits.

Some schools, including *maternelles*, send home the lunch menu two months in advance, with *suggestions du soir* for each evening. How comforting to know that if your four-year-old has feasted on salad, a saucy *daube* with *pommes Parisienne* (potato balls), baguette slathered with goat's cheese and fresh fruit for lunch, all they will need for dinner is a salad of grated carrot, followed by stuffed cabbage, and *crème brûlée*.

A number of schools have their menu posted to an outside notice board for all to read. This way the citizens of France can keep an eye on the gastronomic habits of the next generation, reassuring themselves that standards and traditions are being upheld and, ultimately, that the future of France is in good hands.

Dinner *avec amis*: Annabelle with Steve and Pam

'Tell me what you eat, and I will tell you what you are.'

Jean Anthelme Brillat-Savarin

Jardin du Luxembourg

We hear a slight rustle of leaves, pigeons cooing and the distant thud of tennis balls. It's early on a Sunday morning when we arrive at the gardens via the organic produce market. A nun crosses the empty park to church and, at this hour, it's peaceful and cool.

Sprawling over 25 hectares in the 6th, the Jardin du Luxembourg is the quintessential Paris park, where locals of all ages come to relax and play. Framed by Montparnasse, St-Germain-des-Prés and the Latin Quarter, the city's largest public park echoes the spirit of the Left Bank. A favourite haunt and place of inspiration for writers and philosophers, its colour and structure also draws artists. George Sands, Honoré de Balzac and the painter Antoine Watteau were regular visitors. Some of *Gigi* was filmed here, and it still looks like a movie set.

The gardens are also a much-loved destination for students from nearby universities who sunbake and read on the trademark green-metal chairs. For children, it's like jumping into a *Madeline* book. Imposing statues enchant around every corner. Sweeping vistas, wide avenues, alleyways of trees and vibrant flowerbeds delight the eyes. Generations of Parisian children have grown up here, exposed to art, culture and history from a young age.

The centrepiece is Le Grand Bassin, a large octagonal pond surrounded by formal terraces with stone balustrades. Today, the gigantic urns are spilling over with pink geraniums. Watching over the glassy pond is a semi-circular sweep of statues of prominent women, mostly queens of France. As well as providing an honourable presence, they also supply Georgie with a captive audience for solo ballet performances. Her favourite is Sainte Geneviève, an angelic woman who saved Paris from the attack of Attila and his Huns in 451 and is the city's patron saint. Each time we visit, Georgie curtsies at her feet and strokes the long stone plaits that trail to her knees.

A harmonious mix of styles, the gardens are formal French in the centre with lines of perfect symmetry. They branch out to become less geometrical and more English with wild, tucked-away corners and a rambling maze of paths.

Make no mistake though, this is a thoroughly civilised park, with rules and codes of behaviour. Footballs, rollerblades, baseball bats and boomerangs are *interdit* (forbidden). So is walking on the grass, bathing in Le Grand Bassin, picking flowers and climbing trees. There are designated promenading areas through the centre and dogs are only permitted to use three gates. Rebels risk the wrath of the *Police de la Senat* and their dreaded whistles!

The gardens originally belonged to the Luxembourg Palace, commissioned in 1615 by Marie de Médicis, widow of Henri IV. Homesick for her native Florence, she ordered the palace to be built to remind her of the Palazzo Pitti, and on the nearest edge of Paris to Italy. By the time the palace was completed in 1631, her son, Louis XIII, had already banished his mother from France. She remained in exile until her death.

The palace slipped through one set of royal fingers to another until the French Revolution, when revolutionaries converted the palace into a factory and then a prison. Later turned over to the state, it now houses the French Senate. A hairdresser, bar, gym and post office reside within the palace, so senators don't have to leave the building.

Adjacent to the palace is La Fontaine de Médicis. The exquisite baroque-style fountain depicts Greek mythological figures and is visible from the end of a tranquil, oblong pond filled with fat goldfish. It is a place of great serenity and calm, where artists love to sketch.

The peace is suddenly disturbed by a bell ringing across the gardens. Children come running from all directions. We join the trail and sweep past Madame with her clanging bell into the small Théâtre de Luxembourg for the eleven o'clock performance of Perrault's French fairytale *Le Chat Botté* (Puss in Boots). The theatre offers one of the best traditional marionette shows in the city, with forty-five-minute *spectacles* of children's favourites. For those who don't speak French, performances are easy enough to follow. At the interval, the bell is rung again and Madame miraculously turns herself into a portable snack bar, marching importantly to the front of the theatre with a tray of plump lemon madeleines and an assortment of *bonbons*.

Sainte Geneviève, the patron saint of Paris

Sailing the toy boats on the pond, Jardin du Luxembourg

We stream out of the theatre and straight onto the antique *manège* next door. Designed by Charles Garnier (who also happened to design l'Opéra Garnier), it's no ordinary carousel. Every time we venture to the gardens the girls take a spin and play the ring game. This is how it goes: first, you make a dash to secure one of the outside horses suspended off a circular frame. Then each rider is given a jousting stick. You buckle up your leather safety belt and wait for take off, with your eyes fixed on the ring man who stands on a platform. His job is to load metal rings into the medieval feeder. Suddenly the carousel quickens and horses gallop through the air. At high speed, the riders lunge toward the dangling metal rings, concentrating on spearing one onto their stick each time they pass. The aim is to procure as many as possible. As the horses slow to a halt, the riders count their rings and jubilantly hold them up for all to see.

Annabelle likes to mooch about on the terrace of the Buvette des Marionnettes sipping *fraise à l'eau* (strawberry cordial) and clicking away with her camera (it's quite possible to snap a French star out with their children). This little wooden kiosk near the carousel offers takeaway baguette sandwiches, ice-cream, crêpes and *barbe à papa* ('papa's beard' or fairy floss), or you can sit down for an open-air, light lunch under the umbrellas. But today we picnic by the pond on full-flavoured tomatoes, a round of *demi-sec chèvre* and organic wholewheat rolls. We also have tiny, *première* apples and eco blueberries bursting with flavour. By the time we have fed our leftover bread to the birds hopping amongst the summer flower beds, the boats have been wheeled out.

No outing to the gardens is complete without sailing the little toy boats on the boating pond; every Parisian has warm memories of this traditional childhood activity. The girls choose their boats, grab a bamboo stick and push their boats off the side of the pond. Whoosh! The gentle summer breeze catches the sails and they scud to the other side, narrowly missing a baby duckling or two. The girls race around to the other side and push them off again. Then they bolt back again and Georgie's boat collides with someone else's and almost capsizes and she bumps into someone running the opposite way who trips her up and she almost falls in then she loses sight of her boat and a little *garçon* wearing Cyrillus bermudas whacks her on the head with his stick without so much as a *pardon*!

Over in the northwest corner of the park, groups of solemn old men sit around chess tables under a canopy of purple jacaranda trees, scratching their chins. It's fun to watch them silently contemplating their next move. *Belote*, a French card game, is also popular. In fact, there's a whole area devoted to games and activities. *Le terrain des jeux* includes pony rides, swings at *le petit bar* (where children line up and pay for a quick to-and-fro) and an enormous fenced playground. It is here that we spend the remainder of our afternoon. Without doubt it's the best playground in Paris, filled with a jungle of bright equipment for under tens, the big hits being a rope Eiffel Tower and a flying fox. For weary parents the small entrance fee is worthwhile. Once the girls are settled, we pull up chairs outside the fence, grab a coffee and a newspaper, and breathe in everyday Parisian life.

By four o'clock on weekend afternoons, locals have come out of the woodwork and the gardens lose their tranquil feel. We head toward the southwestern exit of the park passing the garden's beehives on the way. Lessons in beekeeping are available and pots of honey can be purchased from l'Orangerie in late September. During winter, the orangery is used to shelter oleanders, magnolias, palms and other potted trees from around the gardens, some of which are hundreds of years old. Next door is a tangle of blossoms and heady perfume. Here in the oft overlooked orchards, hundreds of varieties of apple and pear trees wind their way up trellising, trained in various espalier styles.

Refreshed after a blissful day in the best backyard in the city, we slip through the far gate and out onto the busy boulevards.

Jardin du Luxembourg
Metro: Odéon/Vavin/St-Sulpice or
RER Luxembourg

Marionettes du Luxembourg
Wed, Sat & Sun.
See *Pariscope* for show times.

Toy boats
Wed, weekends, & daily during summer.

'Of course I have played outdoor games. I once played dominoes in an open-air café in Paris.'

Oscar Wilde

A mural of the old Les Halles market,
Le Cochon à l'Oreille café

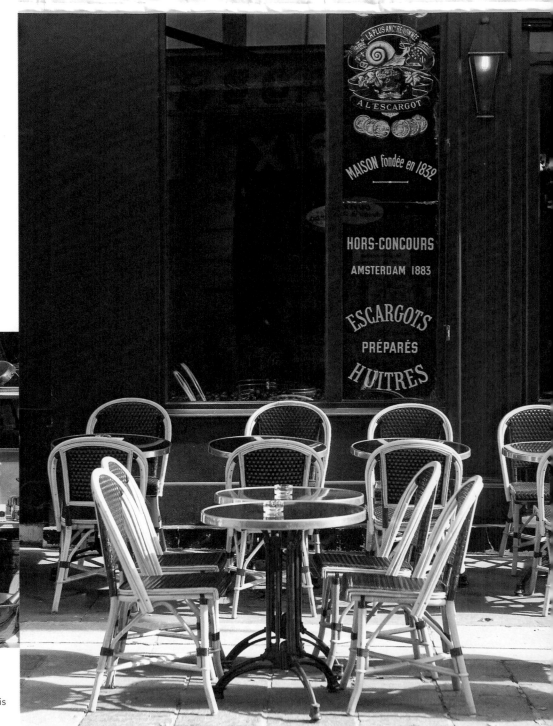

La Revolution Française

Now in 7ème (year 5), Georgie is studying the French Revolution. She is also having nightmares. *Le contrôle* (test) is tomorrow. She is about to throw the foolscap folder full of gruesome facts, dates and key figures (Danton, Robespierre, Marat, Louis XVI, Marie-Antoinette) out the window. She also has to learn by heart the Declaration of the Rights of Man, *l'Assemblée Constitutionnel* and the definition of *la Monarchie Constitutionelle*. But at ten, it is not so much the workload that triggers her lurid nightmares as the grisly films she watches every Friday, showing graphic footage of guillotining and guards kicking heads around.

During the French Revolution, Louis XVI's dying wish was supposedly for a final taste of Brie.

'It is legal because I wish it.'
'Has God forgotten all I have done for Him?'
'I am the State.'

Louis XIV, the Sun King (1643–1715)

Dead Famous

It seems only logical that patriotic Parisians should choose to end their journey at the termination of the city's clockwise snail pattern that starts centre stage in the 1st. In a quiet corner of the 20th, **Cimetière du Père-Lachaise** is considered one of the most hauntingly beautiful places to rest in the world.

The cemetery was named after Father François d'Aix de la Chaise, the confessor of Louis XIV, and rambles over 40 hectares. It's a fascinating place to visit, a peaceful paradise filled with thousands of leafy trees and a labyrinth of cobbled lanes that meander over hills and past elaborate tombs with soft moss roofs. Especially in the springtime when the first daffodils are out, the trees are in bloom and fresh flowers lay on the tombs, it exudes a heavenly tranquillity. On *Toussaint* (All Saints' Day) in November, when the French commemorate their loved ones who have passed away, you'll find it strewn with chrysanthemums.

L'Escargot Montorgueil boasts an ornate 1870s décor

But come on a gloomy winter's day when the trees are bare, the cats slink by and the tombstones have more of a wayward lean, and it can feel a little forlorn. There are grave concerns about vaults that have fallen into disrepair as families have died out, giving several spots a somewhat ghostly aura.

As navigation can be a challenge, it's wise to purchase a map at the entrance. Follow the street signs for a who's who of French history, strolling past tombstones littered with scribbled notes, love poems and gifts left in homage by admirers. Just ensure that you leave when you hear the bell ring before the gates are locked at six o'clock, or you are in for a quiet and eerie night.

Countless great figures have secured a place of eternal rest here, from musicians, artists and dancers to political and literary giants, making the cemetery one of the city's best free museums, packed with prestige. Among the venerable residents are Yves Montand, Victor Hugo, Molière, Delacroix, Proust and Jim Morrison, who has the dubious distinction of 'most popular tomb'. Paris's much-loved Little Sparrow, Edith Piaf, resides here, along with playwright and poet Jean Cocteau, who died within hours of Piaf while preparing a speech about her for radio. One born on a street corner and the other to bourgeois parents, both artists inspired a nationwide outpouring of deep grief. It is said that the French bury their politicians but mourn their artists.

Fans of Balzac can pay their respects to the novelist and to the prominent characters from his novels, who are buried in fictitious graves nearby. Chopin's body is topped with a glorious marble angel, but his heart lies in a church in Poland, in accordance with his will. The Polish composer and pianist died of tuberculosis at his flat on Place Vendôme in 1849. Oscar Wilde's tombstone is covered with lipstick kisses. The handsome, naked and anatomically correct angel of death that sits flamboyantly atop his grave was bequeathed by an anonymous lady admirer. Its rather large private parts were broken off in the 1920s (supposedly by students) and later seen in a nearby café – although there were whispers at the time that the cemetery director used them as a paperweight.

If you're dying to become a permanent Parisian at Père-Lachaise, there are just a couple of little catches. First, there's a very long waiting list and second, to secure a plot one must have lived in Paris, or plan to die in the French capital, which is not so easy to orchestrate – although it can be arranged.

Cimetière du Père-Lachaise
16, rue du Repos, 75020
Tel: 01 43 70 70 33
www.pere-lachaise.com
Metro: Père Lachaise/Philippe Auguste/Alexandre Dumas

*'For me, singing is a way of escaping.
It's another world. I'm no longer on earth.'*

Edith Piaf

Les Moules

Come September, the fish markets are laden with mountains of mussels that are noisily scooped into tins and sold, strangely, by the litre. Cafés and brasseries are busy cooking up *moules frites*, serving fragrant bowls of mussels in a myriad of ways. Blackboards boast *moules marinières* (mussels steamed with shallots and wine), *moules à la provençale* (mussels with tomatoes, garlic, olive oil and wine) and cream, curry, and Roquefort mussels. Enhanced by a fresh baguette and a carafe of wine, digging into a bowl of mussels is an inexpensive and delicious way to pass an evening.

In the markets, look for the superior, fat *moules de bouchot*, grown on wooden pillars (*bouchots*) out of reach of predators and free of sediment. They are identifiable by their small shell and yellow-orange flesh. Grown slowly, their full flavour is attributed to being underwater at high tide and exposed to the maritime air at low tide.

Although France's mussel-growing is concentrated in Brittany, the most prized mussels are from Normandy. *Moules de bouchot de la baie du Mont-St-Michel* (*bouchot* mussels from the bay of Mont-St-Michel) are nurtured in the waters in front of the ancient Benedictine abbey, and farmers claim they have been using the same growing methods since the ninth century.

A Cook's Tour of Old Les Halles

Heavy wraps and scarves have suddenly made an appearance on the streets and the leaves are starting to turn yellow. It's hard to believe that just five weeks ago we were wearing light summer dresses. Windswept, Sharon, Iris, Karen and I continue east along rue St-Honoré and turn into rue du Louvre towards Les Halles. The vibrant **rue Montorgueil market** is jumpstarting into gear as we walk through. Jovial merchants hurl greetings and hose down the cobbles. The old metal shop signs clatter in the wind. Further up, the doors of a butcher's truck are flung open. White-hooded men sling sides of lamb over their shoulders and stride into *la boucherie*.

Caught between the glamour of the Opéra and Tuileries quarters to the west and the avant-garde Centre Pompidou to the east, this ancient street has a fascinating history. Vibrantly depicted by Claude Monet in *La Rue Montorgueil à Paris, Fête du 30 juin 1878* to commemorate the end of the World Fair, the street was originally home to the city's oyster market, when fresh shellfish were transported into Paris via the northern boulevard Poissonnière during the dark early hours. With a down-to-earth scruffy charm, it remains the final crumb of the old Les Halles, the vast wholesale produce market that fed the French capital and defined the neighbourhood for eight centuries.

Les Halles was a way of life for many, an exhilarating rough and tumble existence centred around food, community and hard work. But by the 1960s, the market was causing chaos and congestion in the surrounding city streets. Murky dealings prospered in its shadows. The escalating rat population beneath the sprawling pavilions was no longer acceptable and Charles de Gaulle ordered its demolition, amid much controversy. Slowly but surely, the pulsing heart of the Right Bank was ripped out along with the leeks and lemons and brawny working-class spirit, and the city mourned.

In 1979, the Forum des Halles, a bland underground shopping centre topped with gardens, claimed the landmark site, squashing not only the last leftover tomatoes but the heady soul of Paris's old market district, changing its face forever. And yet, enough vestiges of the intoxicating days remain to fleetingly recall the past. If you listen carefully, you can still hear the whispers of the old markets in the ancient streets that once flourished on Les Halles' grimy rim. Steeped in its own juices, this authentic quarter of Paris that Emile Zola so passionately referred to as '*le ventre de Paris*' (the belly of Paris) continues to play an important role in feeding the city.

A peppering of age-old restaurants and specialty shops survived the big clean up, along with a crop of professional kitchenware stores that have long supplied the restaurants and cafés of Paris. While designer clothing stores and flashy cafés are slowly replacing wholesale food shops, the neighbourhood still offers cooks a chance to lose themselves amongst heavy cauldrons and gigantic soup ladles in search of a souvenir with quintessential French flavour. For the gourmand, it offers a feast for the senses and a unique taste of Paris, past and present.

Before we start exploring the area, we sit and contemplate St-Eustache, an impressive Gothic and Renaissance church standing stoically at the base of rue Montorgueil. Modelled on Notre-Dame and considered the district's solar plexus, it has watched over Les Halles since its completion in 1637. Here, Louis XIV took his first communion, Mozart performed as an infant prodigy and Molière's funeral service was held in the middle of the night. Just as importantly, St-Eustache was the church of the merchants and a testament to the prosperity of the area and its market.

Inside, we find it dark and, save a few souls sheltering from the wind, empty. References to food, as one would expect, are present. In a side chapel, a clay sculpture modelled by Raymond Mason in 1969 shows a procession of grieving merchants laden with fruit and vegetables leaving their beloved market: it is a poignant memorial. Just inside the Place René Cassin entrance, a stained-glass window offered by *La Société de la Charcuterie Française* features pigs, sausages and pies, along with the patron saint of *charcuterie*, St Antoine. An annual mass is also held here in memory of pork butchers who have passed away during the year.

The wind is bracing as we push open the door of **Le Cochon à l'Oreille** nearby. Snug and authentic, this enchanting café is filled with local workers and the ghosts of old Halles. Birds fly in a frieze around the tiny room and tiled murals depicting everyday scenes of the market in its heyday cover the walls. On the ceiling a faded quote translates to 'The belly of Paris has migrated its heart to Les Halles.' As we finish our *café crèmes*, simple, honest *plats du jour* are being scrawled on the blackboard ready for lunch: *saucisse aux lentilles* (sausage and lentils) and *coq au vin*. Comfort food for a chilly day.

Revived, we take a closer look at the now lively rue Montorgueil and, behind the twenty-first-century bustle, we find fragments of an intriguing past. At number 38, it's impossible to miss the enormous golden snail perched above the once very fashionable **l'Escargot Montorgueil** restaurant with its ornate 1870s decor. Snails were considered poor man's food in France until the introduction of pesticides elevated them to a farmed delicacy. While snails from different areas of the country vary in size and taste, *l'escargot de Bourgogne*, the plump Burgundy vineyard snail, remains the culinary star.

Old Les Halles: a unique taste of Paris, past and present

6, rue Coquillière 75001 Paris · 01 40 13 77 00

Les Halles centrales de Paris

Next, we poke our noses into **Stohrer** at number 51, a pastry shop with personality where the ceilings and walls flow with garlands of flowers and cavorting women. The oldest *pâtisserie* in Paris is crammed with excellent *tourtes* and quiches, luscious fruit tartlets, rich chocolate éclairs and Paris-Brests. Apparently created to commemorate the first bicycle race from Paris to Brest in the late nineteenth-century, these ring-shaped cakes (representing the bicycle wheel), are made of *choux* pastry filled with praline cream and sprinkled with flaked almonds. Specialties include *le baba au rhum* (sponge cake soaked in rum syrup) and *le puits d'amour* (flaky pastry hollowed out and filled with jam or custard cream). We choose a pastry each, sample bites all round, and keep strolling along the cobbles.

At number 59 we find references to the street's fishy past. **Au Rocher de Cancale** still boasts its façade of wood and plaster, and at ground level, one corner is cut away to unearth a sculpture of oysters clinging to a rock-bed. The restaurant was opened in 1846 and is named after the seaside village of Cancale in Brittany, well-known for its briny oysters. It was also here that France's famous gastronome and first restaurant critic, Grimod de la Reynière, made his name. Waiters from the best establishments in Paris would dash dishes over for him to taste, pontificate over and create fancy names for.

Another vibrant place not to be missed is **Ahga, Les Halles Courses**, an authentic Moroccan souk cluttered with tagines, lamps and slippers. Preserved lemons, dried fruit and sweets made from rosewater sit next to jute bags filled with exotic grains and aromatic spices poured into pointy peaks.

On the shabby base of rue Montmartre, we find more surprising jewels for the keen cook. **MORA**, a professional cookware store founded in 1814, boasts a vast range of baker's equipment. **La Bovida** stocks everything from industrial crêpe machines to elegant cake boxes and Le Creuset cookware, while next door **Comptoir de la Gastronomie** supplies artisanal *charcuterie*, smoked salmon from the Baltic sea, pure Ibérico de Bellota ham and quality regional produce. Just over rue Étienne-Marcel, **A. Simon** stocks an enormous variety of china, glassware, serving dishes and cutlery. Among us we snap up a set of dachshund-shaped knife rests, a dinner plate from l'Avenue (a chic restaurant in the Triangle d'Or neighbourhood) and a set of snail pincers. The adjacent kitchen and *pâtisserie* store is stocked with a huge selection of chocolate and madeleine moulds, and tins for *petits fours*.

With our feet growing weary and the sights and smells making us hungry, we have time for one more stop before lunch. We lose ourselves for longer than intended in **Librairie Gourmande**, a bookshop consisting of two floors devoted exclusively to cookbooks. Most titles are naturally in French but there's also an English language section with translations of the classics.

Lunch time! We head west along rue Étienne-Marcel to the opulent Place des Victoires. Hidden on the edge of the sleepy Place des Petits-Pères is **Chez Georges**, a bustling traditional bistro where simple classics are served in a setting of faded grandeur. A zinc bar, worn leather banquettes, a mosaic floor and large antique mirrors along the length of the long, thin dining room add to the ambience. We take a while to decipher *la carte*, which is handwritten in purple ink with wines scribbled down the side. Resisting the garlicky snails, I indulge in *salade frisée aux lardons, œuf poché* (curly endive salad with bacon and a poached egg) followed by sole simmered in Pouilly wine, and finish with a generous slab of *tarte Tatin*, a caramelised, upside-down apple tart served with *crème fraîche*. Afterwards, we peek into **Au Panetier**, a tiny Belle Époque bakery on the square, to admire the wood-oven bread and the painted parrots that grace the walls.

We walk off lunch by meandering back through the gardens of the Palais Royal, before tackling the cream of the crop of professional cookware stores, **E. Dehillerin** on rue Coquillière. A veritable rabbit warren, it has been selling to chefs since 1820. Heavy copper saucepans, cast-iron snail dishes and fish kettles are crammed floor to ceiling in the Aladdin's cave basement, and all of them can be shipped worldwide. Upstairs it's all pastry and chocolate moulds, intriguing utensils, crêpe and omelette pans and kitchen knives. There are wooden spoons as big as boat oars and sturdy wooden pepper-grinders made by the trusty mechanics at the Peugeot car company.

Another Les Halles institution on rue Coquillière is the colourful **Au Pied de Cochon**. Open twenty-four hours, it originated to serve merchants who arrived at night and worked through the early hours, but soon became known as 'the' place for a fortifying post-theatre bowl of onion soup. *Soupe à l'oignon* is still their specialty along with lavish seafood platters and, for the intrepid gourmet, *tentation de St Antoine*: pig's tail, ear, muzzle and trotters thinly veiled in a *béarnaise* sauce. **La Poule au Pot** is another sure bet for the old Les Halles tradition of onion soup and a deep tureen of *poule au pot*.

Diagonally across from E. Dehillerin behind a private courtyard is **Verrerie des Halles**. We buzz to unlock the gate. This wooden-floored warehouse furnishes cafés, bars and restaurants with classic French glassware, cutlery and crockery. The girls pick up a typical wine jug for *le vin de table*, and some old-fashioned *glace* and *crème brûlée* dishes, while I settle for a set of traditional onion soup bowls. We nearly have enough equipment to open a Parisian bistro!

Cradling my Peugeot pepper-grinder and soup bowls, I hurry home in the cold, inspired to create my very own piece of France – infused with the spirit of old Les Halles.

Rue Montorgueil market
beginning at rue Rambuteau
Metro: Sentier/Les Halles

CAFÉS/RESTAURANTS
Au Panetier
10, Place des Petits-Peres, 75002
Tel: 01 42 60 90 23

Au Pied de Cochon
6, rue Coquillière, 75001
Tel: 01 40 13 77 00
www.pieddecochon.com

Au Rocher de Cancale
59, rue Montorgueil, 75001
Tel: 01 42 33 50 29
www.aurocherdecancale.fr

Chez Georges
1, rue du Mail, 75002
Tel: 01 42 60 07 11
www.chez-georges.com

La Poule au Pot
9, rue Vauvilliers, 75001
Tel: 01 42 97 48 75
www.lapouleaupot.fr

L'Escargot Montorgueil
38, rue Montorgueil, 75001
Tel: 01 42 36 83 51

Le Cochon à l'Oreille
15, rue Montmartre, 75001
Tel: 01 42 36 07 56

A. Simon
48–52, rue Montmartre, 75002
Tel: 01 42 33 71 65
www.simon-a.com

STORES

Ahga, Les Halles Courses
21, rue Montorgueil, 75001
Tel: 01 42 33 72 39

Comptoir de la Gastronomie
34, rue Montmartre, 75001
Tel: 01 42 33 31 32

E. Dehillerin
18–20, rue Coquillière, 75001
Tel: 01 42 36 53 13
www.e-dehillerin.fr

La Bovida
36, rue Montmartre, 75001
Tel: 01 42 36 09 99

Librairie Gourmande
92, rue Montmartre, 75002
Tel: 01 43 54 37 27

MORA
13, rue Montmartre, 75001
Tel: 01 45 08 19 24
www.mora.fr

Stohrer
51, rue Montorgueil, 75002
Tel: 01 42 33 38 20
www.stohrer.fr

Verrerie des Halles
15, rue du Louvre, 75001
Tel: 01 42 36 86 02

Julie calls, mortified.

On the weekend, she and Mark had been invited – as the guests of honour –
to Mark's boss's house.

'For some reason, Mark had in his head that the party started at four
o'clock, so we thought five o'clock would be an appropriate time to arrive,'
she tells me. 'When we walked in, it was difficult enough that we were
the only non-French guests, but then we noticed that no one had a drink.
Oh, Jane, you know how the French are very particular when entertaining.
Did you know that on more formal occasions it is customary not to serve
drinks until everyone has arrived?'

'What time did the others arrive?' I ask cautiously.

'Three o'clock!' she shrieks.

Bon Chic

Just before nine o'clock on a fresh November morning, Annabelle and I arrive at her school building and climb the foyer stairs together. In front of us is a perfectly groomed mother with perfect hair wearing a chic little Dior knit dress. Her daughter, in a valiant attempt to stuff an entire *pain au chocolat* into her mouth before disappearing into the inner sanctum of the school, drops half of the pastry on the stairs. Her perfect mother bends over to retrieve it and gives us an eyeful of lace-trimmed stockings and black suspenders.

Hard as I try, I find it impossible to imagine this scene on a Monday morning at East Adelaide School.

'I don't understand how a woman can leave the house without fixing herself up a little – if only out of politeness. And then, you never know, maybe that's the day she has a date with destiny. And it's always best to be as pretty as possible for destiny.'

Coco Chanel

Beaujolais Nouveau

You soon discover that learning French does not happen by osmosis as you walk the streets, as one is led to believe when you arrive in France. If you don't live with a French speaker (or have a French lover), a frightful amount of constant hard work and discipline is required to improve, and this mostly involves being cooped up in language lessons or hitting the books at home. When you're only in France temporarily, this can pose a dilemma. With the routine of ordinary Parisian life taking a large chunk out of your day, do you spend your precious spare time learning French or discovering Paris?

Sharon is all for discovering Paris, nobly working her way through the enormous list of museums featured in the *TimeOut* Paris guide.

'I suppose I could speak fluent French if I really set my mind to it but there are just too many wonderful things to do,' she bemoans.

Sharon maintains that it's quite possible to get through most days with the phrase '*Vous prenez la carte bleue?*' (Do you take *carte bleue* debit card?). And yet, when elements of *la vie parisienne* and the French language get too hard, even she will admit that it's necessary to knuckle down and learn the fundamentals: shopping and restaurant French. She found her answer in a teacher prepared to help her practise her grammar – while simultaneously practising her shopping at Le Bon Marché and her food knowledge in the surrounding cafés.

One day, after Sharon and her teacher plonked themselves down in a café off rue de Sèvres, she realised with excitement that it was Beaujolais Nouveau Day – an annual event that celebrates the arrival of the new Beaujolais wine. How could she possibly let such an important tradition pass without partaking in it? Her teacher was all in favour.

'*Quelle bonne idée!*' she applauded.

They both enjoyed a glass of the fruity red wine while Sharon learnt all about the traditions of Beaujolais Day (in English). She learnt that Beaujolais Nouveau is made from Gamay grapes in the picturesque region of Beaujolais, just north of the gastronomic capital of France, Lyon, and that all grapes are hand harvested. Sharon's teacher stressed that this fresh, light wine should be drunk almost immediately, meaning before Christmas.

With urgency, they sampled another. Sharon learnt (in English) that Beaujolais Nouveau was made to celebrate the end of the harvest and was never intended to be a pedigree wine, rather a quaffing wine sold and drunk in the same year. Despite criticism that the wine is overrated and that it has been the fall of high-end producers in Beaujolais, it has enjoyed spectacular success. Originally a local tradition, with clever marketing Beaujolais Nouveau Day gained so much popularity that it caught the world's eye.

By her third glass, Sharon was brimming with knowledge. She learnt (in English) that French law dictates that bottles cannot be released earlier than the third Thursday in November and that, in the Beaujolais region, locals are so eager for this day to arrive that the uncorking ceremony is held on the stroke of midnight, when wine stores around the region throw open their doors. At one minute past midnight, millions of bottles start their journey to the capital for immediate distribution around the globe by truck, plane, helicopter and rickshaw . . . and the race is on to see who can be the first to serve the Nouveau Beaujolais in Paris, New York and around the world. Barrels are rolled onto footpaths, *caves* are decorated with vine leaves, vendors don straw hats and red-and-white balloons bob in the breeze. Sweeping banners announce *le Nouveau*

Beaujolais est arrivé, and Parisians everywhere take *une petite pause* to head to the nearest café for a taste of the new season's wine.

As the pair tasted a Georges Dubœuf, the largest producer of Beaujolais Nouveau and a relentless promoter, Sharon's teacher said (in English), 'I hope my company never tests you on your French.'

By the end of the two-hour session, whoops, lesson, Sharon was full of French tradition and wine – if a touch scanty on the intricacies of the French language.

Small Paris Museums

Hidden in historic mansions and secluded in greenery, the countless small museums of Paris offer a refreshing alternative to the long lines at the Louvre. Their manageable size means they can be enjoyed in the space of an hour or two, creating a delightful diversion in a busy day. Intriguing and intimate, they range in style from classic to quirky to downright eccentric. As well as museums devoted to fashion, art and history, there are museums dedicated to Edith Piaf and Baccarat china, a fan museum, a museum of money, and even a post office museum.

Musée Jacquemart-André

Crammed with Rembrandts, Botticellis, eighteenth-century furniture and *objets d'art*, this splendid mansion retains the feel of a private home and is a favourite address of discerning art lovers. Former owners Nélie Jacquemart and Edouard André devoted their lives to art, travelling to Italy to acquire masterpieces. Upon Nélie's death, the mansion and the finest private collection of art in Paris were bequeathed to l'Institut de France.

Upstairs, the impressive museum houses such treasures as Ucello's *St George and the Dragon*, while downstairs was once the setting for many a society reception. With the aid of the audio guide, it's easy to imagine hundreds of coaches delivering the elite of Paris to Edouard and Nélie's doorstep to be received into *le grand salon* where a thousand candles flickered and music was played by the best musicians of the day.

Once the formal dining room, the tearoom is one of the most beautiful in Paris, slung with eighteenth-century tapestries and red velvet drapes. Sip tea and enjoy a pastry under the ceiling painted by Tiepolo before slipping along the street to Les Caves Augé, the oldest, most revered wine shop in town.

Musée Maillol

Dina Vierny was Aristide Maillol's principal model and muse, and the inspiration for his bronze female nudes. In 1995 she opened this elegant museum in homage to him. The artist's sculptures, paintings, drawings, engravings, sketches and prints are displayed here alongside changing exhibits from Vierny's extensive private collection of twentieth-century paintings.

Musée Rodin

Escape the busy streets and enter one of the most peaceful gardens in the city. Auguste Rodin, widely regarded as the greatest sculptor of his time, lived and worked here and nearly 400 of his works are displayed in the eighteenth-century townhouse and large grounds. Especially in the springtime, it's a true oasis in the heart of Paris with over 2000 rosebushes and rows of leafy lime trees. Restored to its original design, the garden features secret paths, a tranquil pond and quiet cool corners in which to contemplate masterpieces such as *The Thinker*, *Balzac* and *The Gates of Hell*.

Musée National Picasso

Built for a salt tax collector, the Hôtel Salé in the Marais now houses the remarkable Musée National Picasso, a successful fusion of modern art with a gracious seventeenth-century mansion. Works by the great Spanish artist are displayed in chronological order. They reflect all phases of his creative career and include paintings, drawings, photographs, illustrations and sculptures. There are also works by Renoir, Matisse and Cézanne.

Maison de Balzac

Just off rue de Passy, fans of Balzac can tour his home and garden, preserved as it was in the 1840s. Memorabilia include letters, first editions and the monogrammed coffee pot that helped the author through the night while slaving away at *La Comédie Humaine*. Balzac lived here when Passy was still a country village, and did so under a false name to avoid his growing band of creditors. To elude surprise visitors, he would slip out the back entrance into rue Berton with its tall, ivy-covered walls. Here, in the stillness, it's easy to picture Balzac

The Musée Jacquemart-André is a favourite address of discerning art lovers

running along the rough-hewn cobbles in his trademark white monk's frock, and to imagine Paris in another time.

Musée du Vin

A few minutes' walk from Balzac's house is the quirky Museum of Wine. For centuries, the friars of the Passy monastery worked the lush garden terraces, orchards and vines that covered this hillside, storing their red wine in the monastery's limestone cellars. Everything was destroyed in the French Revolution but in 1950 the cellars were finally restored and used for wine storage by the Eiffel Tower restaurant, before eventually becoming the Musée du Vin. Visitors are invited to follow a trail of curious antique winemaking tools and drinking utensils (including an ingenious 'coach glass' designed to avoid spillage on rough roads), before finishing with a glass of wine. Admission to the museum is free if you stay for a hearty lunch in the atmospheric cellars.

Children playing outside the Musée National Picasso

Musée Jacquemart-André
Un palais éblouissant,
une collection unique

vendredi 22.03.2002

1 X P.Tarif   8,00 E

Musée de la Poupée

Children adore this private collection of handmade dolls (*les poupées*), a short stroll from the Centre Pompidou. Tucked at the end of a quiet lane, the magical museum tells the story of dolls from 1800–1919. Presented in chronological order, the dolls reflect the fashions of their time and the materials available. They come alive against a backdrop of beautiful Parisian scenes. The museum also boasts an assortment of doll houses, toys and teddy bears. There's a doll shop and a hospital too, should your antique doll be in need of emergency surgery.

Patrimoine Photographique

This sumptuous Marais mansion, adorned with stunning bas-reliefs of the four seasons and the elements, was built for a notorious gambler who later lost it all in a single roll of the dice. Inside is a gallery devoted to the photographic heritage of France where regular, temporary exhibitions by French and foreign photographers are held. Slip through the poky back door (on the southwest corner of Place des Vosges) into the secluded courtyard with its clipped hedges and orangery. The grounds alone are worth the visit.

Musée Marmottan-Claude Monet

Housed in a former hunting lodge on the edge of the Bois de Boulogne, this most pleasant of small museums boasts the world's largest collection of Monets, including a stunning series of his water-lily canvases. Among its 300 paintings are works by Berthe Morisot, Sisley and Pissaro, and sculptures from the Impressionist and Post-Impressionist periods.

Musées des Parfumeries-Fragonard

Just steps from l'Opéra Garnier, perfume lovers can explore the world of fragrance in the house of Fragonard and discover 3000 years of perfume-making history. The museum extends over two locations, a Napoléon III mansion on rue Scribe and Théâtre Capucines on the adjacent boulevard. Both offer free guided tours. On show is an exquisite collection of perfume bottles, antique lipstick moulds, powder boxes, laboratory utensils and a mini factory. A boutique selling luxurious French scents completes the experience.

'A girl who doesn't wear perfume has no future.'

Coco Chanel

Maison de Balzac
47, rue Raynouard, 75016
Tel: 01 55 74 41 80

Musée Jacquemart-André
158, blvd Haussmann, 75008
Tel: 01 45 62 11 59
www.musee-jacquemart-andre.
com

Musée Maillol
61, rue de Grenelle, 75007
Tel: 01 42 22 59 58
www.museemaillol.com

Musée Marmottan-Claude Monet
2, rue Louis-Boilly, 75016
Tel: 01 44 96 50 33
www.marmottan.com

Musée National Picasso
Hôtel Salé
5, rue de Thorigny, 75003
Tel: 01 42 71 25 21
www.musee-picasso.fr

Musées des Parfumeries-Fragonard
9, rue Scribe, 75009
Tel: 01 47 42 04 56

39, blvd des Capucines, 75002
Tel: 01 42 60 37 14
www.fragonard.com

Musée de la Poupée
Impasse Berthaud, 75003
Tel: 01 42 72 73 11
www.museedelapoupeeparis.
com

Musée Rodin
Hôtel Biron
79, rue de Varenne, 75007
Tel: 01 44 18 61 10
www.musee-rodin.fr

Musée du Vin
5, square Charles Dickens, 75016
Tel: 01 45 25 63 26
www.museeduvinparis.com

Patrimoine Photographique
Hôtel de Sully
62, rue St-Antoine, 75004
Tel: 01 42 74 47 75

Georgie and Annabelle in the gardens of the Musée Rodin

Le Cours de Français

With the crisp November days starting to draw in and winter around the corner, the last place I want to be this afternoon is cooped up in the apartment with a French textbook. Paris is just outside in the soft sunlight. Besides, the clock is ticking louder now, and I want to embrace everything in this wonderful city before it's time to go home in a few short months. Not that anything is certain these days. We have become puppets on a corporate string. When Margueritte arrives for my weekly French lesson, I decide to take a leaf out of Sharon's book and ask if we can take a tour of *le marché* instead.

'You could show me some of your favourite produce, give me tips on how to order and cook various foods and I could extend my food French,' I say, keen to persuade her. 'Besides, I'm sure to remember more with the visual cues of the market.'

'*Bien sûr*,' she says without hesitation, flicking her shawl back over her shoulder. '*On y va!*' (Let's go!)

I'm sure she is tired of textbooks too.

We pass by *le chocolatier*, stopping to admire *les chocolats d'automne* moulded into corn, mushroom and walnut shapes.

'You must always buy the very best chocolate you can afford,' advises Margueritte. 'Life's too short to eat bad chocolate. In fact, I always spit out chocolate that's mediocre: it's not worth wasting the calories.'

Everything in this city is about quality, not quantity. The French really know how to taste life.

As we walk on, Margueritte's love of food and the smells and sights of the market push her into overdrive.

'Buy the big oysters if you want to cook them,' she says, pointing to oysters on beds of ice.

'Oh, look at those lovely snails – just pop them on a bed of rock salt in a hot oven until the butter has melted, about ten minutes,' she continues.

As we pass the fruit and vegetable stall she picks up a brown onion.

'See how thick the skins are this year,' she muses. 'My mother has always said that if the onions have rugged up it's going to be an extra cold winter.'

'I hope she is wrong.'

'No . . . she is never wrong . . . *Le boucher*,' says Margueritte, moving on, 'likes to think of himself as an artist who prides himself on recommending cuts and recipes and giving cooking tips.'

As she speaks, a mincer on the wall behind the counter swallows up her words and a piece of beef with a loud rumble.

'You see that,' says Margueritte, 'customers choose the piece of meat they want and it's minced right before their eyes. There's nothing better than a good *steak haché* rare; it is not so much a burger made from an inferior cut, but fine, freshly ground steak.'

Margueritte goes through the display cabinet giving me a lesson on *les viandes*. I learn about specific cuts and the effects of marbling on taste and texture.

'Meat is aged only briefly in France,' she says, pointing out top-quality Charolais and Limousin beef and *Chateaubriand*. I don't let on that I know a little about meat, having grown up on a sheep and cattle property.

'Keep your eye out for *l'agneau de pré-salé*,' she continues. 'It's very tasty – a true *trésor gastronomique*. Incomparable to other lamb, although so is the price. Unfortunately it is hard to find.' Grazing on pastures that are frequently flooded by the sea, the most famous *pré-salé* is *le grévin*, hailing from La Baie du Mont-St-Michel. The high salt content results in a tender and juicy meat, and the abundance of herbs contributes to its distinct flavour.

'There are chickens and there are Bresse chickens,' says Margueritte, moving on to a bird with blue feet. She goes on to tell me that *poulets de Bresse* are the only chickens in the world protected by an AOC (*appellation d'origine contrôlée*), with strict and precise guidelines defining the zone, breed and rearing conditions.

'They are the world's best,' she says, proudly. 'Top of the pecking order.'

The nineteenth-century epicure and gastronome Brillat-Savarin described *poulet de Bresse* as 'the queen of chickens and the chicken of kings'. Unfortunately, demand for the birds is so high they rarely make it out of France. These rich-flavoured, white-fleshed chickens with yellow fat are reared on small farms around Bresse in the Rhône-Alps. Fed on a mixture of grains and milk, they happily roam the meadows, spending their last days in a wooden box to rest and fatten up.

'The one you see here is the most common variety,' says Margueritte, 'the distinctive Bény, with pure white feathers, a single red crown and aristocratic blue feet, making it a mascot of France.' I take a closer look and see that a distinct *tricolore* seal adorns the bird's neck and a metal ring identifying the breeder is placed around the foot, adding weight to its authenticity.

My mind wanders to butchers' shops in Australia. One will rarely see meat or poultry for sale with any part attached that could inadvertently remind the customer that it was once a live creature. We find it distasteful. By the time a bird or animal is displayed behind the sanitised glass counter, it has generally been transformed into something unrecognisable – something edible. In France, people often prefer to purchase animals and birds that still wear feathers or fur, faces and feet. A rabbit really is a rabbit – with a fluffy cottontail to prove it.

I bump into my neighbour Greg, who is stocking up for a visitor arriving tonight. 'Our ninety-third house guest,' he says, 'and people wonder what I do all day! We're pretty well booked up until the summer.' Having lived in Paris for just over two years, he definitely wins *le prix d'or* (gold prize). I leave him to collect his meat and his thoughts.

At *la charcuterie* across the way, Margueritte motions me towards what looks like a slab of smoked bacon: 'This is *poitrine fumé*. If you get homesick for an English breakfast, ask for this very thinly sliced. Mostly it's cut thickly for lardons.'

Further down the street a man is selling a variety of smoked sausages. We sample a couple and I buy a few slices. 'I still never know what do with a sausage,' says Margueritte. 'There are so many varieties and so many ways to cook them. I'm forever calling my mother.'

If Margueritte has no idea, I have no hope! I turn to leave, my head swirling with new words and recipes, but Margueritte has other ideas.

'Oh look, *le fromager* is selling five crottins de Chavignol on promotion,' she says, urging me to join the queue. She explains that this excellent goat's cheese has been produced since the sixteenth century in the village of Chavignol near Sancerre, and is protected by strict AOC laws.

'I don't know if I need five cheeses, Margueritte. Two would probably do.'

'*Non, non, non,*' demands Margueritte. 'You must buy *cinq*. Be sure to tell *le fromager* if you intend to cook the goat's cheese. You will be given only the moistest, freshest cheese so it won't dry out during cooking.' She explains that crottin de Chavignol is one of the few cheeses that can be eaten at various stages of maturation, becoming harder, drier and fuller in flavour with age, and developing a blanket of blue mould.

We move up the queue. I watch on as *le fromager* cuts a thick wedge from a giant wheel of Beaufort, a popular, hard French cheese from the Alps that complements both fruit and salmon.

Margueritte launches into a dissertation on the virtues of *le fromage de chèvre* and the various ways in which she cooks it, reciting a recipe for tomatoes stuffed with goat's cheese as we inch up the queue.

'Push little purses of cheese into the prepared tomatoes and be sure to sprinkle with *des herbes de Provence* before cooking. I usually serve them with salad and *magret de canard fumé* (fillet of smoked duck),' she says.

I have suddenly become very hungry.

'And of course the cheese goes particularly well with a glass of Sancerre.'

I have reached the front of the queue.

'*SVP Monsieur*, ten of the goat's cheeses on special and a big slice of Beaufort.'

'If I had a son who was ready to marry, I would tell him, "Beware of girls who don't like wine, truffles, cheese or music."'

Colette

La Poste 1

Ask any resident about the postal service in France and, after an initial speechless pause, they will launch forth with their latest frustrating tale. Many foreigners will procrastinate for days rather than confront the growing pile of unsent parcels in the hallway. Finally, when the pile gets too high to ignore and relatives at home are wondering whether you've forgotten their birthday, it's time for a dreaded trip to La Poste.

The first test to pass on entering La Poste is to choose the right *guichet* (counter) as different counters offer different services, which also vary depending on the size and organisation of the particular post office. If this seems too difficult, make a beeline for the counter marked *Toutes Opérations* (All Operations). During busy periods, this queue will be the longest and people will constantly push in front of you but at least you will usually not be turned away at the end of your pilgrimage. You may, however, have to leave to be somewhere else on time with your packages still in tow.

La Copine

Discover I have no taste, bad taste, *de mauvais goût* . . . Françoise is over for tea.

'Do you really have to keep a desk in here? Can't it go down there somewhere?' she says, gesturing to the out-of-sight bedrooms.

'There is no room. You are forgetting our apartment is smaller than yours, Françoise.'

'And that IKEA bookcase can't go there next to that beautiful marble fireplace.'

'Yes, yes, I know it's not ideal,' I say, trying to justify myself, 'but a lot of our furniture is in storage in Australia. We were only going to be in Paris for a couple of years, remember, and really, we could go home at any minute.'

'That sofa must go on an angle so you have more room to move,' says Françoise. She pushes and pulls it around. 'Now, doesn't that look better?' She laughs and says, 'Oh, you must be thinking, what kind of a friend is she?'

I bite my lip.

'Once you are friends in France,' she explains, 'you are allowed to tell your *copine* exactly what you think of her clothes, her house, her cooking. Isn't that what friendship is all about?'

'To a degree,' I mutter.

'You need good friends to tell you what you can't see yourself. So take it as a compliment.'

Especially in Paris, a guarded politeness often excludes you from the homes of neighbours, and French friendships, like a bottle of good Bordeaux, age slowly. By Australian standards the French are terribly private, tending to cultivate a small, very select group of friends. Once you *are* friends, however, there is a high level of commitment and expectation. This discerning approach to friendship does have merit. Like a carefully chosen collection of exclusive Hermès scarves, French friends are enduring, dependable, of consistently high quality and always there when you need a lift.

Unless, of course, they are tied too tightly.

La Poste 2

It was with trepidation that Teresa, heavily pregnant and with Christmas beating at her door, climbed the steps of La Poste carrying a tower of Christmas cards. She passed the first test with flying colours. Juggling her stockpile with her keys balanced precariously on top, she dived straight into the short line at the *guichet* designed for customers with a large amount of mail requiring a large number of stamps. She watched the long All Operations line flashing past next to her with only a glint of remorse before she was finally served.

'*Bonjour, Madame,*' said the attendant. 'Would you like *des beaux timbres* (fancy stamps) on your mail today?'

'No, just ordinary ones will do,' said Teresa.

'Well, I am not selling ordinary stamps today, only fancy ones,' replied the attendant. It seemed he had been bestowed this special status for the day. 'You will have to join the All Operations line to purchase ordinary stamps. Next please.'

With her jaw starting to clench, she joined the All Operations line. Eventually she came up for air at the counter.

'Madame, you should be in the queue for a large amount of mail,' said the attendant.

'He apparently only sells fancy stamps and I don't want fancy stamps, just ordinary ones,' explained Teresa, only just containing herself.

'One moment please,' said the attendant, as he sauntered over to his colleague for a little chat. In a few moments he was back. 'I'm afraid there has been a misunderstanding, Madame. You did not, I believe, understand that you could buy lovely fancy stamps for the same price as ordinary ones. There is no extra charge. They are very nice to send overseas,' he said.

'OKAY THEN!' screamed Teresa, 'GIVE ME FANCY STAMPS.'

'I'm sorry, Madame, but I don't sell fancy stamps. You will have to return to your original queue. Next please.'

Defeated, Teresa flew out of the queue, dropping her keys from the top of her perilous pile. No one batted an eyelid.

A woman in the queue finally said, 'Madame, you have dropped your keys.'

'I know,' Teresa said, smiling through gritted teeth. Fearing a landslide, she asked the woman if she would mind picking them up for her.

'*Elles sont pour vous, Madame,*' said the woman, surprised. 'They are for you, they are yours!'

Turning crimson now, Teresa stooped as best she could with her large belly to pick up her keys, inducing the predicted snowy landslide of letters onto the wet floor followed by an unpredicted flood of tears. And then, muddy letters in hand, she escaped from La Poste and headed home.

Greg 1

I bump into Greg at *la boucherie, encore*. He tells me he brought along a recipe for stew that called for a top sirloin cut of meat.

'So I asked the butcher for some top sirloin,' he says. 'Naturally, he asked me what I was going to do with this fine cut of meat and I replied proudly that I was going to make a very nice stew for the family. I heard a collective gasp as *le boucher* and his customers alike reacted to my outrageous plan to turn a perfectly good cut of meat into a stew. And then he refused to sell me the sirloin for this purpose! He did, however, recommend a more suitable cut to stew,' he adds, holding up a parcel.

'Bye,' he says, retreating home to make the stew. 'I'll let you know how it turns out . . .'

La Poste 3

A strong cup of coffee later, Teresa felt a little better, strong enough in fact to face the Monoprix supermarket to pick up a few groceries so that the whole morning wasn't wasted. After quickly grabbing her supplies, she arrived at the '10 items or less' checkout in time to see a Frenchman and the checkout operator in a wild, feverish exchange: fists banging, shoulders shrugging, mouths pouting. Now, the minimum payment amount for transactions by credit card varies in France, but in some supermarkets, like Monoprix, it is just 5€, which is very convenient – but not quite convenient enough for some. The Frenchman's groceries came to 4.90€, surely near enough to 5€, or so he thought.

'*Non, Monsieur,*' said the checkout operator, 'it is a minimum of 5 euros. I'm sorry but I cannot accept your card.'

'*C'est ridicule!*' shouted the man. '*C'est stupide!*'

'It is our rule,' she replied loudly.

The queue squirmed behind him, growing longer. After all it was Christmas time and everyone was in a hurry.

Le boucher prides himself on recommending cuts and recipes

The checkout, as anywhere in the world, was smattered with rows of chocolate bars and *bonbons*. A sideways stretch and a nimble flick of the wrist would have effortlessly brought down a tin of *pastilles*, pushing the amount over 5€: situation resolved. His wife even offered to slip him the cash.

But no, it was the principle of the matter.

'You give me no choice,' he announced to the checkout operator and to the queue behind him. '*Je vais à la banque.*' (I am going to the bank.)

So off went the proud Parisian down the street while Teresa, the flourishing line, the checkout operator and the proud Parisian's wife waited patiently. Until, that is, someone snapped and a verbal brawl erupted between the wife, the queue and the operator. After the post office episode, Teresa had no intention of changing checkouts. Eventually the Frenchman returned, paid, and left with his wife who was now giving him a mouthful for throwing her to the dogs. The queue stepped back into line (until next time) and Teresa dashed to school just in time to pick up her girls for lunch.

But it is not only foreigners who sometimes find dealing with Parisians difficult. A pre-film advertisement for *Le Parisien* newspaper at the local cinema shows an elderly woman with a couple of items waiting patiently in the supermarket checkout line. Along comes a brash young Parisian with a burgeoning trolley and pushes right in front of her. The old woman looks at the checkout operator and they both shrug their shoulders in resignation. The punch line of the ad roughly translates to: 'It's better to read *Le Parisien* every day than to deal with Parisians every day.'

Julie calls, stuffed.

She has spent the morning prostrate on the couch, recovering. Mark's French relatives were up from their winery in Bordeaux and yesterday the family had been invited for Sunday lunch at their country house in Fontainbleau, 70 kilometres from Paris. Elise and Madeline were especially excited at the prospect of playing in a garden and running in the woods after lunch. Julie explained how they sat down *à table* at one o'clock, starting with Grandma's thirty-year-old pickled eels, which were raised on the Bordeaux property. The girls had gingerly tasted their first glass of Champagne, sprinkled with gold shavings. They proceeded through the afternoon with various delicacies, including dead ants (passed around in a crystal bowl) that Mark's uncle had recently brought back from Caracas. Lunch finished at ten o'clock with dessert, then coffee. The girls were excused from the table earlier, but, even so, by the time they made their escape it was dark.

Les Soldes

Ready, set, go! The day has finally arrived: the official launch of the winter sales. Locals wait with tapping toes for the biannual January and July sales; this morning, boutiques around Paris will open their doors to a stampede of shoppers. For days, platform walls in *les stations de métro* have been covered with bright posters from all the major department stores and hundreds of boutique windows are almost entirely hidden behind huge paper *SOLDES* signs. Yes, we too were confused the first time we were witness to the sales phenomenon.

'How can everything in the windows already be sold?' asked Georgie.

(N.B. *Solde* translates to 'sale' not 'sold'.)

January also means the start of the fashion shows with presentations of the couturiers' upcoming collections running through February. But today, for fashionistas, shopping takes precedence.

The string of exclusive boutiques on rue St-Honoré is jam-packed with chic bargain hunters. A long queue of jewel-encrusted women, none of whom looks vaguely in need of new clothes, waits patiently outside the Gucci store. Their eyes are fixed on the man in black who unlocks the door with a deadpan face, lets in a few fortunate customers, and then wields his power by slamming it shut again.

Around the corner on boulevard de la Madeleine, a branch of Decathlon (the French sporting-goods chain store) has become a running preview for the forthcoming February holidays. Ski pants, gloves and hats are being pulled on in the aisles. Sleds zoom across the floor. Ice-skates are laced up with dreams of shiny rinks. With grand reductions all round, Parisians are buying by the truckload.

But to really experience sales mania, the place that epitomises it all is boulevard Haussmann. Footpaths are seething with people and life. There are displays of magic saucepans, miraculous vegetable graters and somersaulting toy dogs. The organ grinder is in his usual spot, the air is filled with music. Next to him sits a little wooden bed. Under the covers a dog and cat lie entwined in a deep sleep.

'How cute,' I hear a tourist say, as she throws a few coins into the bowl. Yet it's interesting to note that each time I chance upon the organ grinder, the dog and cat are always in the same deep, comatose sleep.

On the ground floor of Galeries Lafayette, the beauty counters of Chanel, Givenchy and Yves Saint Laurent are presenting numerous *petit prix* offers. Downstairs, there are 3000 square metres of shoes. Upstairs in women's fashion, exclusive brands that usually cost *les yeux de la tête* (eyes from your head) or *la peau des fesses* (skin of your bottom) are reduced by up to half.

But it's the lingerie department that I find most thrilling, with a mood of quiet but serious pampering. Tables are graced with hundreds of pretty little boxes filled with luxurious lingerie in every style and colour, for every occasion. Like quality scarves, feminine frills and lace are seen as an investment, and play a major role in *la séduction*. As Veronique Vienne wrote in *The Art of Being a Woman*, 'The famous French expression '*vive la différence*' takes the sting out of the disparity between men and women by highlighting the contrasts rather than the inequalities between the sexes.'

Women of all ages are holding up lingerie to themselves in the mirror, prodding and parading. Sales assistants are busy singing the praises of a Prada g-string and a silk chiffon ensemble, their contorted fingers stretching scraps of frothy fabric into aesthetic poses.

But I can't keep my eyes off the couples.

Men carefully examine styles and fabrics with their partners, holding flouncy *negligées* up to the light and delicate *slips* to their cheeks to confirm their softness. In hushed tones, a lengthy debate flourishes on the virtues of a Chantal Thomass *bustier*. This is serious business. Even more astounding is that nobody seems the least bit coy. It's as natural as checking out the features of a new family car.

In fact, the only males who appear uncomfortable are two Japanese men who have lost their way.

'*Excusez-moi, Madame,*' one of them blurts out to a sales assistant. 'Which floor are we on?'

'You are on the third floor – in *la lingerie* department,' she answers, at which they turn into a wobbling, giggling mass of bright red jelly and shoot off down the escalator.

As a promotion to celebrate the refurbishment of the Galeries Lafayette lingerie department some years ago, free lessons in striptease were offered by a couple of professional striptease artists to teach the skill of undressing in an elegant way. The phone rang off the hook. While the striptease classes exist no more, the store holds a free half-hour fashion show in the Salon Opéra on the seventh floor of the Coupole building most Friday afternoons at three o'clock, showing the latest trends in haute couture and prêt à porter.

Reservations are required. Email: welcome@galerieslafayette.com.

'One of the most captivating qualities of Parisian women is their self-confidence. They wear it like a fine couture gown, perfectly fitted to their body, their age, their style. It shows in the way they carry themselves, and the way they interact with others. What makes them so confident is their keen awareness that being attractive has very little to do with superficial looks.'

Heather Stimmler-Hall, *Naughty Paris: A Lady's Guide to the Sexy City*

Bon Voyage

Having seriously miscalculated the time it would take to physically set up house and emotionally settle everyone in, time flies by before I really get down to pursuing my dream of writing. Besides, we seem to be away on holiday *a lot*. While school terms are taxing, they are balanced by a hefty number of holidays, totalling around fifteen weeks per year. Tim is equally blessed with an exorbitant amount of annual leave – on average seven weeks per year buffered by *jours fériés* (public holidays).

We use this time wisely, renting *un gîte* in Provence, a villa in Tuscany, a traditional quinta in northern Portugal and a thatched roofed cottage in the Devon countryside. Not to mention trips to the Loire valley, Alsace, Scotland, Turkey, Venice, Positano, Pompeii . . .

As Australians, we treasure every trip, considering ourselves ever so lucky. A fleeting two-hour flight, even a two-hour drive, transports us to an exciting new country with a different culture, language, landscape and cuisine. For many Europeans, of course, jaunts like these are perfectly plausible on a regular basis. Airfares are relatively inexpensive and planning where to go next becomes an occupation for some, although fortunate French families also have *une résidence secondaire* in the country where the extended family gathers several times a year. Often it has been passed down the generations.

With all these adventures, my enthusiasm for travel and food writing explodes. Eager to document all the wonderful sights, tastes and places, soon I have a stack of notebooks, serviettes, menus and brochures amassed, covered with comments. I pore over the food and travel magazines at WH Smith on our weekly sojourn, dissecting styles, structure, grammar and content. Finally I get around to putting some of it on the computer. I type up the notes I jotted down on our day trip to Les Halles, shape them into a story, run back to fact-check the details, and email it to *The Age* in Melbourne. I send off a number of pitches and even take a photography course with Iris at WICE, a 'non-profit association providing cultural and educational programs in English for the international community in Paris'. Together we spend hours clicking the black-and-white columns of the Palais Royal, the sleek lines of La Défense and Montparnasse metro station.

www.wice-paris.org

Amalfi

Tuscany

Venice

Greg 2

I bump into Greg at *la boucherie, encore*.

'My stew was delicious,' he says, his attention focused on what the butcher is doing. 'From now on, I have decided to clear everything with him before I attempt any new meat dish.'

He explains that he is buying ingredients for dinner to entertain his wife Colette's French cousins whom she hasn't seen since she was fifteen years old.

'Wanting to make a good impression, I asked *le boucher* for his advice on what to serve. He seemed ever so proud to be asked his opinion. He responded with a lot of questions. Who are they – family, friends, colleagues or strangers? I replied that they were French cousins of my wife's from the Alps, near Grenoble. He suggested *brochettes traditionnelle*: kebabs with lamb, beef and sausage served with rice pilaf and a dish of mixed vegetables. Then he asked for twenty minutes to prepare *les brochettes* . . . I've been watching him select the cuts of meat, cut them into perfect cubes and place them in order on the skewer with great care. He's also prepared a marinade and seasoning packet for me. Believe me – I am going to follow his instructions to the letter. I don't want to disappoint him!'

Having picked up his meat, Greg says goodbye and proceeds to visit *le cavîste* (wine merchant) next door. He is a man on a mission.

La Viande

For the Australian in France, meat can be difficult to decode. It is not just a case of simple translation – French cuts often differ from Australian cuts. If in doubt, do as the locals do and tell the butcher what dish you intend to prepare. Simply request '*Un bourguignon pour six personnes, SVP*' (*bœuf bourguignon* for six people, please), for instance, and the butcher in his infinite wisdom will choose the meat required, chop it into correctly sized cubes and add any garnishes. This is much easier than trying to figure out which cut is equivalent to Australian chuck steak. The method works particularly well for more complicated dishes like *pot-au-feu*. Instead of torturing yourself translating and documenting amounts of beef, veal shank, marrow bones, oxtail (and perhaps Polish sausage, pieces of chicken and gizzards), all you need to say is, '*Un pot-au-feu pour six personnes, SVP.*'

N.B. I have learnt to be very careful when ordering *porc* on a menu: there are many, many parts to a pig . . .

Musée de Cluny

An early morning chorus of birds has woken the still, sleeping courtyard and most of our building. It is the first week of March and the girls are up and ready to start the third and final trimester of the year. Miraculously, two weeks of vacation have shaken off the winter. In *le métro*, the coughs and colds of February have been put away with the gloves. As we crunch through Parc Monceau to school, I notice that it too has awoken from its long sleep, but as yet it is a tapestry half completed. Splashes of colour are embroidered here and there: the first yellow jonquils in long, swirling drifts, cherry trees with tight pink buds and tiny, purple crocuses. A man is sweeping the gravel in the playground with a broom. It is like a newly raked bunker. I restrain Georgie from jumping the fence and running about to mess it all up. We crunch on, past *au pairs* pushing prams and past spotless little treasures with bobs and bows running towards *l'école* in coats with velvet collars. Opposite the school, the magnolia tree that shivered all winter has burst into glorious bud, its pale violet flowers stretching skyward.

We have now been in Paris for almost three years, and as each month passes I'm better acquainted with the rhythm of the seasons. Once again, Tim's contract has been extended. For how long who knows, but now that we're settled, I'm grateful to have the time to really enjoy Paris, and to write. For a food and travel writer, Paris is an excellent place to be. It is stimulating, inspiring and in the beating heart of Europe. There is a never-ending source of stories right on my doorstep.

I kiss the girls goodbye, quickly drop into Le Vigny, then zip to the Marais. *The Age* has accepted my pitch on the quarter. Watching the clock, I race around the ancient streets, peering into gardens and down alleyways. By two o'clock I'm back to pick up Georgie who is finishing early today; it's a perfect opportunity to spend a cultural afternoon together.

With the city bathed in the promise of spring, it seems disheartening to take the metro. We grab *un sandwich jambon* each and two strawberry tartlets in little boxes, and ride the 84 bus past St-Augustin, before skirting around the Madeleine and shaking over the cobblestoned Place de la Concorde, site of the guillotine. We cross over the Seine into the heart of the Left Bank, pass St-Sulpice, snake across the top of the Luxembourg Gardens and hop off as the Panthéon rises before us. In the blink of an eye, we have taken a tour of Paris.

From here, it's a quick walk along the front of the Sorbonne to the **Musée National du Môyen Age**, a romantic Gothic castle better known as the Cluny.

The former abbey sits atop a Gallo-Roman bathhouse and is set in a garden inspired by the Middle Ages. The museum is filled with treasures:

- The Golden Rose of Basil, a long-stemmed bunch of roses made of gold for the Pope in the thirteenth century.
- A headless angel.
- An angel's head.
- A narwhal's horn. (The narwhal, a cousin of the whale, lives in the Arctic and has a huge spear of spiralling ivory protruding from its face. A Viking explorer found a narwhal and took home its horn, starting the legend of the unicorn.)
- The stone heads of the Kings of Judah (circa 1220), unearthed during renovations to the Galeries Lafayette department store.
- Medieval sculptures, paintings, stained-glass windows and religious artefacts including a monk's misery seat depicting scenes of everyday life – monks could not possibly put their bottoms on a biblical scene!
- The headstone of Nicolas Flammel, the medieval bookseller and public scribe who allegedly discovered the secret of alchemy. Found in a nineteenth-century marketplace, his upside-down headstone was being used as a chopping board for spinach.

The highlight, however, is the celebrated fifteenth-century *The Lady and the Unicorn* tapestries, *La Dame à la Licorne*. Discovered by George Sands in a *château* attic and brought to light by her writings, they are worth the trip alone. Hanging in their own dimly lit circular *salon* to preserve the fabric, they evoke an atmosphere that is at once harmonious, mysterious and magical. There are six tapestries in all, ablaze with rich colours. The first five are allegorical representations of the senses. The sixth is named *To My Own Desire* and its true meaning, although vehemently debated, remains a mystery – like the power *The Lady and the Unicorn* possesses. In each tapestry a beautiful woman with flowing, golden hair is standing on a floating blue island. Flowers are raining into the deep red background. She is flanked by a lion and a unicorn and her surrounds are alive with scampering rabbits and foxes, partridges and leopards. Tall trees are adorned with holly, oranges and acorns.

Georgie is mesmerised by the tapestries' incredible beauty. Spellbound, she sits down to contemplate them further, squashing her strawberry tartlet. She talks about them incessantly for the remainder of the afternoon and devours

The Musée National du Môyen Age
(better known as Musée de Cluny)

a book about them in the evening. It would be impossible to live in Paris without developing a sense of history and an appreciation of art. Everything is permeated with beauty, and everywhere art overlaps life.

Musée National du Môyen Age
6, Place Paul-Painlevė, 75005
Tel: 01 53 73 78 16
www.musee-moyenage.fr

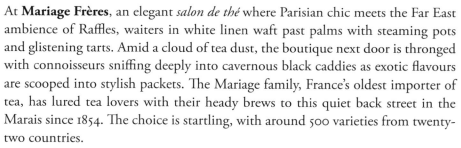

'If you are lucky enough to have lived in Paris as a young man, then wherever you go for the rest of your life, it stays with you, for Paris is a moveable feast.'

Ernest Hemingway

The Historic Marais

At **Mariage Frères**, an elegant *salon de thé* where Parisian chic meets the Far East ambience of Raffles, waiters in white linen waft past palms with steaming pots and glistening tarts. Amid a cloud of tea dust, the boutique next door is thronged with connoisseurs sniffing deeply into cavernous black caddies as exotic flavours are scooped into stylish packets. The Mariage family, France's oldest importer of tea, has lured tea lovers with their heady brews to this quiet back street in the Marais since 1854. The choice is startling, with around 500 varieties from twenty-two countries.

I study the thick menu and find perfumed teas sprinkled with flowers, green tea with Moroccan mint, even *thé de Pâques*, evoking the taste of *crème brûlée*.

'Which is your favourite?' I ask the waiter. '*Ça dépend*,' he pouts, tweaking his white bow tie, 'on the hour, the season, the mood . . .'

Like Mariage Frères, the historic Marais quarter on the Right Bank offers an exhilarating bouquet of aromas and flavours. The neighbourhood has something for every time and taste. Life, art and culture pour from its overflowing cup. Swamped with boutiques, lively bars, bistros and galleries, the ancient village is also home to the most notable examples of pre-revolutionary Paris, providing an opportunity for the savvy traveller to effortlessly combine culture with commerce.

Add a fairytale dusting of lavish *hôtels particuliers* (private town mansions) and the Marais is the best of Paris distilled into a strong, seductive brew that will leave you thirsty for more.

The area claims most of the 3rd and 4th, bordering Les Halles and extending to Place de la Bastille. Lying just outside the original 1180 city wall, the district began as marshland (*marais* meaning marsh), scattered with kitchen gardens. Gradually growing in popularity, the area reached its peak in the seventeenth century when Henri IV built Place des Vosges, and it became *à la mode* with country gentry desiring *un hôtel particulier* in Paris.

But then came the Revolution – the aristocrats lost their beautiful mansions along with their heads, and the Marais fell into ruin. By the Industrial Revolution, artisans and the working class had moved in, mansions were partitioned into workshops and many more were destroyed. While a clutch of mansions remain privately owned, thanks to a preservation order many have been restored to their original grandeur and converted into small, intriguing museums.

This inspiring neighbourhood draws a creative crowd and an eclectic bunch of young professionals who dally on the café terraces and live in the apartments above. It is also home to gay Paris. By the nature of its residents, the Marais is not an early riser. Weekend mornings are particularly quiet, with no more activity than a reluctant trek to *la boulangerie*. But by Saturday afternoon, footpaths throb as locals emerge to meet friends for a drink, slip into a museum or scan their favourite stores. Sunday, too, the streets are alive, the Marais being one of the few quarters open for Sunday trading.

Comprising a rich ethnic mix, this unique pocket also houses the remains of the old Jewish quarter. Jews first settled here in the 1300s, with a large influx from Eastern and Central Europe arriving at the turn of the twentieth century. Sephardic Jews from North Africa moved in more recently. The community's main thoroughfare is the lively rue des Rosiers, a jumble of kosher butchers, bakeries, delicatessens and grocers. Orthodox Jews yarn on the street. Crooked stairways lead to hidden synagogues. Along the length of the narrow street, falafels dripping with hummus are constructed at lightning speed and poked through takeaway windows to waiting hands. Come for Sunday lunch to really soak up the atmosphere. **L'As du Fallafel** makes delicious falafels and homemade lemonade to go, while **Chez Marianne**, an attractive corner restaurant adorned with ivy, is a much-loved stronghold of Jewish food and Middle Eastern mezze. After tea, I stop by **Sacha Finkelsztajn**'s for a square of dense, dreamy cheesecake (in the name of research) and admire the giant trays of *pavot* (poppyseed) strudel

Photographie, Yolande Finkelsztajn

SACHA FINKELSZTAJN
DE PERE EN FILS DEPUIS 1946

MAISON FONDÉE EN
1854
THÉ
QUALITÉ
SUPÉRIEURE
MARIAGE
FRÈRES
MF

LES MEILLEURS CRUS
LA GRANDE TRADITION

BREAKFAST EARL GREY
Thé du matin à la bergamote
Bergamot morning blend

The Marais offers an exhilarating bouquet of aromas and flavours

and pastries dripping with honey. Known as *la boutique jaune*, the yellow shop has been in the same family for three generations, serving delicious Yiddish specialties since 1946.

On rue des Francs-Bourgeois, I tumble into a world far removed from freshly baked bagels. Footpaths buzz with locals juggling shopping bags. One of the major streets slicing through the area, it's crammed with stylish boutiques, jewellery and gift stores. After a bit more scouting about, I plonk myself down at **Camille**, an authentic bistro (and my personal favourite in the quarter), which offers a traditional *plat du jour,* classic dishes and regional wines by the *pichet*. While I wait for my *salade Niçoise*, I take the opportunity to write up a few notes. Gradually I am becoming more confident with my French, questioning *le pâtissier* and *le fromager* and bowling up to *le patron* in hotels and boutiques. I am also becoming more inquisitive and inquiring in search of a story, following medieval alleyways, venturing through doorways and delving into quarters and establishments I may not have otherwise discovered.

After lunch I explore the swag of skinny side streets surrounding rue des Francs-Bourgeois, where original boutiques sit next to small art galleries, before losing myself in the maze of exquisitely decorated rooms at **Musée Carnavalet**. Built as a private mansion in 1545, it now houses the Museum of the City of Paris. Included in its astonishing collection of treasures are a reconstruction of Marcel Proust's bedroom and the original Fouquet jewellery shop. Off rue des Francs-Bourgeois at the base of rue Veille du Temple is a sprinkling of lively cafés and bars. On balmy evenings, the terraces are packed with an arty crowd. *Motos* jam the narrow footpath outside **Au Petit Fer à Cheval**, a tiny, vintage café with a horseshoe-shaped bar.

East of the bustle I take a pause in Place des Vosges, the oldest public square in Paris and the jewel of the Marais. Once the site of society weddings and public duels, the central garden is now a tranquil setting of chirping birds, cool, clipped lime trees and trickling fountains. Locals laze on benches and classical music drifts from string quartets. Victor Hugo lived in the largest townhouse on *la place*, where he wrote a good part of *Les Misérables*. **La Maison de Victor Hugo** is open to the public and features reconstructions of his rooms, books and drawings.

The maze of streets surrounding Place des Vosges is full of pleasant surprises and tucked away *restos*, but that's enough for one day. There will always be something more to discover, to write about, for the Marais's bewitching blend has a way of leaving you craving just one more sip.

The sculptured gardens at Musée Carnavalet

Metro: St Paul/Hôtel de Ville
Bus: 96, 75 & 29.
The 29 bus is an excellent sightseeing route. Hop on at Opéra Garnier and off again at Opéra Bastille, riding past the Centre Pompidou and through the heart of the Marais.

CAFÉS/RESTAURANTS/ SPECIALTY STORES
Au Petit Fer à Cheval
30, rue Veille du Temple, 75004
Tel : 01 42 72 47 47

Camille
24, rue des Francs-Bourgeois, 75003
Tel: 01 42 72 20 50

Chez Marianne
2, rue des Hospitaliers-St-Gervais, 75004
Tel: 01 42 72 18 86

L'As du Fallafel
34, rue des Rosiers, 75004
Tel: 01 48 87 63 60

Mariage Frères
30, rue du Bourg-Tibourg, 75004
Tel: 01 43 47 18 54
or 01 42 72 28 11
www.mariagefreres.com

Sacha Finkelsztajn
27, rue des Rosiers, 75004
Tel: 01 42 72 78 91
www.laboutiquejaune.com

MUSEUMS
La Maison de Victor Hugo
6, Place des Vosges, 75004
Tel: 01 42 72 10 16

Musée Carnavalet
23, rue de Sévigné, 75003
Tel: 01 44 59 58 58
www.carnavalet.paris.fr

Greg 3

I bump into Greg at *la boucherie, encore*.

'How was your dinner with Colette's cousins?' I ask.

'It was a big hit!' he replies. 'The ties between cousins across the Atlantic have been re-established over a meal. Oh, and by the way, the wine merchant asked me exactly the same questions as *le boucher*. I left with a selection of wine that fooled Colette's cousins into thinking I am much more knowledgeable than is the case.' He is distracted for a moment, watching the butcher prepare his *côtes de veau*.

'I knew how to cook before coming to Paris but I have learned to *love* to cook here,' Greg continues with zeal. 'The wide selection of fresh regional produce available and the handful of willing 'coaches' in the neighbourhood make it an adventure every time I open a recipe book.'

I am sure Greg is not alone: it is hard not to be seduced by a city ardently passionate about food and the daily market ritual. Paris has made Greg into a cook.

'Must go,' he says, heading to the fruit and vegetable market. 'Our 105th guest is arriving this afternoon.'

Château d'Aynac

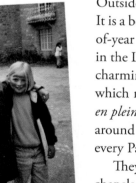

Claire and Annabelle

Outside the gilded gates of Parc Monceau are two buses full of little waving hands. It is a beautiful May morning and Annabelle is leaving on her 10ème (grade 2) end-of-year school trip. The destination is Château d'Aynac, a sixteenth-century castle in the Lot, a fertile valley in Central France where the River Lot winds its way past charming villages, fortified castles, gorges and forests. It is a *classe verte* (green) trip, which means these Parisian kids get to shake off their shackles and run outdoors *en plein air*. They ride horses and participate in nature-based activities, sing songs around the bonfire and learn how to handwash their socks (an essential skill for every Parisian child).

They also visit nearby Rocamadour, a breathtaking cluster of medieval houses, chapels and towers built up from the base of a cliff. A religious sanctuary, it became a centre of pilgrimage following the discovery of an undecayed body in an ancient grave in 1166. It was speculated that this was the body of the early Christian hermit Saint Amadour who, according to tradition, chose this place for his devotions to the Virgin Mary. The discovery unleashed a spate of miracles, heralded by a bell above the mysterious black Madonna in the chapel of Notre-Dame de Rocamadour.

As wonderful as their trip promises to be, it is with hesitation that I wave back to little Annabelle, for this is no fleeting weekend camp but a ten-day sojourn. *La directrice* has decided that seven is the age to start the separation process. The rules are unbending. There is to be no contact between parents and students for the duration of the trip, except in an emergency. Such a gentle transition, don't you think? All students have in their possession ten stamped envelopes, already addressed to their families. Every day, they are to write home about their adventures.

Each morning, Madame Gardienne knocks on our door and delivers a card from Annabelle. It says nothing except 'I MISS YOU XXXX' in enormous letters. Beside myself, I spend ten days wondering just how homesick she is. When she arrives home, she is elated after a wonderful trip. I question her about the cards and ask her if she was homesick.

'No,' she says, 'I just thought that's what you would want to hear.'

Julie calls, bruised.

She has just been knocked to the ground by a debonair sixty-something man with a hanky in his top pocket.

'Whatever happened?' I ask with apprehension.

'Well, I had accidently bumped into him outside the florist on rue de Passy a quarter of an hour earlier,' she says. 'It was obviously unintentional and I apologised profusely – "*Pardon Monsieur, excusez-moi, je suis desolée*" – but he seemed very put out. He evidently watched my movements and lay in wait. Anyway, I ran a couple of errands and started to walk home. Suddenly, in the very place we had collided, I see Monsieur Hanky charge at me out of the corner of my eye while hurling abuse. Before I know it he gives me a walloping hip and shoulder and bowls me right over! He got a good run up from inside the florist.'

'How rude!' I exclaim. 'What's his problem, I wonder? Maybe he's suffering *une crise de foie* (crisis of the liver), that very French malady from too much rich food, wine and cheese.'

'Don't know, don't care, but I've just been to WH Smith to buy *The Complete Merde: The real French you were never taught at school* – "a saucy guide to survival in everyday French". It's time to fight back.'

Normandie

With a string of May long weekends marked on the calendar, we hire a car and drive out of the city with the throngs, heading northwest to Normandy. A region with picture-book scenery and a rich cuisine, it's the land of milk and honey, making it hard to believe this same area was so badly scarred by war.

A slow three-hour drive from Paris brings us to the Côte Fleurie, a stretch of coast sprinkled with chic resorts and fishing villages. It's not until we stop at the seaside town of Deauville that we realise we have left our hotel book behind, with not only the name, address and phone number of our *auberge*, but also the name of the village it is in. We do remember, however, that the village starts with an A. Surely there can't be many little villages in the Norman countryside starting with an A? We decide to enjoy the day and worry about that later this afternoon.

On the glamorous beachside boardwalk, Les Planches, we pass all the new-season fashions. It seems the only acceptable beachwear for women is striped navy-and-white t-shirts with navy or white Capris. Also a must is loads of gold jewellery, a fake tan, and a fluffy little white dog to complement your new loafers.

Bright umbrellas are lined up on the sand in perfectly straight rows. Deckchairs and changerooms are also for rent. There are cafés, and play centres with swings and trampolines. What, I wonder, would the French think of a typical Australian beach, with its stark natural beauty and lack of amenities? At 15°C it's too cold to swim but the girls run and paddle in bare feet, relishing the sand between their toes. It's the first time they've stepped outside the front door *sans* shoes since Tuscany last August.

Along the coast we find Trouville, renowned for its fish market, and further west, Cabourg, dominated by the white Belle Époque Grand Hôtel that looms over the seafront. Marcel Proust spent many summers here and used the resort as a model for Balbec in *Remembrance of Things Past*.

We start thinking about lunch and soon find that every menu posted outside cafés and restaurants along the Côte Fleurie features fresh local seafood and abundant shellfish, along with a prolific medley of crêpes: shrimp crêpes, scallop crêpes, smoked salmon and lemon crêpes . . . exhausting in their variety. For dessert, there are crêpes filled with apple, Calvados and cream; apple, ice-cream and cinnamon; apple, chestnut cream and honey . . .

After lunch we drive inland to the Pays d'Auge, an enchanting rural area of Normandy with the cathedral town of Lisieux its capital. Spotted Norman cows graze peacefully on lush pastures and orchards of flowering apple trees spill down valleys. A rich agricultural area noted for its dairy and apple production, the idyllic countryside is woven with hedgerows, gently rolling hills and thatched cottages. Down backroads, cream roses cascade down high stone walls. Long leafy driveways lead to half-timbered manor houses. Now all we have to do is find the hotel.

The girls are singing French songs in the back of the car as the sun slowly fades. Why is it that men would rather drive in circles for an unlimited amount of time than stop and ask for help? Asking for directions seems to be the definitive sign that they have failed in life. Women often have the gene required for navigation missing. This is a bad combination.

After visiting various towns starting with 'A', we finally hit the jackpot at Annebault. Pulling up at the small family *auberge*, I am just thankful to have somewhere to lay our heads on this busy long weekend.

On Sunday morning, we follow the cider and cheese trails that wind along the country roads. The most famous of the region's soft white cheeses was developed in the village of Camembert. The Pays d'Auge is also noted for Pont l'Evêque (bishop's bridge), a square cow's cheese dating to the Middle Ages, and Livarot. All three carry the AOC quality label – as do *beurre d'Isigny*, a rich butter made in the region and *crème d'Isigny*, a superb, full-bodied cream. Many dairy farms along *la Route de Fromage* welcome visitors for sampling and sales. Cider-makers offer cider and Calvados apple brandy and, occasionally, distillery and cellar visits. The Pays d'Auge is also granted AOC quality status for its cider and Calvados.

Bayeux, Normandy

A tangle of wood hyacinths and yellow primroses decorates the meadows. There is an occasional cluster of blood-red poppies, the symbol of remembrance. World War II has certainly has left its mark on this beautiful region. There are monuments everywhere: on the roadsides, in front of churches, in town squares. British and American war cemeteries are scattered throughout the area: rows and rows of identical white tombstones of sons and fathers and brothers. The scale of the war is brought home. Of the hundreds of villages in Normandy, only a few were left unscathed. Most were razed.

We drive along the Côte de Nacre, the site of the D-Day Allied landings in the early hours of 6 June, 1944. American, Canadian, English, Scottish and French flags fly in every tiny village along the coast. We stop to see the evocative remains of Mulberry Harbour, the artificial port towed across from England, at Arromanches-les-Bains. Massive cement caissons were sunk to form a semi-circular breakwater. On this overcast May day the grey seas are choppy and we try to imagine the harbour in full swing, the warships, and the thousands of troops coming out of the water. 135,000 men were brought to shore via Operation Overlord, the biggest military operation in history. By the end of D-Day, 10,000 people had lost their lives. The landings were followed by the 76-day Battle of Normandy, which led to the liberation of France from Nazi occupation.

Later in the afternoon, we drive to Bayeux, the first town in Normandy to be liberated by the Allies and one of the few towns left unscathed by war. We have come to see the famous eleventh-century masterpiece, *The Bayeux Tapestry*. Embroidered on a linen background 70 metres long and 50 centimetres high, this giant, medieval comic strip tells the epic story of the invasion of England by William the Conqueror, and the Battle of Hastings in 1066. Stitched with woollen yarn in eight different colours and still in remarkable condition after nine centuries, this tapestry of extraordinary richness is both an unparalleled work of art and an historical document. Commentary is in primitive Latin script and records details of almost all aspects of eleventh-century life. Georgie, who has recently studied the Battle of Hastings, particularly likes the scene where Harold King of England is finally defeated, an arrow piercing his eye and killing him instantly.

After an action-packed day, we dine in the restaurant at the *auberge*. We choose a set menu of classic regional dishes: fish soup followed by *poulet vallée d'Auge* served with a slightly chilled Chinon red. This delicious chicken dish in a cider and Calvados sauce brings together Normandy's apples, butter and cream. Next, a cheese trolley is wheeled to the table laden with an assortment of superb local cheeses. We finish with a classic *tarte aux pommes à la Normande* (apple tart), coffee and a welcome digestive of Calvados, *bien sûr*.

Before heading home on the Monday, we take a detour to Honfleur, a quaint seaside town where life centres on *le Vieux Bassin*, the Old Dock. St Catherine's Quay on the dock's western side is bordered by a row of tall seventeenth-century houses, stacked together like a set of coloured pencils. Small art galleries are poked in here and there between restaurants and shops selling Calvados. Appreciated for its changing light, this picturesque port has long been a magnet for painters and photographers. Sisley, Pissaro, Renoir and Cézanne visited often and the town is proud of the Musée Eugène Boudin, dedicated to the work of the seascape painter who was born here.

Just before midday we sit down at a sunny terrace table overlooking the water and no sooner have we ordered than we hear the sound of distant bagpipes. On the other side of the harbour there appears to be a parade of some kind. On further investigation we discover we have unwittingly stumbled upon – and scored prime viewing seats for – the Honfleur Seafarers' Pilgrimage, a traditional Pentecost festival that has been celebrated since 1861. As we savour *gratin de St-Jacques* (gratinéed scallops served in the shell), a procession of sailors, fishermen and floats trail past us punctuated by bellowing brass bands. Toddlers wave from inside vast buoyant boats thronged with pink crêpe-paper flowers while older children, sporting colourful hats with scarves around their waists, precariously balance model ships on wooden trays.

The annual festival is held to renew the town's links with its maritime history. On the Sunday of Pentecost, decorated local fishing boats gather in the old harbour. They then proceed out to sea before coming together in a circle in the Seine Estuary to be blessed by a priest.

The last boat passes and the music dies down. We finish our lunch, marvelling at our luck and the huge platter of seafood set high above the adjoining table, and drive reluctantly back to Paris.

La Dictée

We jump off the 30 bus at Trocadéro and order *un coca* on the terrace of Café Kléber. Now that summer's here, we frequently stop by on the way home from school. The waiters have got to know us and they dote on the girls.

As we sip our drinks, Georgie mentions that she received a bad mark for her *dictée* today and that Madame had measured her head with a tape measure in front of the class again. News to me.

'Why?' I ask. Nothing surprises me anymore.

'Oh, just to see if my brain has shrunk,' she answers, unperturbed.

La Boulangerie

I often poke my nose into bakeries when I'm out and about, no matter where I am in the city or what the time of day. I can't resist the smell of warm buttery pastries in the morning and the sight of fresh baguette sandwiches in toppling towers at lunchtime. They come in many guises, from the rustic bakery with provincial décor and communal table to the charming classics with etched glass windows, whimsical wrought-iron bread racks and chandeliers. Even the pretty paper bags, printed with pastoral scenes and flowers, put a smile on my face.

In Paris, bread is taken seriously. *Le pain* plays an important role in daily life and *la boulangerie* is indispensable. The best are owned by dedicated, sleep-deprived *boulangers* who make and bake on the premises, with ovens firing all day long. Most bakeries, however, time their batches to come crackling out of the oven around 7 a.m., just before lunchtime, and around 7 p.m. Parisians buy

Prix Du Pain

St Clément	4,60	le Kg
baguette	0,90	euro
demie baguette	0,45	euro
Pain	1,10	euro
-demi-pain	0,55	euro
baguette à l'ancienne	1,10	euro
-demi baguette à l'ancienne	0,55	euro
petit campagne	1,00	euro
-campagne moyen	1,90	euro
-grand campagne	3,20	euros
-complet petit	1,80	euro
-grand complet	3,20	euros
pain de mie	2,20	euros
pain bié	2,00	euros
morvandiau	5,90	euros le kg
Pavé des petits Pères	5,90	euros le kg
St Fiacre	5,50	euros le kg

fresh bread for each meal and one can generally tell a good bakery by the smell of hot bread and the long line of clued-up locals lurking at the door. Sometimes, it feels as if my days are spent bringing home the bread.

The iconic baguette is the bread of the Parisians; a classic, slender loaf derived from the French word for wand. The real thing will be moist and chewy with a crackling, crisp golden crust, and the crumbs inside (*la mie*) will be creamy in colour with large, irregular holes. A good baguette should also have strong diagonal slits across the top for the gases to escape as the bread bakes. Beware of mass-produced baguettes made from frozen dough or fabricated off-premises. If you're handed a pale, limp baguette with a white cotton-wool centre, you've wasted your dough.

The price of a standard baguette is regulated and determined by weight. After all, isn't a baguette every day the right of every Frenchman? Margueritte tells me there's been an increase in cheap factory-made bread over the last twenty-five years, but also a renaissance in artisanal breads, with the younger generation turning away from flabby fakes towards the traditional wholegrain loaves and rustic baguettes favoured by their great-grandparents. These trademarked varieties, often made from stone-ground organic flours, are prepared to strict old-fashioned methods and have fanciful brand names like *rétrodor*, *pain passion* and *flûte Gana*.

A short lifespan means the baguette must be consumed soon after purchase. Good baguettes, with no preservatives, will be as hard as a plank in six hours. All attempts to revive them will fail. Resuscitation techniques such as spraying with water and warming in the oven *ne marchent pas* (do not work). Nor does microwaving. Do not attempt to wrap a baguette in plastic in the hope of extending its shelf life or in an effort to soften. The bread will suffer a slow and sweaty demise by suffocation. In August, when it's hot and humid, your wand will lose its magic in around two hours. It will turn into a tough leather belt. You can order half a baguette if you wish ('*Une demi baguette, SVP*'), which will save you throwing out the other half when you arrive home in the evening.

Along with the ubiquitous baguette, *la boulangerie* sells bread in all shapes and sizes, made from a variety of flours. Plump country-style *boules* sit next to soft brioches and loaves showered with nuts, bacon or pumpkin seeds. And then, of course, there are the pastries . . .

Quel désirez-vous?

- ❧ *Chapeau*: small, round loaf topped with a little hat.
- ❧ *Chouquettes*: crispy rounds of light choux pastry sprinkled with sugar crystals, ordered by weight.
- ❧ *Croissant aux amandes*: originally created as a way to use day-old croissants, this addictive breakfast treat is filled with dense almond cream and sprinkled with sliced almonds.
- ❧ *Escargot au chocolat*: pastry filled with chocolate, rolled into a snail shape.
- ❧ *Ficelle*: very thin, string-like baguette, delicious when studded with bacon.
- ❧ *Fougasse*: flat ladder of bread that can be bought plain or with fillings such as olives or goat's cheese and sundried tomatoes.
- ❧ *Pain à l'ancienne*: bread made using traditional methods.
- ❧ *Pain aux céréales*: wholegrain loaf.
- ❧ *Pain aux raisins*: sweet, sticky swirl of soft dough scattered with raisins.
- ❧ *Pain de campagne*: hearty round country loaf dusted with flour.
- ❧ *Pain de mie*: slightly sweet white sandwich loaf.

Since Marie-Antoinette's alleged callous reply to being told that the people had no bread during the French Revolution, "Well, then, let them eat cake!", bread has had enormous political significance in France. From 1789 to the present, no French government would dare allow the price of bread to climb out of reach of the poorest family.'

Ross Steele, *When in France, Do As the French Do:*
The clued-in guide to French life, language and culture

Le Médicin

Just two weeks after arriving in Paris, Georgie fell ill. With a raging temperature, extreme malaise and an inflamed throat, she could neither eat nor swallow. Having no idea about the medical system, I slipped down the stairs of our hotel and asked the receptionist what I should do.

'I'll call SOS Médicins straight away,' she replied sincerely, picking up the phone. 'The French take ill health very seriously. They will come immediately.' Sure, I thought sarcastically, but within ten minutes a stern-looking man in a black leather jacket and knee-high bike boots knocked on the door, holding a *moto* helmet in one hand and a doctor's bag in the other. He poked and prodded, wrote out numerous prescriptions and gave me the bill – all without saying a word.

I blocked the door as he tried to leave, blurting out question after question in English. 'Has she got tonsillitis? Aren't you going to take a swab? What are the prescriptions for?' I got the feeling that I was well out of line questioning a doctor, but persisted. Finally, when he realised I wasn't about to give up, he said, 'She has a sick throat.'

'I am a registered nurse, specialising in paediatrics,' I said, hoping this would persuade him to offer more information, but he just looked at me as if he was thinking, 'So what!'

'What is this script for?' I persevered, pointing to something very foreign in terrible French handwriting.

'For her cough,' he replied.

'But she hasn't got a cough,' I said, becoming irritated.

'She'll probably get one soon,' he sneered.

Exasperated, I closed the door.

Another time, in the dead of winter, we took Georgie to be seen by a delightful French paediatrician at the American Hospital of Paris, a long taxi-ride to the suburb of Neuilly-sur-Seine. He offered us kittens free of charge. What he couldn't offer us was a good, English-speaking paediatrician in the 16th who does house calls, a civilised part of the French medical system that avoids ripping the sick from their beds when it's -2°C outside, giving them pneumonia as well.

'Beware of paediatricians in the 16th. They tend to prance around in fancy ties and charge the earth,' he said. (More confirmation that we have picked a *très cher arrondissement*, but no point moving now – we'll be home before we know it.)

After a rash of medical mishaps and cultural misunderstandings, I learn my lesson. Simply put, there are certain subjects that you need to be able to discuss in your native tongue. At the top of the list are matters requiring gynaecologists – followed closely by hairdressers. Trying to tiptoe your way through unknown territory and foreign vocabulary is fraught with danger and usually an expensive waste of time. You either come out clueless, or with platinum blonde hair. To prevent further embarrassing appointments consisting of much gesticulation and drawing of body parts, I come to the conclusion that only an English-speaking doctor will do.

So the next time Georgie wakes with a high temperature and ear pain, my heart sinks. In no mood to face the taxi ride to the American Hospital with a sick child, I scout around and find the numbers of two paediatricians recommended to me by Jocelyn, a doctor herself. (In France, children often visit paediatricians directly.) Neither is available. With half of Paris on *les grandes vacances* it will be near impossible to find a doctor left in Paris with a high level of English, an appointment available and a surgery within *le périphérique*. I think how easy this would be in Adelaide: quick call to local surgery, whack patient in car, drop in at pharmacy next door, home within the hour.

I nip down to the pharmacy on the corner (identifiable by a green cross that is illuminated during opening hours) and ask for advice. A valuable source of healthcare information, your knowledgeable pharmacist (who often has a degree in homeopathy and natural medicine, and sometimes a medical degree as well) will provide the names of doctors, nurses and paramedical professionals who practise in the quarter. Just as importantly, they will administer first aid. They are also trained to identify *les champignons*: an age-old tradition requires all pharmacists study mushroom taxonomy. With the aid of an official chart picturing poisonous species, they will inspect and declare whether your fungi are safe *pour manger* (to eat) or are *dangereux*. Sometimes they will even dispense advice on preparation and cooking. Before you don your rubber boots for an autumn foray in the woods, however, there are rules to follow. Mushrooms must be cut at the base with a knife (all other tools are forbidden) and be carried in a wicker basket so spores can disperse and propagate.

I wait while the pharmacist phones several paediatricians and general practitioners, going well beyond the call of duty. At this stage I don't care if they speak only Arabic, but each time she shakes her head. Finally she shrugs her shoulders and says, '*Je suis désolée*, everyone is away on vacation.' If she can't find one, I have no chance so I go home and pray for a miracle. It's best not to get sick in August.

When the miracle doesn't happen, I am about to pick up the phone and take my chances with SOS Médicins again when Françoise rings. She's home from holidays. I relay what has happened.

'I'll call you back in five minutes,' she says.

'I've booked you in with my paediatrician just down the road,' she informs me when she calls back. 'He's going to squeeze you in.'

'*Merci mille fois*, Françoise,' (Thank you a thousand times) I say, elated. As anywhere in the world, it's who you know.

Françoise walks us down and 'presents' us.

'This way you will be well looked after,' she says. The doctor is *charmant*, handsome and speaks perfect English to boot. Georgie adores him. He pats children on the head, kisses the babies and charms the mothers. At last, a kind doctor around the corner with whom I can communicate on a medical level. Only two drawbacks: the visit and drugs cost more than a new winter coat, and in true French style, he loves drugs – the more the better.

His diagnosis is a pedestrian case of otitis media for which he gives me a handwritten prescription that looks like a war zone. I stare at it, hoping something familiar will jump out, but I only recognise the odd word here and there – and that's after successfully deciphering doctors' atrocious handwriting in hospitals for years. In my defence, it is *en français* with foreign trade and generic names.

While waiting in the pharmacy for my script to be filled, I notice an entire shelf devoted to *les tisanes*: herbal teas for various complaints. All products are well stocked except three where the shelves are completely bare: anti-wrinkle, anti-age and cellulite. French women are human after all! The pharmacist puts my stash of drugs on the counter and gives me a lightning-quick rundown of dosages, routes and times, which, unfortunately, I don't quite get. Sometimes there are personalised instructions on packets and bottles, and sometimes, as in this case, not.

I go home and pull out my trusty paediatric prescribing reference guide and look up active ingredients. I work things out for myself, drawing up a drug chart for the cocktail of antibiotics, ear drops, nasal sprays, vitamin supplements, pain relievers and anti-inflammatory suppositories (a mode of administration of which the French are particularly fond). I wonder how many times suppositories have been given orally, nose drops put in ears, and bottles of antibiotics made up with the wrong amounts of water.

By the time Georgie has eventually taken her mountain of *médicaments*, darkness has crept through the house. A whole day spent doing not much more than going to the doctor. Maybe tomorrow will be a better day.

La Zone Sinistrée

It is September 11. The news has just broken that a plane has flown into the North Tower of the World Trade Centre. It is pick-up time at school and the international wives are panicking. On top of the horror and shock at the event that has just occurred, everyone is trying to remember where their husband is. I, for one, know that Tim is in the United States . . . somewhere.

'Catch me on my mobile if you need me,' he had said as he strode out the front door.

We hurry home and turn on the television, aghast like the rest of the world at the events that are unfolding. I try Tim's mobile. It is impossible to get through.

'Where's *Papa*?' asks Annabelle. 'Is he in Manhattan?'

'*Je ne sais pas*,' (I don't know) I answer, truthfully.

Several hours pass and then we receive a phone call from Tim's secretary. Finally someone had got through to the office in France.

'Is *Papa* safe?' whispers Annabelle.

'Yes, *Papa* is safe.'

'Where is he?'

'Midtown Manhattan.'

Julie calls, tormented.

She has just experienced a harrowing day. After her last disastrous attempt at cooking dinner for her French relatives, she decided to prove she really could cook and invited them over for a proper Sunday lunch. She explains that she woke with the sun and was down at the market just as the first rabbits with cottontails were being hung from hooks. She sat contentedly at a nearby café sipping her morning *café crème* as merchants with bleary eyes stacked leeks into rows and poured fleshy *cèpes* into baskets.

Then she got down to business. Nothing was going to go wrong with this lunch. At *la boucherie* she ordered a thick slice of gutsy grouse and juniper terrine to slather on crusty bread and chose the two plumpest saddles of hare to roast, which would go nicely with a full-bodied bottle of Bordeaux, she thought. At *la fromagerie* she selected a creamy St-Marcellin (a superb cheese with a soft, silky texture) and a firm farmhouse Cantal, a cow's milk cheese from the Auvergne, dating back to the Gauls.

Notre-Dame

Then she bought some wild mushrooms to sauté with the hare, potatoes for a creamy *gratin dauphinois*, some vegetables and an assortment of simple salad leaves to toss in vinaigrette. Lastly, she popped into her favourite bakery where she deliberated over a wafer-thin, spiced apple tart and a fragrant pear tart. Finally, she decided on *une grande tarte aux poires*, which was beautifully boxed and tied with ribbon. Then home she went with her basket full of goodies, swinging her tart from its ribbon in joyous anticipation. She arranged flowers and set the table feeling confident that lunch would be a success.

'Everything went well,' says Julie, 'for a while. They loved the terrine, devoured the field salad, raved about the hare and approved of the wine. Being rather full we lingered over the cheeses with a bottle of Châteauneuf-du-Pape, so I served the children their dessert in the kitchen. But oh, you won't believe what happened next!' she wails. '*Une catastrophe!* I didn't know that the tart had ground almonds in it, nor that one of the children, little Cloelia, was severely allergic to almonds. Just my luck!'

She painfully unravels the spiralling sequence of events. It all happened so fast. Cloelia had staggered into the dining room with a navy blue face and promptly collapsed unconscious. Cloelia's mother, her face draining quickly of colour, had raced into the kitchen, saw the pear tart and, realising what had happened, proceeded to run around the apartment screaming, '*Vite, vite, les Pompiers!*'

Now, as *les Pompiers* are the fire brigade, Julie and Mark became more than a little concerned about her psychological state and the outcome of the situation. So when Cloelia's father dialled 18 for *les Pompiers*, they were beside themselves. A scuffle broke out as they tried unsuccessfully to stop the call and dial for an ambulance instead. But even as Julie and Mark were still screaming in English and the remaining conscious relatives still shrieking in French (one reverts to one's native tongue in times of stress), they heard sirens approaching and, within the blink of an eye, two burly firemen appeared at the door, accompanied by trained paramedics. All ended well and Cloelia was carted off to hospital.

Les Pompiers try to keep response times to less than five minutes and are highly regarded by the French, who readily call on them in case of medical emergency. If the situation is life-threatening, *les Pompiers* will call SAMU (*Service d'Aide Médicale Urgence*), who will provide ambulance back-up.

'Another good impression on the French relatives,' Julie laments.

'Julie,' I say gently, 'go out for dinner next time.'
'I don't think there will be a next time,' she says, with a sigh.
N.B. Call: 18 Fire; 17 Police; 15 Ambulance; 112 SOS (all services).

La Circulation

We zoom around the city in our rented Renault Twingo. It's the Sunday before Christmas and the stores are open today, *ouverture exceptionelle*, to cater for the pre-Christmas rush. Georgie is dropped off on the Champs-Élysées for a birthday party and we watch as she runs towards her friends, past white-gloved doormen and shoppers laden with boxes.

We stop here and there buying gifts and running last-minute errands. The luxury Hôtel de Crillon sits resplendent, draped in garlands of gold. Place Vendôme sparkles. We whiz past the Jardins du Trocadéro where a magic wand has been waved, transforming the gardens into a winter wonderland. There's a little assistance, however, from the snow cannons that fire out tonnes of fluffy white snow every day and the hundreds of imported fir trees that help create the scene.

We cross the river to Le Bon Marché department store where discreet posters urge shoppers to enter into the New Year with good taste. How can one resist? A dash to **La Grande Épicerie** on the ground floor reveals all the trimmings of a decadent French Christmas. Locals stock up on golden tins of *confit de canard*, caviar, *foie gras* and Veuve Clicquot Champagne, for purchase by the bottle or the carton – the popular option judging by the number of bright orange boxes riding in trolleys amongst the milk and Maxim's chocolates. For the food lover, a trip to the best grocery store in Paris ranks as high on the excitement scale as climbing onto Santa's knee does for a child.

We sweep past pyramids of panettone, bottles of Bordeaux, mountains of luscious dried fruits and miles of *marron glacé* (candied chestnuts). Further on are hundreds of *fromages de fête*, soft skeins of fresh spaghetti, pink opened-mouthed fish on beds of ice, and smoked duck for unexpected visitors. We grab a few goodies and *un gâteau à la broche*, a Christmas-tree-shaped cake that's cooked on a turning spit over a wood fire . . . but what did we actually come for again?

La circulation (traffic) is building up as we drive around the Arc de Triomphe and up to the 17th. Annabelle is playing in her first piano recital with eight

adorable little girls, hosted in Teresa's beautiful apartment. We are so lucky to have found Grahame, our dedicated Australian piano teacher who zips around the city on the metro to teach these *jeunes filles* in the comfort of their own homes.

The parents sip Champagne and listen to *Au Clair de la Lune* and *Le Chèvre Noir*. Annabelle is playing *J'ai du Bon Tabac* ('I have some good tobacco') – a children's classic in France. From the balcony, we look down onto rue Courcelles, strung across its breadth with dainty white lights like a thousand pearl necklaces. People walk by with bouquets of flowers and bulging bags. A film crew is setting up at the end of the street with six trailers and a newly built tower.

After a perfect afternoon we pick up Georgie on the Champs-Élysées. Along its length, the trees are wrapped snugly in reams of toile, which theatrically changes colour from mauve to blue to pink with the aid of dramatic lighting. Georgie waves her friends goodbye and jumps in, wearing a pair of 3D glasses.

'Have a look through these,' she says excitedly, snatching them off her face and giving them to Annabelle. She explains that Sephora, France's leading chain store devoted to cosmetics, fragrances and skincare, is handing them out at the door of their hangar-sized space on the avenue, telling shoppers to glance at the lights.

Annabelle squeals in delight: 'All of the lights along the road have turned into pink and yellow hearts!'

Like the rest of Paris, we head for home – but *la circulation* is overwhelming, the Arc as busy as we have seen it. There's no way around it. Tim puts his foot to the floor and zips into the flow but the next thing we know, every vehicle on the roundabout seems simultaneously to screech to a halt. *Zut!* We are caught in the gridlock. If you can imagine a circle the size of a football oval, filled with stationary cars, buses, *motos* and vans at every conceivable angle to each other, you have the picture. There we stay for half an hour.

Tempers fray and fist-fights erupt on car bonnets. The horns become deafening. *Motos* try to squeeze through the traffic to escape the standstill, their drivers punching side mirrors when cars don't inch out of the way. We happen to be one of those cars, but this particular *moto* driver has other ideas.

He spits venomously on the windows.

'*C'est dégoûtant!*' Annabelle cringes, ducking for cover.

Thankfully the windows are up. We lock the doors and continue to watch the drama unfold around us . . . and the spit slide slowly down the glass.

Just as we think we may be in for a long, cosy evening, *la police* converge from all directions and gradually help the traffic out. We escape the Arc and crawl down avenue Kléber, after our now not-so-perfect afternoon in the city of contradictions.

La Grande Épicerie
38, rue de Sèvres, 75007
Tel: 01 44 39 81 00
www.lagrandeepicerie.fr

L'Email

Late one January evening, I finally pluck up the courage to email a feature story on Paris produce markets to the editor of *Australian Gourmet Traveller*.

I awake the next morning to a reply that, as a new writer, you dream about:

Dear Jane,
This is a lovely piece and I would be very interested to view
the photographs that go with it. If photographs are plentiful
and of good quality, I would be interested in running this piece.
I look forward to hearing from you re pictures.
Kind regards,
Judy Sarris
Editor
Australian Gourmet Traveller

I am over the moon and wake up everyone in the house.

But did I really say 'I have a series of shots relevant to the article that you are welcome to view'? What was I thinking? Why did I say that? Probably because I didn't really expect such a fabulous response!

I look at my photos and panic.

As soon as the clock strikes nine, I call Brooke's French husband, Vincent, a professional photographer born in the 10th and raised between Opéra and Pigalle. I ask him if he's interested in doing some shots.

'*Australian Gourmet*?' he confirms. 'What do you want?'

Très chic: impeccably dressed Parisian twins

Raclette au Mont d'Or

Margueritte arrives for a lesson and pulls a cheese enveloped in bands of fragrant spruce from her bag.

'There's nothing like Vacherin Mont d'Or in winter, and this one is exceptional,' she says, shoving it under my nose. 'It's made from the milk of cattle that graze on the Swiss side of the Jura Mountains. The spruce flavours the cheese and helps to keep its shape. I bought it from Fromagerie Barthélémy, one of the best *fromageries* in Paris.'

We spend half the lesson talking about how Margueritte prepares Mont d'Or. She relays a simple recipe that resembles Swiss raclette, a kind of fondue, and I write it all down in French. First you slit the soft, loose crust in several places and pour a little white wine underneath. Then let it sit for a while in its circular wooden box, before placing it in a moderate oven until the cheese is warm and runny and the wine absorbed, infusing its flavour (twenty minutes or so). Peel off the crust and plunge a tablespoon into the raclette. Serve with boiled potatoes, some *pâté* and cornichons, a fresh baguette and a glass of red.

The following day, I check out **Fromagerie Barthélémy** and find a staggering melange of highly regarded unpasteurised cheese. At all serious *fromageries*, cheese is unpasteurised. No self-respecting *fromager-affineur* would carry anything else, shuddering at the thought of plastic impostors. This unassuming, shoebox-sized shop supplies prominent French politicians and some of the most flamboyant dinner parties on the Left Bank. Roland Barthélémy is *un maître fromager affineur*, an expert at personally selecting farmhouse cheeses and ripening them before sale. All the cheeses have been lovingly turned and washed in the cellars below before being presented in the shop just in time to explode with flavour. A superb seasonal selection from all over France is offered, including the finest raw milk Camembert and Brie. Travelling cheese aficionados can request selections hermetically sealed in odour-free bags to be enjoyed at a later date.

Fromagerie Barthélémy
51, rue de Grenelle, 75007
Tel: 01 42 22 82 24

Une Baguette, SVP

It is a Tuesday evening in the abyss of February. We heave open the door of l'Académie Américaine de Danse de Paris and fight our way down rue Rousselet against a bitterly cold wind. The girls are beginning to drag their feet after a long day of school and ballet, and I am dragging two astonishingly heavy school bags. The dog wee is frozen on the street. Homework is yet to begin and dinner is a long way off. Straight ahead in the darkness, little squares of light shine from Tour Montparnasse, the only skyscraper in the heart of Paris.

A bicycle bell pierces the air as a man rides by with a steaming, slender baguette – an instant hot water bottle. Towards the end of the street is the unmistakable aroma of freshly baked bread.

As we reach the corner, the line is already out the door at *la boulangerie*. Annabelle counts out the change. We join the line of locals. Some are weary on their way home from work, while others have left their apartments purposely to arrive just as the batch of hot baguettes is pulled from the scorching oven. Tall country quiches and lemon tarts line the counter to our right. Orange gateaux and glistening pastries beckon to our left, but as we shuffle through the bakery all we hear is, '*Une baguette, SVP, deux baguettes, SVP.*' They are walking out the door like bundles of kindling.

As Annabelle shyly asks for '*Une baguette, SVP*,' I feel a sense of belonging – a part of the ebb and flow of Parisian life. There's a certain solidarity that springs from daily rituals. From knowing that others, too, are cold and hungry, that others are buying their bread and scurrying home.

Walking down rue de Sèvres towards Vaneau metro station, we tear off chunks of baguette, the steam swirling into the crisp night air. For a moment, the wind no longer feels bitter – and it's the moments that count.

We pass cafés and people sipping their evening *apéro*. *Le fruitier* is packing up his outside stalls. **Fromagerie Quatrehomme**, one of the Left Bank's premier cheese stores, is still full of poking, sniffing customers, and pungent aromas pervade the street. Owned by the lovely Marie Quatrehomme, the store is well known for its Comté and St-Marcellin. I stop to buy a disc of soft and creamy Brie de Meaux *pour manger tout de suite* (to eat immediately) and receive a perfectly ripe specimen. Always advise 'when' you intend to eat the cheese you purchase and it will be chosen accordingly. This is vital for soft cheeses, such as Brie de Meaux. Loved by Charlemagne and made in the region of Brie, this ancient French cheese is sold on a straw mat. It is especially popular in winter.

I look forward to slathering it on a piece of baguette (if there's any left) later this evening and washing it down with a glass of smooth, full-bodied St-Émilion as I help the girls recite their poems and verbs.

The doors snap shut on my coat as we squeeze onto a crowded train full of coughs, and tumble out again at La Motte Picquet-Grenelle to change to line six. From here to Passy station the train is mostly high above ground and I peek through tall French windows into cosy *salons* with amber lamps and bookcases. We rush by the glowing Eiffel Tower and over the shadowy Seine.

If I am going to be cold, tired and hungry, it may as well be in Paris.

Fromagerie Quatrehomme
62, rue de Sèvres, 75007
Tel: 01 47 34 33 45

Le Chocolat

The inviting aroma of *bœuf bourguignon* mingles with warm *tarte Tatin* as we push open the door to a favourite family dining spot in the 7th. It's lunchtime on a Sunday in February and snow is looming. Waiters dash by with bowls of steaming onion soup, plates of *poulet fermier d'Auvergne* and profiteroles with chocolate sauce. Cups of strong black coffee are delivered to contented customers, each accompanied by a solitary square of smooth bittersweet chocolate – that mandatory morsel that brightens every Parisian's day.

We are ushered to a cosy table with a red-and-white chequered tablecloth and peruse the menu. To our left, an apricot poodle, who appears to have recently undergone a set and blow-dry at the dog salon, sits patiently with eyes transfixed on his elderly mistress. She mops up her gravy with a slice of baguette and savours her *pichet* of red wine. To our right, the empty table is filled by a couple with a snow-white Maltese. Our *plats* arrive and just as we reach for our knives and forks, growling comes from our left. The poodle has spied the Maltese.

With a lithe leap, the poodle clears our table, narrowly missing a bottle of Côte de Beane, and lands on the surprised Maltese. A harrowing dogfight erupts, but nobody seems particularly interested or surprised by the spectacle. Madame drains her glass of red and slowly struggles to her feet, plunging her foot into the poodle's water bowl before whipping him with her serviette and pulling him off the Maltese. Reprimanding her beloved with a sharp tongue and a slap, she assures him that today he will not have the pleasure of receiving his treasured daily treat – that indulgent square of smooth bittersweet chocolate.

Bon Courage

It is the last day of the trimester before winter vacation and time for the report cards again. Annabelle's class is interrupted by a knock on the door, whereupon *la directrice* strides in, armed with a stack of orange *carnets de correspondance*. She proceeds to hand them out, commenting on each pupil as she goes. She finishes with the phrase that has begun to sound like a broken record: '*Courage, je compte sur vous*' (Courage, I am counting on you), before striding out again. This is the French way of saying, 'Yes, you can do it. We have faith in you.' It keeps the bar at a high level, while acknowledging the pupils face a challenge. Indeed, for children struggling with the system, a certain amount of *bon courage* is needed just to get through the day.

The main school campus is a converted stone apartment building with small classrooms and desks lined in rows. There is no school playground, library, gymnasium, art or music room, and no space large enough to accommodate the whole student body. Accordingly, there is no sports day, swimming carnival – and no real notion of school community.

Assemblies, achievement awards and school house systems do not exist. Neither does show and tell. Excursions and cultural activities are rare, and *informatique* (computer class) is once a fortnight. Health and safety issues, environmental awareness and life skills of all kinds are deemed extracurricular. The lack of a school newsletter, parent/teacher interviews, social functions and parental involvement on all levels makes it doubly hard for newcomers to integrate and get a feel for what goes on behind the closed doors.

And so you start to get the picture of the typical French primary school, where providing a holistic education that meets individual learning and developmental needs in a nurturing environment is not the priority. Rather, the exceptionally disciplined and rigorous education system is singularly focused on churning out intellectuals.

The ultimate aim is to be accepted into one of France's elite tertiary schools or *grandes écoles*, a feat that practically assures a bright future. To gain entry, however, students must first pass the tough French Baccalauréat (*le bac*).

Training for this gruelling academic marathon starts early, with enormous pressure put on young children to perform.

Consequently, after easy outdoor lives in Australia, our first years in Paris involve a steep and emotional learning curve. In winter, the girls go to school in the dark and come home in the dark. Quickly, we learn that in France, fun is never used in the same sentence as education.

Our greatest challenge is grasping that the system is founded on negative reinforcement. Despite the enormous amounts of extra work initially required to bring Georgie up to a satisfactory French standard (often six or seven hours of homework on the weekend), no encouragement was given to her, no empathy or leniency was shown. With the slip of a few accents she often achieved a negative grade and a page of red ink. She longed for a 'good try' sticker and a pat on the back.

The years corresponding to our grades 4, 5 and 6 (8ème, 7ème, 6ème) are relentless and rigorous to the extreme; they are the years when students learn by heart all of their grammar and vocabulary. Immersion into the straight French section after this age would, I suggest, be highly stressful for a foreign child. In fact, at our school *adaptation* is only offered until 7ème; thereafter, newcomers must commence high school at a campus where English is the main language of education and French is taught daily.

We soon notice how age and personality affect the adaption process. Georgie, a sensitive, creative eight-year-old, struggled to adjust to the system whereas five-year-old Annabelle took French school life and her 9 a.m.–4.30 p.m. day in her stride. In hindsight, she moved to France at just the right age. She also speaks French without the slightest hint of an Aussie accent.

The system esteems 'linear learners' who are highly articulate with a linguistic and logical-mathematical intelligence but makes no allowances for children with different learning styles and other kinds of intelligence. Students with special needs are not catered for and simply *redouble* (repeat) the year, which is common in France. But on a positive note, unless students reach a certain high benchmark they are not admitted to the next year-level. Those who pass really deserve to.

At times, behaviour regarded as acceptable by French parents is not to us, just as aspects of the laid-back Australian education system would astonish the French. But, at the end of the day, in order to adapt to a new culture, you must accept its ways. The extremely rigid and prestigious *système éducatif français* has been in place for generations and no amount of jumping up and down is going to change it. It is seen as sacred and fiercely defended against outside influences. Threats to topple its exalted standards are taken seriously. Consequently the curriculum has seen very little change in decades.

This year, Georgie commenced *collège* (the first four years of secondary education running from 6ème to 3ème). A French acquaintance discovered Georgie had been jogging in sport class and said, 'Yes, that's right, I did a term of *le jogging* in *sixième* too.' Almost forty years ago.

Physical education is offered regularly (one morning a week) from 6ème onwards and includes sports such as European handball, table tennis and squash. The lack of team sport, however, together with fierce classroom competition and an individually orientated curriculum, helps shape individualists in the workplace with little understanding of solidarity, open communication and teamwork – and fosters a very private society.

Visual and performing arts also have a token presence and pupils are encouraged to pursue these frivolous activities out of school hours. A chance to express oneself through drama and creative writing in class time is rare, and tuition is under tight control. The lack of creative subjects leaves a lot of time for maths and French, with roughly a third of the week devoted to learning the intricacies of the French language. In kindergarten there is a serious emphasis on language skills with an escalating focus on grammar, conjugation, literature, poetry and the memorisation of texts.

Without exception, everything is strictly graded. Testing is continuous. Even in junior primary, grades are taken seriously. Although pen-and-paper examinations are not necessarily the best way to test pupils' performance, they do, however, give parents concrete information about their child's progress and a keyhole look into what's going on behind those closed doors.

Savoir Vivre

It is merely part of a Frenchman's *liberté* to break mundane rules created by some bureaucrat. Far more important are aesthetics and good living. These ideals symbolise the unspoken rules that really count and can't be broken.

The art of living well, *savoir vivre*, encompasses following the conventional norms of polite society with good manners and etiquette. It's an elusive blend of *savoir faire* (worldliness, sophistication, knowing how to respond to situations with savvy choices) and *joie de vivre*, the joy of living. This culture of beauty and elegance extends to all corners of French life.

From an early age, children are taught how to attain aesthetic perfection in every area of their daily life. Much time and effort is spent civilising *les enfants*, reinforcing good manners, style and the appropriate etiquette for every situation. Girls will have been dabbed behind the ears with good French perfume as a baby and learn from an early age when to extend a handshake or offer a cheek. Generally, French children have impeccable manners in public, are respectful, keep conversations low, and can sit perfectly still for hours in restaurants without any sign of petulant behaviour. These traits, I am proud to say, have been adopted by our girls after enduring many a long lunch, along with highly disciplined days at school.

The whole community appears to take an interest and a role in cultivating the next generation, and people have no qualms about correcting parent or child. Advice is delivered by well-meaning strangers to keep standards high. One summer day I was stopped in the street by an elegant grandmother tottering on dangerously high heels and dragging a microscopic terrier. She frowned before reprimanding me for dressing the girls in jelly sandals: 'They are for the beach, dear, not for the streets of Paris!' On another occasion, the girls were scolded for picking up the odd *frite* with their fingers by a concerned *grand-mère* who shook her head and wagged her perfectly manicured finger as she left the café. I do suggest, however, that codes of behaviour differ by *arrondissement*, with conventions being much stricter in the conservative 16th than perhaps in the bohemian Montmartre.

Older women in Paris, in my experience, are revered and respected; as matriarchs they are put on a pedestal, their opinions valued. (In Australia they often become invisible.) Impeccably dressed in chic coats accessorised with classic scarves, bags and jewellery, their style harks back to another era. Often, I am reminded of my country grandmothers who dressed up with pride to go 'to town' once a week and to church on Sundays.

By the time French girls blossom into women they have learnt the rules that matter. They exemplify *bon goût* (good taste), which has little to do with the latest fashions. Not only do they innately know how to dress and what looks good together, they will wear matching underwear every day and possess lingerie for every occasion. They will not step out of their apartment without being perfectly coiffed, manicured and dressed. They are always seen at their best and they will never 'let themselves go'. (Trackie pants are for exercise only and are never worn on the street.) *Les femmes* intuitively know how to tie a scarf and throw a cardie over their shoulders so it drapes just so. Their clothes are carefully chosen and flattering: the classic white shirt, the little black dress and the well-cut *pantalons*.

French women exemplify *bon goût* (good taste)

And if their *pantalons* are not quite well-cut enough they will have them taken in a centimetre. There are rules to follow, however. It is *coquette* to have the back of your pants tight – but never the front. This can sometimes pose a problem, one which only your trusty tailor can rectify.

Even at her tender age, Annabelle seems to have developed instinctive good taste, absorbing what she sees on the street. She has taken it upon herself to act as her father's fashion consultant, picking out his ties in the morning with great pride and pleasure.

French girls also acquire a natural eye for interior design. A flair for style occurs almost by osmosis. Growing up seeing their mothers and grandmothers create table settings with enough elegance and detail to rival the best homeware stores in the city, they attain a talent for *l'art de la table* and are equipped to dress a table for any event.

When invited to formal dinner at a private Parisian home, young French women are also well acquainted with the unspoken rules. Unlike foreigners, who have to tiptoe through the social mire, they already know NOT to bring wine to someone's house to drink on the night. It is not BYO. Choosing the wine is the host's job. They will also know NOT to arrive on time (that's rude), NOT to offer chrysanthemums (reserved for cemeteries) and that a woman does NOT pour the wine, even if she is single and the hostess.

They will never cut the 'nose' off a cheese during the cheese course, *mais oui* (one must always keep the shape), and they will only break bread with their fingers. Instinctively, they will know to keep their hands on the table at all times during a meal, NOT on their lap (no hanky-panky, please), but their elbows off the table. They will stick to safe subjects like food and wine, and *le calendrier Parisien*. Lastly, they will know to leave their napkin on their chair NOT the table when they go to the loo, and NOT to fold their napkin at the end of the meal.

'Style is a simple way of saying complicated things.'

Jean Cocteau

Roving Gourmet on the Left Bank

While most of Paris's temples of gastronomy shimmer across the river, the gourmet appeal of the Rive Gauche lies in simpler pleasures. Here you'll find comfortable cafés and bistros and the *crème de la crème* of small specialty stores owned by passionate artisans devoted to keeping French gastronomic traditions alive. From heavenly chocolate shops to breathtaking *pâtisseries*, the Left Bank's pantry is richly stocked.

Although many of *les bonnes adresses* are concentrated in walkable pockets, seeking out the best is not always a matter of convenience. It's more about the adventure. Buy a good map, put on your walking shoes and rove the streets. It's the best way to see Paris. Investigate long queues. Sample here and there, and, most importantly, allow time to linger because distractions are numerous. Keep in mind that streets perpendicular to the Seine are numbered from the river, while streets parallel start their numbering from the east (increasing in the direction the river flows).

South of boulevard St-Germain, amongst the chic boutiques and antiquarian bookshops, you'll find the outstanding *pâtisserie* **Gérard Mulot**. It's a magnet for neighbourhood celebrities who pop in for their morning pastry. Come early to sample Monsieur Mulot's exceptional croissants and sugar-topped brioche.

Nearby is the sensational *pâtisserie* and chocolate shop that Parisians can't get enough of, **Pierre Hermé**. The queue in his sparse, contemporary boutique never seems to dwindle as passionfruit and white chocolate *macarons*, intense lemon tartlets and innovative cakes filled with feather-light mousses float out the door.

North of boulevard St-Germain, weaving through the narrow streets heading towards the Seine, it's all art galleries and interior fabrics. In springtime, when the cherry trees are in flower, or on a warm summer evening, squeeze into a wicker chair on the terrace of the bohemian café **La Palette**, order a glass of wine and soak up the spirit. A rendezvous point for struggling artists for generations, the back room attracts an edgy crowd from the nearby École des Beaux-Arts and dealers from the surrounding galleries.

Stylish boutiques line rue Jacob. Blink and you'll miss **Huilerie Artisanale J. Leblanc et Fils**. The Leblanc family has been producing some of the finest artisanal table oils in France since 1878, and until Anne Leblanc opened this store, devotees had to travel to Burgundy to pick up a stoneware bottle of Leblanc pistachio, walnut or olive oil to drizzle on their goat's cheese or splash on their salad.

Artisanal loves from Poilâne; typically French dark chocolate
from Debauve & Gallais; a bust of Delacroix

The tiny shop is just steps from the charming Place de Furstenburg, a calm corner lit in the evenings by a central antique candelabrum. It's often featured in French films. Behind heavy wooden doors is the small **Musée Delacroix**. The French Romantic painter moved here in 1857 to be closer to the Church of St-Sulpice, where he painted the three striking murals that can still be seen today.

Another pocket bursting with treats is the scramble of streets dipping into the 7th, around the Sèvres Babylone shopping district. On rue du Bac, amongst the antique and curiosity shops that clutter the stretch from boulevard St-Germain to rue de Sèvres is **Ryst-Dupeyron**, a thoroughly civilised wine and spirits store in historic premises. The charming Nathalie, great-granddaughter of the founder Joseph Dupeyron, will welcome you. A large oak table is set with an array of bottles ready for tasting: port, Scottish whisky and Monsieur Ryst's vintage Armagnac, a collection that dates back to 1868. There is also a fine selection of old Bordeaux and Champagnes. Striking personalised labels can be created while you wait, and deliveries to your hotel can be arranged.

Lovers of typically French dark chocolate should make a detour to **Debauve & Gallais**. The store opened as a pharmacy in 1800 dispensing full-flavoured chocolate rich in cocoa, which was thought to be beneficial to the health. Baudelaire and Simone de Beauvoir were fans, as were the kings of France. Delicacies include *pistoles de Marie-Antoinette* and chocolate shavings, an old-fashioned luxury. Selections are beautifully boxed and sealed with the King of France coat of arms. The perfect gourmet gift – if you can resist the temptation to eat them yourself.

Look for a long line of loyal customers on rue du Cherche-Midi and you'll discover the revered *boulangerie* **Poilâne**. Inside, bread racks are piled high with walnut, rye and raisin breads and rustic designer loaves baked in ancient wood ovens beneath the shop. Thousands of Poilâne sourdough loaves are served in cafés and brasseries across the city every day and flown fresh to select restaurants and supermarkets around the world. Many surrounding cafés serve their *croque monsieurs* on Poilâne bread.

On a side street crossing rue du Cherche-Midi is Vincent's favourite *boucherie-triperie,* **J.-P. Bajon.** This traditional shop with its sawdust-strewn floors, original fittings and sausages hanging in the window has been family-owned since the 1930s. Specialties include poultry, high-quality beef and lamb from the mountainous Aubrac region, and *pâté maison*. There's even a bowl of sliced *saussison* on the counter for hungry children.

Within walking distance of the Eiffel Tower in the 7th is **Au Bon Accueil**, a true *petit bistro de quartier*. From the tiny terrace you can see the tower light up at the end of the street. This is just the place for an intimate, sophisticated dinner, with excellent *cuisine du marché* and an interesting wine list. (Be sure to reserve a table in the front room.)

Nearby is **Marie-Anne Cantin**'s *fromagerie*. The dedicated Cantin, one of Paris's key figures in the fight to protect traditional methods of cheese-making, supplies a host of prestigious addresses including the Assemblée Nationale, Hôtel de Crillon and Hôtel de Bristol. Underneath the pretty shop, 130–150 different

Marie-Anne Cantin's *fromagerie*

types of unpasteurised cheese, selected from the best farms in the country, sleep on beds of straw. Stout rounds of Epoisse with brick-red rinds and inky-blue Roqueforts slowly develop their character. The specialty of the house is St-Antoine, a triple-cream cow's milk cheese with a delicate flavour, ideal with Champagne. Marie-Anne and her husband, Antoine Dias, offer two-hour tasting sessions on how to choose, eat, present and store cheese.

Steps away on the bustling open-air market street rue Cler is the ever-popular **Café du Marché**, a lively spot known for its good-value fresh market *salades* and *plats*. Enjoy lunch here or, alternatively, join the faithful throngs at **Davoli,** a deliciously tempting French-Italian *charcuterie*. Pick up a few slices of ham or a thick wedge of country terrine to add to your cheese from Cantin, grab a baguette and some fruit to complete your feast and spread out a picnic on the green expanse of the Champ de Mars.

Musée Delacroix
6, rue de Furstenberg, 75006
Tel: 01 44 41 86 50
www.musee-delacroix.fr

CAFÉS/BISTROS/ RESTAURANTS
Au Bon Accueil
14, rue de Monttessuy, 75007
Tel: 01 47 05 46 11
www.aubonaccueilparis.com

La Palette
43, rue de Seine, 75006
Tel: 01 43 26 68 15

Le Café du Marché
38, rue Cler, 75007
Tel: 01 47 05 51 27

GOURMET & SPECIALTY STORES
Davoli
34, rue Cler, 75007
Tel: 01 45 51 23 41
www.davoli.fr

Debauve & Gallais
30, rue des Sts-Pères, 75007
Tel: 01 45 48 54 67
www.debauve-et-gallais.com

Gérard Mulot
76, rue de Seine, 75006
Tel: 01 43 26 85 77
www.gerard-mulot.com

Huilerie Artisanale J. Leblanc et Fils
6, rue Jacob, 75006
Tel: 01 46 34 61 55
www.huile-leblanc.com

J.-P. Bajon
29, rue de l'Abbé-Grégoire, 75006
Tel : 01 42 22 58 41

Marie-Anne Cantin
12, rue du Champ de Mars, 75007
Tel: 01 45 50 43 94
www.cantin.fr

Pierre Hermé
72, rue Bonaparte, 75006
Tel: 01 43 54 47 77
www.pierreherme.com

Poilâne
8, rue du Cherche-Midi, 75006
Tel: 01 45 48 42 59
www.poilane.com

Ryst-Dupeyron
79, rue du Bac, 75007
Tel: 01 45 48 80 93
www.vintageandco.com

Enjoy a moment of peace in the garden of Musée Delacroix

La Poste . . . encore

Grahame arrives to give Annabelle her piano lesson with steam coming out of his ears. Putting down his briefcase, he launches into the latest tale of injustice delivered by La Poste.

After a twenty-minute shuffle, he was at the front of the All Operations queue when his phone rang. Expecting an important call from his lawyer, he answered, asked him to hang on for a minute and put the phone in his top pocket.

'Seven stamps, *SVP*.'

'*Non*,' said the attendant, a grouchy bottle-blonde who he'd seen down the park playing *boules* with the guys.

'*Excusez-moi?*' said Grahame.

'*Non*,' she glared.

'*Pourquoi pas?*' (Why not?)

'I don't serve people talking on mobiles.'

'But I'm not on my mobile, I'm on hold.'

Folding her arms crossly and continuing to glare she said, 'I don't care. Switch it off or I'm not serving you.'

With the task of buying stamps now having taken almost twenty-five minutes, Grahame appealed to her sense of duty and justice.

'But I just want seven stamps.'

'*Bof*,' she said, puffing out her cheeks and turning towards the next customer. No one behind said a word.

'Okay then, please get your *responsable* (supervisor).'

'*Non*,' she said, indifferently. The queue started to squirm. Finally realising Grahame wasn't going to go away, she dawdled over to find her *responsable*. A couple of minutes later, he poked his head through the window.

'She doesn't have to serve you if she doesn't want to,' he informed Grahame. The queue started to revolt.

'Is there a notice that says you will not be served if you are on the phone?'

Monsieur Responsable got all sanctimonious and clarified that it was more a question of politeness.

Grahame was about to explain, *encore*, that he wasn't actually on the phone, when it occurred to him that he was wasting his time, *encore* – more than thirty minutes on seven silly stamps!

Stamp-less and furious, he marched out of La Poste.

'How exasperating,' I say, as he pulls up a chair to start the lesson.

Fortunately, he explains, his lawyer overheard it all. Grahame and his French partner, Pierre, have an appointment with the bottle blonde and Monsieur Responsable on Friday morning.

'*Bravo!*' I applaud, but underneath we both silently acknowledge that while his appointment may give him a chance to air his grievances, it won't bring about any change. It is simply another vagary of Parisian life, of the reality of living here. Over time, you learn to accept, reluctantly, that the *responsables* will fiercely back up their colleagues even if they're clearly in the wrong. You become acutely aware that French *fonctionnaires* (civil servants) may choose to give you an extra-hard time if they notice that you have an accent or can't fight well in French.

And yet the longer I live here, the more I find that the frustrating side of French life and the city's sharp angles are adequately compensated for by the allure of the capital and its mysterious power of seduction. Exasperating and exhilarating in equal measures, it is never dull.

Grahame picks up his briefcase, and I wish him *bon courage*.

Mai

The horse chestnut trees along the Seine are alight with pink and white candles, the parks are a riot of colour, and statues glisten in the sun. Everyone is out and about. The city is in full bloom and the weather gorgeous for the arrival of my favourite month in Paris.

Today is 1 May, *Fête du Travail* or Labour Day, and street corners, markets and parks are flooded with vendors selling small, fragrant bouquets of *muguet* (lily of the valley), traditionally bought for family and friends to bring them luck and happiness. On this day, anyone can pick the wild flowers and sell them without a licence, provided they are more than 50 metres from a florist shop. Tim even scored a bunch from *le fromager* with his cheese.

The rhythm of the French year runs like clockwork and there is always something to anticipate and cherish. At first I found life in France a little too formulaic, but as time passed, the unyielding rhythm of the days and the seasons started to have a surprising effect on me. I began to embrace and relish the patterns, looking forward to the fat chocolate fish that swim in schools across the windows of *chocolatiers* around 1 April, and to the chocolate bells at Easter time. Now, I soak up tradition, flipping pancakes on Candlemas and booking *les grandes vacances* months ahead to secure a good *gîte*.

For the keen cook and food lover, the arrival of various fruits, vegetables and produce in the markets marks the months and seasons, and indeed the passing of the year, as plainly as turning the pages of your kitchen calendar. Every month is cause for new celebration.

In May, tiny wild strawberries, *fraises des bois*, become plentiful and sweet. These delicate, intensely perfumed berries are extensively depicted in medieval art, having grown for centuries in woods all over Europe. Violet artichokes from Provence make an appearance and so do apricots from Spain, while posies of red baby radishes beg to be dipped in melted butter and rolled in salt from the Camargue – I can already hear their crunch. Shoppers fill their baskets with blades of chives and *bouquets d'herbs* (posies of freshly picked mixed herbs). Such a clever yet simple idea for when you want just a little of this or that: an aromatic kitchen garden on your bench top.

Wild asparagus from the Marne also arrives, their tender tips attached to pencil-thin stems. As spring goes by, stalks of fat white asparagus from Landes overtake *l'asperge verte*, and fragile bunches of blackcurrants appear. By the end of May, fresh almonds hit the markets, zipped in soft green velour jackets. There is *dorade* (sea bream) from the Mediterranean with shimmering silver skin, and mackerel and frogs' legs.

In *les fromageries*, glistening bowls of thick *crème frâiche* beckon alongside baskets of brown eggs and enormous pats of raw, straw-coloured butter, rich and nutty from the new spring grasses. I can see my grandmother now, her wooden pats and nimble fingers moulding yellow butter into blocks ridged with salty lines. Bought in a slab, *bon beurre* (good butter) is best appreciated as a simple *tartine*, spread thickly on a length of crusty baguette.

Fresh market salads are on every spring menu and the array of delicate greens is astounding. The eternally popular *mâche*, a dark, small-leafed salad green with a mild flavour, is the first to arrive. There's no better way to eat it than tossed in good vinaigrette and topped with walnuts and Roquefort, the famous sheep's milk blue aged in the limestone caves of Roquefort-sur-Soulzon in southwestern France. And then there's mesclun, rocket, watercress, romaine, sorrel . . .

The markets are also abuzz with the arrival of the first new-season cherries and the streets are soon running blood red. As an Australian, I associate cherries with Christmas – and Christmas with family. Suddenly I am very homesick. To lift my spirits, I pop into Le Vigny for coffee. With cherries raining down all over Paris, an American woman new to the city tells us about buying a small bagful at the market. She was so proud she had actually 'understood' the vendor when he blurted out the price that it wasn't until she got home and converted her *carte bleu* receipt that she realised in horror her shiny new cherries had set her back $US35!

Her husband was not a happy man and returned them that evening.

When he suggested to the vendor that he was taking advantage of unknowing foreigners, the vendor protested wildly, exclaiming, 'But these are some of the very first cherries in all of Paris, picked by hand on the sunny slopes of Provence, packed with excruciating care by my brother-in-law in Toulouse and immediately driven in the cool of the night to Paris. A Parisian would be so delighted and proud to taste them they would not think twice.'

'Well, I am not that Parisian yet!' the husband shouted.

Champagne

On a cool June morning, Tim and I pull up at Brooke and Vincent's flat on rue Mouffetard. The produce market is just stretching awake as we pack Vincent's photographic equipment into the boot and head out of town; it is exciting to anticipate the next few days. Vincent and I have received a commission from *Gourmet Traveller* for a feature on the Champagne region, which requires a tightly packed four-day familiarisation tour, courtesy of the French tourist board. Tim and Brooke are tagging along, and the girls have been left in the capable hands of Lyn Lyn (their adored Filipina babysitter), with the promise of an Asian feast.

In ninety minutes we are there, and immediately start on appointments in and around the legendary towns of Reims and Epernay. Way below their bustling streets we are plunged into a dark, undisturbed world where infinite bottles age in hundreds of kilometres of cellars carved from chalk. Here, most of the *grandes marques* Champagne houses can be found, each with an individual spirit and distinct personality. We take impressive guided tours of dramatically lit caves and listen to copious explanations of *méthode champenoise* winemaking.

In Reims, I interview Prince Alain de Polignac, oenologue at **Pommery**, who likens his fine collection to a fashion house with specific styles for different occasions. We meet with members of the **Taittinger** family who pride themselves on understated elegance, and slide into a Disneyland-style automated car for an exhilarating sound and light show at **Piper-Heidsieck**. The Champagne of cinema, it possesses a fresh, glamorous spirit. Marilyn Monroe loved to start her day with a glass – and once took a bath in 350 bottles of it.

By the time we tick off the Belle Époque **Perrier-Jouët** and the imposing **Moët & Chandon** along avenue de Champagne in Epernay, we have been steeped in history.

Yet despite the fame of the larger houses, they're not the only ones making bubbles. Thousands of small producers carve out a livelihood from as little as one hectare, and most welcome visitors into their homes for an intimate tasting, providing a glimpse of French provincial life. We gradually settle into the pace of the countryside, meandering through the corduroy hills along *la route touristique*, past roses in bloom, farmers and hilltop churches. High in the Montagne de Reims, we find ourselves in the heart of some of the most prestigious vineyard country in the world. Tim has acquired the title of official chauffeur and, at Vincent's regular request, brakes for photos along the way. We watch and wait while Vincent disappears over a fence or trudges through a field in search of that one great shot.

South of Epernay, in the Côte des Blancs, vineyards scurry down a steep incline past rustic Chardonnay villages, while north is Aÿ (home of **Bollinger**) and the picturesque village of Hautvillers. It was here that the seventeenth-century Benedictine monk Dom Pérignon was accredited with putting the bubbles in Champagne.

'Come my brothers, quick,' he reportedly said, 'I have drunk the stars.'

The rolling plains of Champagne fall into golden crops and peaceful streams to the south and swell into the wild hills of Ardennes to the north. Deep forests brim with deer, wild boar, pheasant and tiny song thrushes. Snails, pigeon, duck and geese are also plentiful and the rivers teem with trout but, oddly, despite the bountiful produce in the surrounding countryside, Champagne claims surprisingly few signature dishes. Regional cuisine is scanty, with borrowed influences. The most recognisable fare is the pink *biscuits roses* found in local bakeries, and *potée des vendangeurs* (grapepickers' stew). Ardennes ham and *truite à la crème* can be found on menus, along with rustic *pâtés en croûte* and andouillette sausages from Troyes.

Yet our trip is punctuated with plenty of fine dining experiences, the finesse and sophistication of Champagne bubbling onto the plate. Perched on a shoulder of the Montagne de Reims with dramatic views over the vines, we enjoy traditional cuisine at the historic **Royal Champagne**. It was a favourite staging post of Napoléon's on the road to Reims, where most of the kings of France were crowned in the majestic Gothic cathedral. Conveniently, our trip coincides with Tim's fortieth birthday and here we celebrate in true regional style, with a glass of Champagne to match each course.

Tired and sticky after another long day of sipping Champagne, eating, interviewing and shooting, we are somewhat behind on our last day. With one dinner remaining on our punishing schedule, Vincent suddenly asks, 'Why is **Les Crayères** not on our itinerary? It's an institution – it can not be left out.'

La carte from the historic Royal Champagne

Les poissons

Effilochée de cabillaud fumé minute par nos soins, oignons roussis, aillade de pomme de terre au persil plat, beurre nantais à la ciboulette	27,50
Sole des côtes bretonnes cuite au plat puis désarêtée, farcie d'une duxelle de champignons, côte de laitue au jus de jambon ibérique, gratin de gnocchis vert et blanc glacé au vieux parmesan	35,80
Saint-Pierre de petits bateaux cuisiné au naturel, aux tomates fraîches, fenouil et citron, risotto à l'encre de seiche poêlé, jus quatre quart	38,50
Homard cuisiné en casserole aux artichauts poivrade, fleur de courgette, oignons cébette et champignons, une sauce au corail pour le saucer	50,90

Les viandes

Cœur de charolais gourmand, mille-feuille de blette au lard pomme de terre farcie au pied de veau et oignons confits, une sauce à la moutarde violette	35,90
Osso bucco de veau, braisé en cocotte, une sautée de légumes à crue liée au beurre d'escargots, jus blond à la moelle	28,50
Pigeon de la « Machauderie » en piccata au foie gras et jambon ibérique, pomme boulangère, artichauts poivrade et tomates confites, jus au Marsala	37,40
Volaille de Bresse cuite en croûte de noisettes en deux services, pour 2 personnes, les suprêmes avec des petits pois à la française champignons et grosses pommes frites avec une salade aux lardons et foie poêlé	73,90

Prix nets en Euros taxes et service inclus

A haven of refinement set in 7 hectares on the outskirts of Reims, Les Crayères' magic is largely attributed to the management of Gérard and Elyane Boyer who are masters of the French *art de vivre*. Gérard is at the helm in the kitchen, and the restaurant is considered one of the best 'tables' in France. Seventeen sumptuous rooms are located in the *château*, decorated with couture fabrics and antiques.

We have a tough decision to make. In one hour we are scheduled for our third Michelin-starred meal in three days. Do we return to **Le Clos Raymi**, our charming boutique hotel, change and freshen up for dinner before tackling a classic menu that will no doubt feature truffles, *foie gras*, snails and Champagne sauces? Or do we go straight to Les Crayères, unannounced, before arriving late to dinner, dishevelled in our day clothes? Given the reputation of Les Crayères, we unanimously decide on the latter option. It is not an ideal situation, but it's the only time we have to squeeze in this esteemed hotel.

We drive through the tall iron gates of the walled property, crunching over the gravel and I gasp at the breathtaking *château* and its immaculately groomed lawns. We enter the bouquet-filled foyer and a blonde woman approaches: Chanel platform shoes, chic orange dress, *beaucoup de style*. She is the flamboyant Elyane Boyer. Deducing that the eloquence of a native speaker will increase our chances of weaselling our way in, Vincent takes the lead. He explains that, unfortunately, we do not have an appointment but wonders if we could perhaps take a few shots outside, have a quick chat, a look around?

'You are with *Gourmet* and you have come here unannounced, at the beginning of service?' Their voices escalate, erupting into an argument that echoes through the foyer. I watch my new vocation evaporate before my eyes. What have we done? Brooke, who is sitting on an antique *chaise longue* a few yards away, motions me to come and sit down.

'Don't worry,' she says, 'just let them go. It's really just a spirited, lively discussion. You'll see – it will turn out all right.' In France, it seems, I never do stop learning what is *normale*.

After another round of 'discussion', Madame realises that we are not with *American Gourmet* but *Australian Gourmet*. She softens for a moment. Then she snaps and says, 'Why weren't we on your itinerary? Why were we left out?' Both agree that there has been an unthinkable oversight and fall silent.

Before we know it, Madame ushers the four of us into the inner sanctum of the hotel, perfume wafting behind her. Impeccable waiters deliver Champagne in dewy ice buckets, corks pop softly and a fabulous terrace shaded by vast white

Vineyards around Oeuilly in the Champagne region

umbrellas stretches out to clipped hedges. We find ourselves in La Rotonde, an exquisite conservatory-style bar with plush chairs and small round tables.

'*Asseyez vous,*' sings Madame Boyer, leaving us in the hands of a polished waiter as we take our seats. An ice-bucket on a stand is placed before us and a bottle of Bollinger is cracked open and poured into glasses. Vincent runs around discreetly taking a few shots while I take in the view, the menu, and the ambience of this amazing place. Through the full-length windows I watch the waiters pouring Champagne on the terrace and the June sun drop into the treetops. Already we are late for our reservation at **Hostellerie La Briqueterie**. It is time to go. We drain our Bolly, farewell Madame Boyer with a *merci mille fois* and brace ourselves for our final Champagne dinner.

N.B. The Boyers have unfortunately retired since our visit.

CHAMPAGNE HOUSES
Bollinger
16, rue Jules-Lobet, Aÿ
Tel: 03 26 53 33 66
www.champagne-bollinger.fr

Moët & Chandon
20, ave de Champagne,
Epernay
Tel: 03 26 51 20 20
www.moet.com

Perrier-Jouët
24–28, ave de Champagne,
Epernay
Tel: 03 26 53 38 10
www.perrier-jouet.com

Piper-Heidsieck
51, blvd Henry-Vasnier, Reims
Tel: 03 26 84 43 44
www.piper-heidsieck.com

Pommery
5, Place du Général-Gouraud
Reims
Tel: 03 26 61 62 63
www.pommery.fr

Taittinger
9, Place St-Niçaise, Reims
Tel: 03 26 85 45 35
www.taittinger.fr

HOTELS & RESTAURANTS
L'Hostellerie La Briqueterie
4, route de Sézanne, Vinay
Tel: 03 26 59 99 99
www.labriqueterie.fr

Le Clos Raymi
3, rue Joseph-de-Venoge, Epernay
Tel: 03 26 51 00 58
www.closraymi-hotel.com

Le Royal Champagne
Bellevue, Champillon-Epernay
Tel: 03 26 52 87 11
www.royalchampagne.com

Les Crayères
64, blvd Henry-Vasnier, Reims
Tel: 03 26 24 90 00
www.lescrayeres.com

'Burgundy makes you think of silly things,
Bordeaux makes you talk about them,
and Champagne makes you do them.'

Jean Anthelme Brillat-Savarin

Julie calls, breathless.

'You'll never guess what happened,' she says.

'No, I'm sure you're right. Are you okay?' I'd seen Julie the previous evening when she stayed for an impromptu dinner with Mark and the girls. They left at ten o'clock to get the children to bed. What could have possibly happened overnight?

Julie explains that they had walked home through the streets of Passy. Exhausted, the four of them had squeezed into their ancient little lift, ready to fall into bed. Slowly it rose, let out a great shudder, then, somewhere between the third and fourth floors, stopped dead.

'We were stuck in a hot, dark lift!' she exclaims.

'*Non!*'

'*Oui!* Feeling around in the dark, we found what we hoped was an emergency button. Mark kept pushing it optimistically hoping that it was actually connected to something.'

'*Mon Dieu*, how frightening!'

'Well, after fifteen long minutes, just as we were really starting to freak out and trying to come to terms with spending the night stacked together like a bunch of hot baguettes, we heard a man's booming voice outside yelling, "*RESTEZ CALME!*" Music to our ears, I can tell you.

'His voice was very unclear and his French fast, but eventually we understood him,' Julie goes on. 'He explained that because we were stuck between floors, he would have to pull us out manually through the top of the lift. So he wrenched off the roof and hauled us up and out, one by one; all very dramatic.

'Just another typical day in Paris,' she sighs resignedly.

Le Chassé-Croisé

The month starts precariously with crossed fingers and a prayer, our fragile lives held in the incapable hands of a Parisian taxi driver. Speeding towards the airport, the fresh morning breeze fast in our faces, we glimpse signs intended to slow him down, to no avail. *Sans* seatbelt, our chauffeur continues oblivious, honking angrily at other drivers for travelling too slowly. We wince as he takes his controlling hand off the wheel for added effect. So it is with drained faces that we arrive abruptly at Roissy-Charles-de-Gaulle to catch our flight to Madrid.

We are by no means alone. A chain of suitcases, hats and bright clothing snakes from the check-in counters. It seems most of Paris is here – almost unrecognisable in beachwear and shorts. We have chosen the busiest weekend of the year to travel. This first weekend in August is well known as a time of pandemonium and planned chaos as *juilletistes* return from vacation and *aoûtiens* leave. It is the most treacherous weekend of the year on the roads; *les bouchons* (bottlenecks and traffic jams) are kilometres long and everyone is tuned into the traffic radio channel, Autoroute FM. Officially the weekend is called *le grand chassé-croisé des vacances* (the mix-up and crossover of July and August holidaymakers).

Such is the highly orchestrated and cyclic rhythm of French life: doctors and artists alike lock their apartments and garrets behind them and migrate south to the sun. August brings the highest annual temperatures and is the most popular month to holiday. Paris apartments become unbearably hot: most are *sans* air-con. All over the city, specialty stores, boutiques, cafés and restaurants batten down their hatches – which is enough in itself to make you want to leave. *Fermé jusqu'à la rentrée* signs are posted on shop windows: closed until 'the return' in September. Until then, Paris is devoid of Parisians.

The city breathes a sigh of relief and basks in its respite. The tourists, in fact, have the place almost to themselves. Those Parisians left behind rattle in their empty cage – sunbaking along Paris Plage (the fake beach set up along the Seine) by day and stretching out on café terraces by night. Queues are shorter, the metro less congested and parking meters are free – the inspectors are all *en vacances*.

Driving back into Paris after our Andalusian adventure, with the Eiffel Tower watching protectively, I feel a surge of belonging and pride that takes me by surprise. After four years, the city feels familiar and comfortable, like a croissant for breakfast and a trench coat in spring. There is a sense of knowing and an acceptance of what lies beneath her flawless skin, a respect for and growing understanding of her ways.

It is as we hurtle across Place du Trocadéro that I realise I am in love with a city and a culture, warts and all.

We pull up at the apartment door, and even Madame Gardienne registers a flicker of endearment. Still leaning on her mop in the doorway and prattling on at the speed of the TGV to anyone passing who will listen, she offers us a pleasant '*Bonjour Monsieur, bonjour Madame, bonjour les enfants*' and, if I am not mistaken, the faint beginnings of a smile.

Hurtling across Place du Trocadéro

Paris,

je t'aime . . .
à la folie

Menthe ⇒ 4ᶠ
Tyme ⇒ 8ᶠ
Ciboullette ⇒ ᶠ
Persil ⇒ 5ᶠ
Basilic ⇒ 7ᶠ
ANETTE ⇒ 6ᶠ
Coriande ⇒ ᶠ
Romarin ⇒ 6ᶠ
l'oseil ⇒ 6ᶠ
Estragons ⇒ 6ᶠ
Pot de Basilic ⇒

Fresh herbs for sale
at rue Mouffetard market

Rose Royale

It's time to celebrate in style! Finally I have in my hands a glossy copy of my first feature published with *Gourmet Traveller* (lead times are terribly long in the magazine world). I leave the girls with Lyn Lyn, who has arrived juggling cartons of noodles from the enormous Asian supermarket **Tang Frères**, and meet Tim at Le Bar du Hôtel Plaza Athénée. On the glitzy avenue Montaigne, the grand **Hôtel Plaza Athénée** drips with exquisite French refinement. Luxurious rooms and apartments rival glamorous dining areas supervised by Alain Ducasse – the star being his own contemporary restaurant, Alain Ducasse au Plaza Athénée. The bar offers lots of bling and a fabulous range of cocktails including a clutch of special creations. I relax on a Regency-style stool under tiny chandeliers suspended on wires and savour an elegant Rose Royale, a delicious blend of fresh raspberry coulis and Champagne. Thrilled, I flick through shiny pages filled with shots of autumn produce and markets . . . and raise my glass to Paris.

Hôtel Plaza Athénée
25, ave Montaigne, 75008
Tel: 01 53 67 66 65
www.plaza-athenee-paris.com

Tang Frères
48, ave d'Ivry, 75013
Tel: 01 45 70 80 00

The Markets in Autumn

Summer holidays are officially over. Leaves spill from the horse chestnut trees along the Seine. There's a nip in the air and chairs are disappearing from terraces, umbrellas are snapped shut and doors slammed on cosy cafés as Parisians prepare for the cooler months ahead. Gone too are the mountains of strawberries and the streams of summer cherries. Stuffed with the fullness of autumn, the French countryside has been trucked to Paris and the open-air markets explode in fiery shades of scarlet, bronze and gold. Shopping baskets now brim with treasures found on forest floors. Stalls swell with cheery *clémentines*. Rickety crates of corn are banged down next to mounds of plums with frosted purple skins and pears with windblown cheeks.

As the weather turns, chefs toss salads from menus, roll up their sleeves with relish and bring down their pots to prepare the first of the season's rich, robust sauces. Restaurants begin to feel warm and homey again, and blackboards announce comforting delights that capture the flavours of fall: *caille rôtie aux figues* (quail with roasted figs), *lapin à la moutarde* (rabbit in mustard sauce).

The French live by the seasons and the rural connection remains strong, with discerning Parisians yearning to draw closer to 'the source'. In a city fiercely passionate about food, *le marché* not only provides a venue for fresh regional produce but also plays an important part in the daily *art de vivre*. The market trip gives locals a chance to meet friends over *un café*, exchange cooking tips with the fishmonger and banter away to the bloodstained butcher. Customers form strong relationships with their favourite merchants, who act as culinary counsellors.

A ramble through the markets provides an interesting way for food lovers to discover Paris and reveals much about the character and habits of those who live in each quarter. There are three types of markets scattered throughout the city: small covered markets, roving markets and merchant streets, each with their own personality and flavour. Generally, covered markets have become more of historical interest than culinary, unable to compete with supermarkets. Open-air roving markets set up at dawn under colourful canopies, only to vanish again around lunchtime. They come alive twice a week, leaving in their wake streets strewn with boxes and broken baguettes. With the help of pecking pigeons and an army of brooms, the cobbles are soon returned to normal.

Straddling the eastern fence of the once noble Marais and working-class Bastille is one of Paris's most fashionable roving markets, the lively **Marché Bastille**. Erected along the broad tree-lined boulevard Richard Lenoir under the protective wing of the Genie de la Bastille, the market draws a mix of urban professionals and creative types from the hip neighbourhoods nearby. Here you will encounter oozing farmhouse cheeses, exceptional seafood at Jacky Lorenzo's (one of the best fishmongers in the city), *escargots de Bourgogne* and the occasional baby goat.

Across town, **Marché President-Wilson** is the smartest, most genteel roving market in Paris. Avenue du President Wilson is transformed into an opulent banquet catering to the 16th. Step into the long aisle of stalls sandwiched between the Musée d'Art Moderne and the Musée de la Mode et du Costume and you'll sweep past huge pans of paella, crêpes on the griddle and speckled quail eggs. With a clientele who demand superior quality, you can be assured the produce is pristine. Many locals do their flower shopping here, choosing from a breathtaking array of blooms.

The eastern end of the market runs into Place de l'Alma, and from here you can stroll over the bridge into the exclusive 7th. Wander down avenue Rapp to the charming rue St-Dominique and lunch at **La Fontaine de Mars**. With its crisp gingham cloths, clanging kitchen bell and traditional southwestern cuisine,

this restaurant defines *vieille* France. It was opened at the turn of the twentieth century and named after the small fountain nearby, commissioned by Napoléon. Tables are always jammed with locals tucking into seasonal bistro fare – try the classic *cassoulet*. Trek further in and you'll discover a very intimate side of old-money Paris. **Marché Saxe-Breteuil**, a large market with a lively country village atmosphere, has set up its canopies under the shadow of the Eiffel Tower since 1873. Bustle past pots of lavender honey, tubs of tapenade, rustic fruit tarts and poodles. Sample some Tomme de Savoie cheese or some olives from Provence. There's also fish transported that very morning from Trouville and geese from the Périgord.

A short metro ride away on boulevard Raspail, the fashionable organic farmers' market springs up on Sunday mornings. Eco-conscious Parisians and local residents from St-Germain converge on the stretch in droves for the **Marché Biologique Raspail**. Farmers load up dewy pears, cider, vegetable tarts and homemade cakes at first light, jump in their trucks and rattle into town. Produce is grown and prepared according to strict organic regulations. Keep your eye out for healthy wholewheat galettes – and celebrities.

In contrast to roving markets, merchant streets consist of stalls that tumble out of specialty shops along established thoroughfares. Weekends are the liveliest time to visit. Locals dally in the cafés, buskers sing and piano accordionists belt out traditional tunes. Late on Sunday mornings, families are out gathering supplies for lunch, along with a baguette, a tart, a bottle of wine and a cheese or two, before slipping behind heavy doors to their apartments. Wonderful aromas float into courtyards and waft down stairwells, and an audible hush falls over the streets as the city settles in for a long Sunday lunch, still a treasured tradition in France.

Just a short walk from the Arc de Triomphe is **rue Poncelet** – a vibrant street in the residential 17th catering to a loyal band of middle-class families. Agile fishmongers squelch about in rubber boots, scooping up mussels and pouring cockles onto dripping ice beds. Frenzied customers at *la boucherie* order plucked pigeons, quails and guinea fowls, while hot roasted rabbits are slipped into bags. The demand is a little slower at the horse butcher (identified by the three sculptured horse heads).

Hunting remains a steadfast tradition; September marks the start of *la chasse*. Field hares grown plump and flavourful on the lush green grasses of summer are cheap and plentiful and by November, venison and wild boar are proudly displayed, dressed in their coats. Larks are on hand for those with the urge to make lark *pâté*.

Sample some cheese from the family-run **Alléosse** at number 13, widely considered one of the finest *fromageries* in Paris. Cheeses are selected personally from the best dairies in France and aged in cellars beneath the shop.

One of Paris's oldest merchant streets is **rue Mouffetard** on the edge of the Latin Quarter. Surrounded by ancient alleyways, this Left Bank area of bookshops, writers and students is devoted to learning. Described by Ernest Hemingway in *A Moveable Feast*, the street has changed little over the centuries, its bumpy grey cobblestones worn smooth with the passage of time.

The street climbs up and along its hilly way from the medieval church of St-Médard past fleshy pig's ears, pearly strings of garlic and North Sea prawns. Ruddy-faced merchants unpack wooden boxes brimming with figs and herbs from the scented hills of Provence and bellow out the day's promotions. Be sure to look up at number 134 to see the mural of forest animals roaming across the four-storey building.

Nearby are the Luxembourg Gardens, now showered in autumn leaves. Winter is just around the corner. Soon, Parisians will dig gloves out of drawers and zip precious poodles into stylish coats. Thoughts will turn to firewood, turkeys with tail feathers, fat geese and truffles – and, once more, the markets will reinvent themselves.

Alléosse
13, rue Poncelet, 75017
Tel: 01 46 22 50 45
www.fromage-alleosse.com

La Fontaine de Mars
129, rue St-Dominique, 75007
Tel: 01 47 05 46 44
www.fontainedemars.com

ROVING MARKETS
Marché Bastille
blvd Richard-Lenoir,
beginning at rue Amelot
Metro: Bastille
Thurs 7 a.m to around 2.30 p.m.;
Sun 7 a.m. to around 3 p.m.

Marché President-Wilson
ave du President-Wilson,
between Place d'Iéna
and rue Debrousse
Metro: Alma-Marceau/Iéna
Wed 7 a.m to around 2.30 p.m.;
Sat 7 a.m. to around 3 p.m.

Marché Raspail
blvd Raspail, between rue de
Rennes and rue du Cherche-Midi
Metro: Rennes/Sevres-Babylone
Tue & Fri 7 a.m to around
2.30 p.m. (regular market
with some organic);
Sun morning (organic market)

Marché Saxe-Breteuil
ave de Saxe, between Place
de Breteuil and ave de Ségur
Metro: Ségur/Duroc
Thurs 7 a.m to around 2.30 p.m.;
Sat 7 a.m. to around 3 p.m.

MERCHANT STREETS
Tue–Sat between 8 a.m.
and 9 a.m.–1 p.m.
then 4 p.m.–7 p.m.;
Sun between 8 a.m.
and 9 a.m.–1 p.m.

Rue Mouffetard
beginning at rue de
l'Epée-de-Bois
Metro: Censier-Daubenton/
Place Monge

Rue Poncelet
beginning at ave des Ternes
and extending down rue Bayen
Metro: Ternes

Le Lait

I arrive at Le Vigny in time to hear Mel, a vivacious Englishwoman new to Paris, tell of her latest misadventure. It began when she popped down to the corner store to buy milk.

She glanced at the due date, 17 September, which was still four days away, bought the milk and headed home.

'That date is still imprinted in my mind,' she tells the group as Serge delivers our *café crèmes*. 'Anyway, I get home, make myself a coffee and pour in some milk. It is obviously off!

'I go straight back to the store and change the milk for a new carton with the same due date. I traipse home again, make a fresh coffee and pour in the milk. It glugs out of the carton!'

So Mel marched back to the store with the milk.

'You again,' said the owner, rolling his eyes.

'This milk is off too,' said Mel. 'It must be your fridge.'

'It is not off,' said the owner, looking at the carton. 'It doesn't expire until 17 September and there's nothing wrong with my fridge.'

'I'm telling you it is off,' said Mel, shoving the carton under his nose.

He didn't flinch, correcting her on her pronunciation of *tourner à l'aigre* (turn sour), before repeating, 'No, it is not off.'

'Okay, then,' cried Mel, '*GOÛTEZ-LE, MONSIEUR!*' (Taste it!)

'Okay,' he said, pouring a little milk into a glass. He called both assistants over for a tasting too. They all sipped the milk before a round of '*Ça va . . . c'est frais.*' (It's good, it's fresh.)

Not a flinch between them.

'*CE N'EST PAS FRAIS!*' cried Mel, fearing a conspiracy. 'What are these lumps floating about in the milk?'

'Oh, just pieces of butter – sometimes you get them in very fresh milk.'

Mel didn't know whether to laugh or cry.

'Realising I wasn't going to get anywhere, I demanded to change the carton for some long-life milk, which, surprisingly, the owner willingly did. Anything but admit that he was wrong. Anything but apologise!'

We put on our coats and depart Le Vigny to start another new year in Paris, leaving our *café crèmes* almost untouched.

Georgie and friend, Zazou, backstage at *The Nutcracker*

Le Petit Problème

In just five years, I have watched l'Académie Américaine de Danse de Paris grow into one of the largest and finest classical dance schools in the city, offering an alternative to the French system and giving l'École de l'Opéra, the prestigious school that feeds into the Ballet de l'Opéra de Paris, a run for its money. Word soon flew around the dance world that a school was achieving excellent results without criticising and screaming at their students. French parents were astonished.

At twelve, Georgie auditions for and is accepted into Brooke's pre-professional program. This means eighteen hours of classical dance a week. It also means changing academic schools to a special *école* that somehow condenses the French curriculum into the morning, leaving the afternoon for students to practise their various aptitudes, such as dance or music.

Georgie and a new Russian boy are the only foreign students in her year-level, and both bear the brunt of being perceived as 'different'. One day after Georgie returns home particularly upset, Tim and I call for a meeting with *la directrice*. When I hand her a copy of a harassment policy from an Australian school to consider, she flicks through briefly before discarding it, saying, 'We do not need a harassment policy at this school as we have never had a problem – until now.'

The children who dance in the chorus at the prestigious l'Opéra de Paris are affectionately known as *Les Petits Rats*.

Julie calls, relieved.

'I think I'll stay away from train stations,' she says.

'What's happened now?' I ask, tentatively.

'Well, I was at Montparnasse station today with a couple of friends and desperately needed to go to *les toilettes*. You know how impossible it is to find one underground . . . Anyway, there was a TGV at a platform nearby, so one of my friends suggested I jump on the train and find a loo. The choice was down to the TGV or the tunnel so I snuck on and ran down the passage.'

'Then what happened?' I ask, smiling to myself.

'Well, I'm sitting on the loo and the next thing I know, the train is making moves to go, and I'm thinking, this is just my luck! I had visions of waving goodbye to my friends through the train window and ending up goodness knows where. So I zip up my jeans, make a wild dash for the door and leap off just before I am whisked away to Bordeaux – so I find out afterwards. Actually it would have been quite a nice little break . . .'

'Julie, just think,' I say, laughing, 'you could have rung Mark from the train and said, "Didn't I tell you I was going away? Must have slipped my mind. Be back late tomorrow evening. Call my mobile if you need me. *Ciao*."'

La Cigarette

An historic quarter in eastern Paris, Bercy is back on the map after a long period of decline. Known as 'the Cellar of the World' in its nineteenth-century heyday, Bercy was once the largest wine-trading centre in Europe, receiving a continual stream of barges laden with barrels from the vineyards of France. I have just spent the afternoon here with Vincent, researching a story on **Chai 33** for *Gourmet Traveller WINE*. This revolutionary bar/restaurant/wine boutique is housed in a converted wine warehouse on Cour St-Émilion, a revamped pedestrian street that runs through the village.

Finishing with half an hour to spare before picking up Annabelle, I stop by a café. I order *un citron pressé*, a glass of freshly squeezed lemon juice that arrives with a pot of sugar, then sit back and watch the comings and goings.

On my right sits a beautiful brown-eyed boy with tumbling curls and his female companion, both all of fourteen. Their table is covered with school texts. They drink coffee and chain smoke, the boy rolling his own like a seasoned professional. They write furiously and discuss earnestly with a discipline I have yet to encounter in Australians of their age. But then, Australians of their age do not have to pass the same stringent exams.

On my left sits an elderly gentleman, exquisitely dressed with a fancy bow tie, hair perfectly in place. His Burberry scarf and coat are taken instantly by a pandering waiter.

'*Bonjour, Monsieur,*' call all the waiters, appearing from around the room to give double-cheek kisses. No doubt the waiters expect his daily visit, sitting him at his favourite table and knowing his order by heart. There is something endearing about having a local where you are known and nurtured, rather than being just another nondescript number.

It appears Monsieur Burberry has come for his four o'clock glass of *vin rouge* and generous slice of quiche Lorraine. But what I find most fascinating about this stylish Parisian is that he seems to be eating, drinking, smoking and reading *Le Figaro* simultaneously. As cigarette smoke curls in the ashtray, he reads the paper, hesitating only slightly to cut off the next mouthful of quiche that is surreptitiously followed by a slurp of wine and a long drag of his cigarette. Then back to the quiche. This routine is adhered to until his plate and glass are empty, his ashtray full and the paper read.

Then he calls, '*L'addition, SVP,*' leaves a generous tip and is helped on with his coat. With a flurry of *au revoirs,* he disappears out the door until his next rendezvous.

www.chai33.com

'If I were King, I would close all cafés, for those who frequent them become dangerous hotheads.'

Charles de Montesquieu

Coq au Vin

The last leaves are hanging on the trees like forgotten washing. The tourists have gone. We rug up and take a bracing stroll along the quay under an ashen sky. Heading east, we pass the Grand Palais, marvelling at the chariots and bronze flying horses that rear courageously over its corners. Across Pont Alexandre III, the Dôme Church is trying to catch some sun on its golden roof. We artfully dodge the traffic on Place de la Concorde and walk on, crunching through the bleak, puddle-filled Jardin des Tuileries before diverting back to the river. Our shoes are soon soaked and our hair frosted with November rain.

Steam rises from a hot crêpe griddle outside a café further down the quay and the girls run ahead to order golden crêpes slathered with Nutella, and cups of hot chocolate all round. Revived, we walk on, stopping to browse the few *bouquinistes* open along the Seine.

It is while I am engrossed in a 1945 edition of *Giselle* that I am jolted back to reality by what I could swear is a crowing rooster. *Un coq* in the centre of Paris? *C'est bizarre!* We follow the crow across the road to discover not only a proud rooster, but clucking chooks, pigeons and quaking quails.

Between Pont Neuf (the first stone bridge in Paris) and Châtelet on Quai de la Mégisserie is a veritable menagerie. Within a 100 metre stretch you can buy virtually any pet, from a rare beige chinchilla to a duck. We find exotic birds in large elaborate cages, fat sandy prairie dogs, wrinkly goannas and squirrels. The girls are enthralled. Seeds have been sown and names are being discussed. Living in a world of uncertainty, not knowing where you will be next year, or next month, makes the question of pets a difficult one. Growing up without a backyard is one thing but, for a country girl like me, the thought of a childhood *sans* pets is unthinkable. And who knows, if our past history is anything to go by, we could be here forever! Steering the girls around to the idea of a couple of nice respectable budgies, we promise them a visit to the Marché aux Oiseaux – the lively bird market at Place Louis-Lépine that turns from a colourful flower market during the week into a jumble of noisy birds on Sundays.

But the question of who buys a rooster in Paris continues to puzzle us. While courtyards are common, gardens are not, and those lucky enough to own a private *château* are unlikely to erect a chook-house by the fountain. There's also

the problem of the neighbours being woken at daybreak. Surely these pampered pets are not allowed inside to roost on the sofa? And if you live in the suburbs, why trek into the heart of Paris for an overpriced chook?

After much discussion, the only conclusion we can draw is *coq au vin*: softly simmered cockerel in a full-bodied red from Burgundy, cooked with bacon, mushrooms and onions, and served with parsley potatoes for Sunday lunch.

Label Rouge

Fermier products are sought after for their superior quality and flavour, having generally been raised or handmade by devoted small producers. When discussing cheese, *fermier* refers to 'farmhouse'; for chickens, it usually denotes free-range. When ordering a hot roast chicken at the market, be sure to ask for '*un poulet rôti fermier, SVP*'. Look for the certified free-range *Label Rouge* when buying eggs and ready-to-cook poultry products (chicken, guinea fowl, capon, duck, goose, turkey and quail), a mark of premium quality. It was created in the 1960s by farmers in the Landes region where fowl roam the forests, and guarantees traditional, free-range farming methods in accordance with stringent specifications.

Le Pull

Françoise knocks on the door.

'I have just bought little Annabelle *un pull adorable*,' she says proudly.

She holds up a sky blue jumper.

'*Merci beaucoup!*' I say in astonishment.

'I hope you like the colour. Anyway, must go and walk the dog. *Salut*.'

I close the door and look at the jumper. It is very generous of Françoise, but just what are the expectations? How do I respond to this benevolent gesture now that we are 'friends', now that we *tu* not *vous*? Am I expected to reciprocate with a gift of equal value for Capucine? In what time frame? Is this a simple one-off act of kindness or have we entered into an unspoken, ongoing and escalating arrangement?

CAN SOMEONE PLEASE TELL ME THE RULES HERE?

During winter, the square in front of Hôtel de Ville turns into a shiny, white ice-rink

Marché aux Oiseaux

Annabelle slips on her new *pull*, tries on numerous scarves until she finds one that matches perfectly, ties it flawlessly with a flourish and, finally, we head to Place Louis-Lépine. We stomp up the steps of Cité metro station and walk right into the middle of a bustling market full of squawking birds and colour. The girls walk up and down the rows numerous times past birds and cages of all shapes and sizes before stopping at a cage containing a bright blue and a sea green budgie. Above is a sign: '*Perruches* 15€ a couple'.

'*Elles sont mignonne!*' (They are so sweet!) exclaims Georgie. Before we know it, we are precariously manoeuvring Lillypilly and Lollipop in a large white cage through the train doors. Really, from the disapproving looks we receive, we may as well have brought a lion onto *le métro*!

'Les chats ont sept vies.'
In France, cats have seven lives. In Australia, cats have nine lives. I therefore conclude that it's better for cats to live in Australia than France.

Le Bricolage

When I was growing up, I don't think my father ever came home from town without a bag of buns from Morris's, our country bakery. My parents are visiting for a few weeks and I see that nothing has changed. Dad is calmly working his way through every item in our local *pâtisserie* and has even developed a routine. He points to what he fancies, holds up one finger, then holds out his palm full of change: it takes more than a language barrier to deter a true sweet-tooth. But today he stands with a twinkle in his eye for a different reason. I have taken him to *le sous-sol* (basement) of **Le Bazaar de L'Hôtel de Ville (BHV)** with a lengthy list of bits and pieces needed for repairs to our apartment. He is in hardware heaven.

On the busy rue de Rivoli, BHV is one of the city's grand old department stores, an institution since 1856. Lacking the glamour of the stores in the Opéra quarter, BHV has built its reputation on home improvements. For fashion and

cosmetics head elsewhere, but if your passion is DIY, make a beeline for *le bricolage* department, affectionately known as the biggest toolbox in Paris.

Part of the fascination is that the entire basement seems so uncharacteristic of Paris, so ordinary and messy, yet oddly still so French. In this enchanting maze with an old-world hardware shop feel, it's easy to lose yourself in the assortment of yawning bidets, truffle hoes, pigeon boxes, scythes and sickles. Strong, burly blokes in paint-splattered overalls zip out their tape measures, and knowledgeable staff are sometimes at your service with pencils tucked behind their ears. It's also the place to learn intriguing new vocabulary that you're unlikely ever to need again. On Saturdays, half of the city's male population seems to be siphoned into *le sous-sol* engrossed in saws and concrete mixers, nuts and bolts.

While my father is transfixed by drill pieces, locks and chains, I amuse myself by wading through the kingdom of antique French door knobs. With styles often named after monarchs, they give you a quick flick through the history of France. Browsing around *le fer forge* (wrought iron) I find horseshoes at bargain-basement prices, cow bells in eight different sizes and an enormous assortment of metal signs including everything from *hommes* and *dames* to imitations of the classic, royal blue street signs.

I eventually locate Dad with one of the staff, attempting to buy a screwdriver using hand actions. With a growing basket of gadgets and gizmos, we trek around one last time to discover we have missed the snares for hares, the village of post boxes and an entire grove devoted to the automobile, with guidebooks and maps of France. We stumble over nets for ferrets, rows of lawnmowers lined up ready to zoom around all those Paris backyards, and a possession that nobody should be without, *un piège à taupes*, a booby trap for moles. It's the kind of place a hands-on man can lose himself in for the entire afternoon.

BHV
52–64, rue de Rivoli, 75004
Tel: 01 42 74 90 00
www.bhv.fr

La Mode

Annabelle is busy contemplating whether to work for Chanel when she grows up, to live like Chanel at the Ritz, or to simply wear Chanel.

Enchantée

Soon after *Gourmet Traveller* publishes my second story, the editor, Judy Sarris, visits Paris on a family trip and I invite her over for drinks with her husband, Stan, and daughter, Bella. I dash about cleaning up and run through the snow to *la fleuriste* for a big bunch of long-stemmed roses. There is something different about French roses. Like the clipped trees that line the Champs-Élysées east of the Rond Point, each one is box-shaped, conforming and perfect. They are so much more composed than the average Australian rose, I think, as I watch them being beautifully wrapped.

Brooke and Vincent join us, and the girls make friends over *une galette des Rois*. We christen the Champagne glasses Georgie and Annabelle recently bought us for Christmas, sneaking down to a bijou boutique on rue de la Tour.

It is while we are sipping our Perrier-Jouët and nibbling our canapés from Lenôtre that I am asked if I'd like to be Paris Contributor for *Gourmet Traveller*.

Are you kidding?

Galette des Rois

While the religious significance of *La Fête des Rois* or Epiphany is dwindling in France, celebrating the day by sharing *une galette des Rois* or Twelfth Night cake with your family is still a treasured French tradition. Epiphany celebrates the visit of the three wise men to the Christ child and falls twelve days after Christmas on 6 January. In France, the Magi are known as *Les Rois Mages* or the Sorcerer Kings.

A peep into any *boulangerie* during the month of January will reveal shelves swamped with the rich and buttery pastry pies. In fact, the French bemoan that *les galettes des Rois* used only to be available for a few special days, but now appear in December and stay well beyond their welcome throughout February.

Filled with frangipane, a soft, smooth mixture of almond cream and *crème pâtissière*, these flaky pies also come flavoured with chocolate, pear or pistachio and are sold with a golden paper crown. Hidden inside each galette is *une fève*. Historically, a broad bean (*fève*) was cooked inside, hence the name, but today it is commonplace to find a tiny porcelain figurine: a king perhaps or baby Jesus, even Tintin or a baker holding a baguette. We now have quite a collection.

To serve the cake, the youngest member of the family hides under the table, calling out the name of the next person to receive a slice. Traditionally, one slice

of the galette is saved for the first homeless person to knock on your door and say, 'I'm hungry'. Whoever is lucky enough to stumble on the *feve* is crowned king or queen. They choose a partner or consort and reign supreme for the rest of the day.

This year, Georgie cut up a galette in her classroom and Iris's daughter Sarah was chosen by the winning king as a consort.

She wept all afternoon.

Julie calls, upset.

'We're leaving,' she sobs.

'What! Oh Julie . . . when?'

'The removalists are coming in the morning and we fly tomorrow night.'

'When did you find out?'

'Today,' she whimpers.

'Where are you going?'

'Not sure yet . . . Maybe Perth, maybe Bahrain . . . the company is sending us to Brisbane. By the time we arrive, we will know where we are going next.'

One of the joys of time offshore is that you're forever finding people and places that touch your heart – but one of the perils is that you're always saying goodbye. Your circle of friends keeps changing. People come and go. Strong bonds are formed quickly through necessity – and then your new friend is gone; a whirlwind goodbye.

And yet, despite the difficult transition of living abroad, the positives far outweigh the negatives. A new culture and language stretches the mind, questions how you view the world, catapults you out of your comfort zone and enables you to appreciate other points of view. Being challenged in new ways every day forces you to grow and adapt and become 'as strong as the Pont Neuf'.

'I'm going to miss you so much, Julie! Will you be okay? What I am going to do without you?'

'Jane, if we have survived Paris I know we will both be just fine.'

Mediterranean Mystery Tour

As the TGV Méditerranée pulls out of the station and slowly gathers speed, we watch Paris disappear under a shower of January rain. Soon, Vincent and I are flying past farmhouses and bare fields dusted with snow. In just three hours we will be in Marseilles with the Mediterranean lapping at our feet and blue sky overhead.

Mixed with our excitement is a growing air of mystery as the train rushes towards the sun, for this is no ordinary voyage or ordinary train. Friends of Hermès from around the world are gathered on board to celebrate the inspiration behind this year's spring/summer theme. Hermès has dedicated its new collection to the vibrant colours, flavours and sensations of the Mediterranean, and the mosaic of countries and cultures that meet its shores. This assignment with *Gourmet Traveller* has been shrouded in mystery for weeks, with the secret destination making the trip all the more enticing.

By the time we race through Avignon we have already eaten our way through Provence, sampling from its herb-scented hills and fertile plains – from *chèvres* and red peppers dressed in oil and thyme, to tiny olives and pasta tossed in pesto. Every dish in this continuous brunch has been infused with the intensity and flavour of *le terroir*.

With great anticipation, we arrive in Marseilles at noon and are whisked to Vieux Port, home of the renowned morning fish market. We board boats and plough out to sea, then gently turn east to moor. But still our enigmatic journey is not complete. Waiting buses drive us toward the Calanques, a strip of turquoise coast furnished with rocky inlets and jagged white cliffs that stretch to the pretty fishing village of Cassis. We alight at the tranquil little port of Calanque de Callelongue.

Within moments of our arrival, *boules* are clinking and glasses are filled with cloudy pastis. The sun is warm on our faces. Over the next couple of hours we eat our way though a lunch of startling imagination. Everything placed before us has a hint of culinary fantasy and is garnished with surprise. We guess the ingredients of dishes delivered without announcement and Vincent happily snaps away.

'On each plate, I have endeavoured to put a little something from both the sea and the countryside around Marseilles,' says the chef. First comes wild rabbit terrine embellished with fanciful treats: a *foie gras bonbon* layered with jelly in a flourish of clear cellophane; an artfully placed spoon cradling a sea urchin. Then a fresh fillet of sea bream scented with rosemary and layered with truffle and ravioli on an artichoke bed. Balanced on top is a caramelised prawn shell. What makes this dish unique is the saffron-infused rouille sauce (conventionally served with *bouillabaisse*) that arrives in individual glass test tubes with cork stoppers. Traditional taste, new look – embracing the spirit of the day.

Jean-Louis Dumas, president of Hermès, welcomes in the 'Year of the Mediterranean' to hearty applause. Glasses are filled with pale gold Muscat from Corsica and dessert is served – a scoop of exquisite orange-flower ice-cream coupled with an elegantly dressed olive cake dancing in a swirl of *clémentine* sauce.

In the late afternoon, we drive back along the coast to Marseilles and visit the exhibition *Méditations Méditerranée*, a poetic portrait of the region filled with changing colour, light and sound.

The chef continues to weave magic and mystery into the evening as we tear back to Paris on the TGV, teasing us with morsels from other, more exotic Mediterranean lands. We bite into Greece, Morocco, Tunisia, Algeria and Spain. One after another, delicious appetisers and seductive platters float past, followed by a heady trail of spicy aromas. There are endless warm savoury pastries and crunchy *kibbehs*, spears of bamboo threaded with juicy *gambas*, garlicky squid, and small glass jars of pickled vegetables. With one precious hour to go, we are tempted with dainty diamonds of *baklava* and ponder a tiny pot of chocolate *ganache*. Bursting at the seams we brace ourselves for almond-flavoured ice-cream in frosty Arabic tea glasses, and dusky pink Turkish delight. Last but not least, a satisfying squirt of lemony liqueur from our very own plastic goldfish. We have come to expect the unexpected.

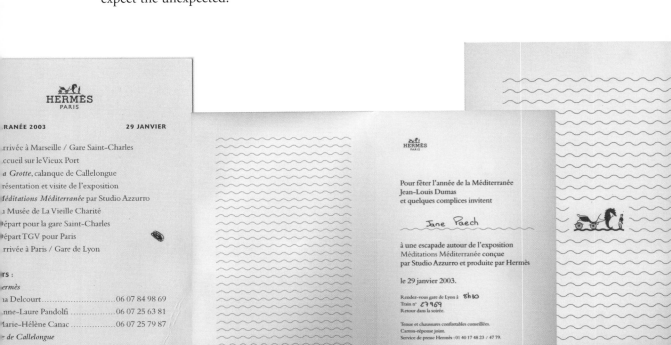

HERMÈS
PARIS

..RANÉE 2003   29 JANVIER

..rrivée à Marseille / Gare Saint-Charles
..ccueil sur le Vieux Port
.a Grotte, calanque de Callelongue
.résentation et visite de l'exposition
.Méditations Méditerranée par Studio Azzurro
.u Musée de La Vieille Charité
.épart pour la gare Saint-Charles
.épart TGV pour Paris
.rrivée à Paris / Gare de Lyon

.rs :
.ermès
.na Delcourt.........................06 07 84 98 69
.nne-Laure Pandolfi 06 07 25 63 81
.Marie-Hélène Canac 06 07 25 79 87
.e de Callelongue
..Grotte   04 91 73 17 79

HERMÈS
PARIS

Pour fêter l'année de la Méditerranée
Jean-Louis Dumas
et quelques complices invitent

Jane Paech

à une escapade autour de l'exposition
Méditations Méditerranée conçue
par Studio Azzurro et produite par Hermès

le 29 janvier 2003.

Rendez-vous gare de Lyon à 8h30
Train n° 27969
Retour dans la soirée.

Tenue et chaussures confortables conseillées.
Carton-réponse joint.
Service de presse Hermès : 01 40 17 48 23 / 47 79.

La Banque 1

6 JANUARY Tim goes to *la banque*. Fills out money transfer for large sum to cover mortgage and various commitments at home; expects sum to be deposited in Australia in seven days.

8 JANUARY Money deducted from French bank account.

10 JANUARY Receive written confirmation that transfer has gone through.

14 JANUARY Contact Australian bank to confirm deposit. No sign of it. Call French bank to advise. They run a trace.

16 JANUARY Mortgage due. Money not found. French bank suggests Australian bank has made an error and recommends calling Australian bank.

17 JANUARY 2 A.M Call Australian bank. They suggest intermediary bank may be holding money and recommend French bank call intermediary bank.

9 A.M. Call French bank to request they call intermediary bank.

19 JANUARY After some investigation, French bank acknowledges money is sitting in intermediary account waiting for Australian bank to clear it. There is nothing they can do. Tim marches into bank and demands to speak to Monsieur Bungler, the man in charge of our account.

He does some more scouting around and confirms, '*Oui, oui*, your money is sitting in the holding bank in Australia. Has been for ten days.'

'You said the money would take seven days to transfer,' said Tim.

'Out of our hands now,' he shrugs.

'Well, whose hands is it in?'

'*Je ne sais pas,*' he mumbles.

Days pass: no word. It's not as if the money has to physically pass from one person to another. How can it possibly take so long? Tired of the whole fiasco, we bury our heads over the weekend, catching a movie in V. O. (Version Originale) on the Champs-Élysées and visiting the Egyptian antiquities collection at the Louvre. In the evening, we dine at Le Scheffer, tucked quietly in *le seizième*.

The Eiffel Tower in winter

Le Scheffer

A million miles away from modern Paris, this authentic neighbourhood bistro is a local favourite. Don't expect an English menu or contemporary touches here. Do expect good old-fashioned French cooking, a warm atmosphere and bags of charm. Monsieur, in his suit and bow tie, pours pitchers of red wine behind the bar. Madame breezes around the room chatting to the regulars and delivering entrées of herring cured in oil with warm potato salad, and succulent bone marrow. A friendly waitress dashes out with piping-hot plates of crispy *confit de canard* with sautéed potatoes, and *steak tartare*, and reels off the desserts to a couple who probably know them by heart: simple classics like *profiteroles au chocolat* and *les îles flottantes*.

Le Scheffer
22, rue Scheffer, 75016
Tel: 01 47 27 81 11

La Banque 2

28 JANUARY Letter in post from Australian bank: Where is your mortgage payment?

29 JANUARY Call Australian bank just after midnight. They ask name of intermediary bank and what currency money is in.

'*Je ne sais pas*,' says Tim with a sigh, hanging up the phone and pouring a stiff Cognac.

9 A.M. Call French bank to try to find out name of intermediary bank and what currency money is in. Discover money has been transferred to an English bank in euros.

30 JANUARY Discover Australian bank does not have euro account with that bank. After much detective work, advise French bank that our money has been sent to wrong bank in wrong currency. Demand they retrieve money immediately and send to the correct bank instead. They admit it was their mistake and promise to fix it!

'The money will be in your account in two to three days,' assures Monsieur Bungler. Mmmm, *quand les poules auront des dents!* (When chicken have teeth!)

At the end of his tether after a long string of similar incidents, Tim talks to a colleague in finance about it.

'Welcome to banking in France,' he smirks. 'You can change banks if you like but there is no guarantee it will be better. *Eh bien, tant pis.*' (Oh well, too bad.)

Picard

Having been raised with farm freezers full of stewed fruit, legs of lamb and freshly podded peas from the paddock, I have always found the notion of bought frozen food and TV dinners unpalatable: a culinary no-no, for lazy cooks only. For this very reason, it took me years to discover **Picard-Surgelés**, France's leading frozen-food specialist. With blinkers on, I would shiver past their clinical storefront on cold nights after ballet, too busy thinking about what to cook for dinner to give Picard a second glance. And then one evening, with time to kill as the girls rehearsed for *Coppélia*, I step across the threshold into an icy wonderland.

Before my eyes is an entire supermarket full of sleek, waist-high freezers. Intrigued, I watch customers peer delightedly through the glass at hundreds of products. Glimpsing into baskets and freezers, I soon realise that this is no ordinary frozen-food store. This is frozen food with style, smashing a lifetime of preconceptions. Clarence Birdseye may have invented the concept of flash-freezing in the 1920s but Raymond Picard elevated it to an art form. Opening his first food store in Paris in 1974, he succeeded in marrying superior quality and convenience. With over 700 chilly retail stores of varying sizes across France and a startling variety of reasonably priced gourmet products, Picard is a hit.

While the vegetables and gourmet pizza are predictably present, it's the surprises that enthral. *Coquilles St-Jacques* with Chablis sauce sit next to mini *boudin blancs*. Further on, I spy roast quail stuffed with artichokes and *girolles* in a mirabelle plum sauce, lamb shanks with figs and orange zest. There's also rabbit, and salmon *en croûte*. Reading the packet of a quiche Lorraine, I am fascinated to find a recommendation for both wine and salad ingredients.

And then there's dessert. An Opéra cake, perhaps, or a pyramid of sorbets: thirty frosty balls in a rainbow of colours and flavours.

I pick up a basket and slide open the glass.

www.picard.fr

La Banque 3

5 FEBRUARY Money still not deposited. *Quelle surprise!* Tim has day off so we storm into head office to get this fixed up once and for all. Monsieur Bungler makes us wait while he chats to colleagues about the fab little bistro he dined in last night. Finally, we are able to tell him that the money has still not arrived in our account. Also tell him we appear to know more about where our money is than he does. Read him riot act and demand to see manager. All his colleagues stop to watch performance (any excuse). Advise manager that if bank forecloses on mortgage, they will be legally liable. Manager *très* patronising but ABSOLUTELY PROMISES money will be in our Australian account by 9 February.

'International transfers can take seven to ten days from France,' he says, trying to reassure us.

Why, when in most countries in the world they take two or three?

9 FEBRUARY Still no money. Mortgage not paid. Next payment due in eight days. Bury myself in *The Sunday Times* and come across this amusing piece of useless information:

'The Banque de France and the Bank of England fulfil roughly similar functions in countries of approximately the same size. The Bank of England employs 6,000 people; the Banque de France employs 16,000.'

Les Égouts

Winter weekends can sometimes prove a challenge in Paris. By February, life becomes one long blur of black-and-white re-runs and we all have cabin fever. The overheated stores are crammed with shoppers, the girls can't face another museum and it's freezing outside.

Craving for something different to do, I pull out our **Paris Walks** timetable. Marked on the calendar for today is a tour of the sewers, *les égouts*. It promises 'an unusual and fascinating view of the underside of Paris'. Well, it may not exactly be a breath of fresh air, but it's certainly something different! We grab our coats and scarves, wait for Annabelle to change her outfit numerous times, and head out the door.

Founded in 1994 by Peter and Oriel Caine, Paris Walks has become one of our favourite distractions. The entertaining two-hour sessions comprise an alluring

mix of history, art and architecture, and are packed with scurrilous gossip and intriguing trivia. The English couple, who have lived in the city for a couple of decades, are walking history books. Due to popular demand they employ a small team of native English-speaking guides, all of whom are engaging, knowledgeable and passionate about Paris. Adding to the appeal is the fact that no reservations are required – you just show up at the meeting point, rain or shine.

We meet Peter at the entrance of *les égouts* and disappear underground with the group. Nowadays, the public are only allowed to tour the Sewer Museum around Alma Marceau where there are no important buildings. Visitors used to be able to glide along the sewers in boats until one day in the 1970s a gang of bandits slinked off their boat under the Palais Royal. Unseen by sewer workers, they drilled their way into the vaults of the Banque de France and escaped with a boatload of gold ingots.

We browse the displays of photos, dredging tools and old lamps. It is dark and damp with gushing water. Peter informs us that the first perilous survey of the system in 1805 turned up the skeleton of Josephine's pet orang-utan – who apparently had better table manners than most of Napoléon's friends.

'Many swords have also been found in the sewers,' says Peter. He explains that swords were a sign of nobility and during the French Revolution they were banned in public places. This did not, however, deter nobles from wearing them. If a policeman was about, the easiest way to dispose of the sword was through a hole in the gutter that dropped down to the sewers.

Today, all street-level rubbish is washed into the sewers through these same holes every morning. It's an easy way to keep the city clean. 'There is now a number to call if you drop a valuable personal possession into the sewers by accident,' continues Peter. 'If you call within ten minutes there is a 95 per cent chance that your keys or ring will be retrieved.'

We continue walking through damp tunnels, which correspond to the streets above. Apparently, if the tunnels were stretched out they would reach all the way to Turkey. We pass the odd sewer worker in overalls and long rubber boots.

'Originally, the boots were made of leather and drenched in urine to make them supple,' says Peter. 'Realising how soft they were, a bootmaker bought up the sewer workers' old boots and used the leather to make the finest women's shoes. Many a lady danced at a ball in shoes recycled from sewer boots – unbeknown to her,' he says with a grin.

We discover there's a four-year waiting list for residents clamouring to become sewer workers. Why would anyone want to work down here?

'The workers are well paid, generally starting at six in the morning (for the breakfast rush) and finishing by lunchtime,' says Peter. 'There's no real danger except the rats, and the workers are inoculated against nasty diseases. The holidays are good, the work is mindless and not physically hard (just smelly), and the workers have twenty minutes of paid time for a shower afterwards.' *Irrésistible!*

We surface into the fresh February air, crossing the Seine at Pont de l'Alma. In front of us is the Flame of Liberty, a giant replica of the flame that burns from the torch held by the Statue of Liberty, and an unofficial memorial to Princess Diana who crashed in the tunnel directly underneath. The history in this city is overwhelming – there are stories to be told on every boulevard and bridge, in every public square – and, as we discover today, deep under every street.

When the Seine laps at the feet of the Zouave soldier standing under Pont de l'Alma, the footpaths along the quays are closed. The statue under the bridge is a rudimentary measuring device for the river's water levels. Severe storms will find the soldier up to his knees, and during the great flood of 1910 he was almost up to his neck in water.

Paris Walks
Peter & Oriel Caine
Tel: 01 48 09 21 40
www.paris-walks.com

'To err is human, to stroll is Parisian.'

Victor Hugo, *Les Misérables*

The Zoave soldier under Pont de l'Alma

La Banque 4

12 FEBRUARY In dead of night Tim is pacing around apartment contemplating most painful way for Monsieur Bungler to die. Also mulling over whether it would be more gratifying to expose bank to the media. I point out neither option would be satisfying because:

Option 1: if Monsieur Bungler is dead he can't ever find our money.

Option 2: French media won't think it anything out of the ordinary, just a simple bureaucratic bungle. After all, they did invent the word.

N.B. *Bureau* means 'office' and 'desk' in French.

13 FEBRUARY Mortgage due in four days. Monsieur Bungler calls Tim at midday. After multiple requests he has written a formal letter of apology on behalf of French bank to Australian bank.

'It's in the post. Would you like a copy faxed to your office, Monsieur?'

'*Tout à fait*,' (Certainly) replies Tim.

'Please give me your fax number,' says Monsieur Bungler.

'And by the way,' slips in Tim, 'the money is still not in our account.'

'*Ce n'est pas possible!* Please give me the number for your direct line and I will call you back *tout de suite*!' (Note: immediately.)

Let's face it, the money is lost.

Five minutes later: Monsieur Bungler attempts to put fax through using phone number and call Tim on fax number.

Three hours later: no word. Monsieur Bungler has no doubt smuggled money into personal bank account and is *en route* to St-Tropez or Caribbean with *une belle jeune fille*. Either that or he's gone to lunch.

2 MARCH After calling Australian bank yet again, Tim sends fax to Monsieur Bungler and his boss:

Dear Messieurs,

Monsieur Smith of the International Department of my Australian bank has checked all possible GBP and EUR intermediary accounts again and confirmed that they do not have 'cover' in any of their accounts. I advised him that you informed me an English bank in Sydney is holding the funds. He told me that there has been no banking operation in Sydney of the bank in question since 1994. It is now more than three weeks since our meeting in your office regarding this problem and more than six weeks since we first advised you that the funds were missing. Clearly, the action taken by you to recover these funds has been ineffective. We find this situation intolerable. Where is our money? Meanwhile we are forced to continue to do the investigative work on your behalf. We require an immediate resolution to this problem or we will be forced to take our frustration to a higher authority.

Yours sincerely,
Très frustrated customers

'That was very restrained,' I mutter. Tim looks at me through gritted teeth, about to explode.

3 MARCH Monsieur Bungler calls. He says it is not his fault, *bien sûr,* but he will sort this out *tout de suite.* (Note: immediately.)
Days pass.

9 MARCH Just as we are at the end of our patience (*à bout de patience*), THE MONEY IS IN OUR ACCOUNT! *BRAVO!* Monsieur Bungler has come through, two months and five days later.

'Bureaucracy is the art of making the possible impossible.'

Javier Pascual Salcedo

Le or La?

'How come *le bonheur* (happiness) is masculine and *la misère* (misery) feminine?' asks Georgie's friend Claire one day. Good question. Come to think of it, why is *le soutien-gorge* (bra) masculine?

Déjeuner au café: Claire and Georgie

Le Bonheur

The first day of sunshine is here after a long and arduous winter and there's a spring in my step. I walk along avenue Paul-Doumer in a little black dress and suede knee-high boots, my new Furla bag from the January sales slipped over my shoulder. I sail past a busload of tourists with smiling faces and loud voices. They are unable to contain their excitement as they explore this beautiful city from the comfort of their large, secure group. It is late March and *les touristes* have tumbled out of the woodwork, craning their necks to gaze at the Eiffel Tower, equipped with clicking cameras and shiny new maps. Striding past the café terraces that hug Place du Trocadéro, I hear them asking awkwardly for coffee and *pâtisseries*. It is my turn to smile. I realise at this moment how much I have learnt about Paris and Parisians, and how much Paris has given me back.

In our early years here, I soaked up information at such an alarming rate that I believed I had fair understanding of the city and its people. Looking back, I had only peeled away the top layer of the onion.

How different is the Paris I know today from my original impression, yet oddly it is still the same. Although I now have a much greater understanding, I continue to marvel at the beauty around me and the art that infuses everyday life. I am still inspired and stimulated every time I open the door to our street.

Six years on, I know the city like the back of my hand, a feat accelerated by a desire and need to scour the streets for research, and consolidated every time visitors come to stay. Yet there is always more to know about Paris, always another layer of the onion. Along with my car-free urban lifestyle comes a natural fitness, and I now have to rein in my normal breakneck pace when acting as a local guide.

Life has finally taken on a degree of normality. We laze about on the weekend rather than rushing out to see the latest exhibitions, and forget to carry our camera. At nine and twelve, the girls are old hands at *le métro*, punching through tickets in record time and dashing for the best seats. Georgie confidently catches

Le Jardin des Tuileries

Springtime, Palais Royal

Georgie catching some rays by the pond in the Jardin des Tuileries

the bus and metro home alone, which works well, except on the occasions when she looks up at the end of an absorbing book to find herself also at the end of the line.

As I turn onto avenue Kléber, I feel on top of the world. A Frenchwoman stops me to ask for directions. I pass cafés and florists and pause to glance up at the intimate **Hôtel Raphael**, with its tasteful red awnings. I am on my way to interview *le Directeur Général* of the elegant **Hôtel Lancaster** as part of a round-up of Paris hotels. With an undisputed reputation for impeccable standards and the highest level of personal service, it is one of Europe's most charming small luxury hotels. Later today I will visit **La Villa**, a contemporary boutique hotel in the heart of St-Germain-des-Prés, and the deluxe **Pavillon de la Reine** on Place des Vosges, where romantic seventeenth-century rooms with wood-burning fires offer twenty-first-century guests the perfect Paris *pied-à-terre*. But first there is lunch at Ladurée on the Champs-Élysées with Pam and Mel.

As I round the Arc de Triomphe I have a sudden, overwhelming sense of belonging – a spiritual moment. Right now, I couldn't imagine living anywhere else. I love everything about the day, the city, my work. Everything feels so right, so comfortable. Finally, I am in control. As the doorman ushers me into the Lancaster, I am exactly where I want to be.

www.hotel-lancaster.fr
www.pavillon-de-la-reine.com
www.raphael-hotel.com
www.villa-saintgermain.com

'*There is never any ending to Paris and the memory of each person who has lived in it differs from that of any other.*'

Ernest Hemingway, *A Moveable Feast*

La Misère

I am sitting on the terrace of Café de la Mairie with Mel, our chairs facing Place St-Sulpice. The fountains are sending rainbows into the air. We sip and talk. Annabelle and Mel's son Jack are riding their silver scooters around the square. Locals are hanging out in the sun under the budding horse chestnut trees.

We have just found out we are to be sent home in December.

Très Français

We arrive at the Jardin des Tuileries armed with Annabelle's bike, Georgie's rollerblades, a picnic basket and a bottle of good old Jacob's Creek (we thought it appropriate as we are lunching with fellow Australians). It's a typical April day, with blue skies turning quickly to grey, short showers and a cool wind. The gardens are alive with striking black, red and yellow tulips.

The children throw down their coats on the track, making goals for an innovative game of soccer and play away happily, dodging the promenaders and the puddles. After a while they grow tired of *le foot* and choose a boat each to sail on the pond, craftily poking and steering with their long bamboo sticks.

Daniel and I stand at the pond chatting, taking in the view. Fresh from twenty years in Sydney but French-Swiss by birth and educated in Switzerland, he confirms what I know only too well: the French school system is all about logic. 'There is no room for free expression, for problem solving or innovation,' he says.

In front of us is the Louvre, more a feat of engineering than creativity. I am reminded of a comment passed recently that an Italian architect will always draw for you an oval or circle, and a French architect a square or rectangle. My eyes scan the structured, disciplined gardens surrounding us, the strong straight lines. To me, that says it all: *très français*. Controlled creativity. Incredibly beautiful but incredibly disciplined.

Sharon and Jemima in the Jardin des Tuileries

Whatever the future holds, I'm grateful that the girls have had an opportunity to experience a new way of viewing the world and to realise that neither way is right or wrong, merely different. It breeds tolerance. And it forms ties. Georgie and Annabelle will have among their memories sailing a boat on the pond at the Jardin des Tuileries with the fountains sparkling and the tulips blooming. Memories will encourage them to return; entwined with that, I hope the bonds with their new friends will remain strong, people being the strongest link in the chain.

Daniel hopes that by bringing his children back to Europe (and by giving them the gift of language), his family ties will strengthen again.

'It only takes one generation to break the link. I have friends still in Europe, but my children do not know them,' he says.

After lunch we play *pétanque* under the linden trees and are fascinated to see tourists snapping away and a Japanese man videotaping us. How odd to be thought of as *très français*, typical Parisians enjoying a day out in the Tuileries.

Luxembourg

My next commission for *Gourmet Traveller* takes me to Luxembourg. Prosperous and well maintained, it's the old Europe of feudal castles, unspoilt woods, neatly pleated vineyards and quiet villages on the banks of rushing rivers. Twenty-five times smaller than Tasmania, this bite-sized country offers a disproportionate sack of attractions.

Unfortunately, Vincent is unable to make the trip as Brooke is due with their first child any day. He puts me on to a friend who is also a professional photographer, also tall and dark, and also named Vincent. Requiring a means to distinguish between the two, I affectionately dub them Vincent I and Vincent II.

'You make it sound as though I am a French king or something,' says Vincent II, with a grin. The quintessential arty Parisian, he flies around the city *en moto* and lives with his partner in Montmartre, where he also has a photographic studio. Starting his career in the food industry as an apprentice at the acclaimed Jules Verne restaurant in the Eiffel Tower, he later decided that while he appreciated the science and art of food, he enjoyed the science and art of photography more.

He agrees to do the four-day Luxembourg trip but, due to previous commitments, can't make it until day two. It appears Tim and I have a night to ourselves. (How does Tim wind up on some of my work trips but I don't get to join him on his? *Une bonne question.*)

We arrive in Luxembourg City with time to see its fortress, set high above the gorges, and visit the market on Place Guillaume before my first appointment. Locals blow the froth off steins of Belgian beer and fill their baskets with German sausages and French farmhouse cheeses before trickling home through the narrow streets for lunch. Nestled contentedly between Belgium, Germany and France, this independent nation is influenced by all three. Ruled by a grand duke, the people of landlocked Luxembourg have a big history and an even greater love of food and wine. We notice that although the capital is more wholesome than hip, a cosmopolitan edge creeps through with an astonishing number of restaurants. Apparently, the Grand Duchy is home to more Michelin-starred restaurants per capita than any country in the world.

This taste for quality also extends to *l'art de la table*. The royal house of **Villeroy & Boch** was founded here in 1748 and its timeless products are still ever-present. Besides featuring on elegantly laid restaurant tables, Villeroy & Boch is sold on the Grand Rue and in a factory outlet centre near the company's spectacular Château de Septfountaines. It is here that we are to spend the night, after a late-afternoon tour of *le château*.

'Have a good evening,' says Monsieur Villeroy & Boch at the completion of his tour, handing us a hefty key. 'I'm off now. I hope you don't mind but you'll be here alone tonight. Make yourself at home and help yourself to breakfast in the kitchen.'

He closes the door behind him.

What? We have the entire *château* to ourselves? We run around and explore, opening doors and peeking into rooms like two kids let loose in a lolly shop. One of the perks of the job is that you often find yourself in places you would perhaps otherwise never be able to access. We change and go into the city for dinner, rushing our meal to come home and curl up in our castle with a cup of tea. It is very dark and ever so still, with the occasional creak. Thank goodness Tim decided to tag along otherwise I would be here *toute seule* (all alone). We climb the staircase and latch the landing door.

www.luxembourg-city.lu/touristinfo
www.villeroy-boch.com

La Grève

2 JUNE Tim and Annabelle arrive at Passy metro station at 8.33 a.m. only to hear an announcement that all metropolitan trains are on strike and traffic *est très perturbé sur le RER* (very disrupted on the suburban train network). A trainload of angry peak-hour commuters tumbles out onto the platform. Gates are locked and stations across the city fall silent. For how long, who knows? Apparently a metro worker was assaulted early this morning and is unconscious in hospital.

Transport strikes (*grèves*) are a common occurrence in France, especially on the coldest, most dismal day in winter, or when there's an important event in town. Typically they involve wages or working conditions. A few years back, *une grève* continued for almost three weeks during December. Stores suffered and residents resorted to rollerblades.

The angry commuters stream up the station steps. Tim and Annabelle, along with Greg and his girls, scurry towards the bus terminus at Trocadéro hoping the buses are still running. Yes! Three stops on, the bus is as tightly packed as *la boulangerie* late Sunday morning and getting scary. The children have little room to breathe as more and more people push their way on.

Then it's time to get off. The doors open but it's impossible to move. The bus makes moves to go. Tim and Greg shout, '*Arrêtez, nous descendons, nous decendons!*' (Stop, we want to get off!) at the top of their voices and try to wade through the crowd. The driver waits for them but just as they are making progress a very large Frenchman (unusual in itself) decides to enter through the middle door and stands there, blocking the exit. The whole bus urges him to move and let the people who need to get off *descend*, but he will not budge. He does not want to lose his spot and face a very long walk to work. Thousands of workers in the outer *arrondissements* will be tackling a commute of at least an hour and a half on foot this morning. A screaming match erupts between the commuters and the large, stubborn man. The girls are now very scared and very squashed. In a show of solidarity Greg and Tim push him off the bus to a round of applause, and exit.

11 A.M. Leave early to pick up Annabelle at midday (of course it is a Wednesday), and walk to Trocadéro in the hope that the buses are still running. Now that peak hour has passed, they may be a little more civilised, I convince myself. A car stops and the driver yells out, '*Pas de bus, pas de bus.*' No buses. They are on strike too. The taxi stand is twenty deep. I walk to school via the Arc. It is totally

jammed: hundreds of vehicles at a standstill. Further on, an angry tow-truck driver is reversing into cars. *Motos* are flying along footpaths and down the wrong side of the road. Drivers are speeding through red lights, pedestrians are running, wiping their brows, and tourists are dragging large suitcases, maps in hand. I pass a fist-fight between two truck drivers. There are continuous sirens, continuous accidents. An eerie energy hovers over the city. Yes, the strike has achieved its aim. Everyone's day has been turned upside down.

12.15 P.M. I arrive late to find Annabelle in the playground of Parc Monceau with Olivia and Steve, who has kindly picked her up. With no way of getting the girls to their ballet class this afternoon, we walk to Steve's. He sensibly lives near the school. Thankfully, Georgie can walk home from her new school.

Plan A: Annabelle will play at Olivia's for the afternoon. Hopefully, the strike will be finished by late afternoon, and Steve will bring her home. I relax with a cup of tea before walking the 3 kilometres back to Passy.

2 P.M. The media releases a statement. The metro worker has died. There is no chance of the strike finishing. The trade union is calling for additional jobs to be created to bolster a human presence in *le métro* and more patrols of camouflage-clad, machine-gun-wielding police to help improve safety conditions.

5 P.M. Plan B: Tim will pick Annabelle up via a pre-booked taxi on his way home from work.

7.30 P.M. Tim is unable to book or hail a taxi. He walks to Steve's. Five secretaries also leave together. One has a car and offers to drop off the others in various *arrondissements*, a task that will take several hours.

8 P.M. Situation remains unchanged. Plan C launches into operation: Tim walks Annabelle home through the still-chaotic streets.

9 P.M. Tim and Annabelle arrive home.

3 JUNE Watch 7 a.m. news. *La grève* continues. *Le périphérique* is already saturated with traffic. The invisible workers of Paris have been thrown into chaos. More than 80 per cent of Parisians live in the suburbs, which extend to twenty-five times the area of the city. The Highway Information Centre reports that

Le métro: a quick and efficient way to navigate the city – unless there is a strike yesterday morning there were 210 kilometres of traffic jams in the Paris area, disrupting millions of people. The girls stay home. Tim walks to work. Pedestrians, rollerbladers and cyclists are already thick on the footpath. The museums have also decided to strike. *Pourquoi pas?* (Why not?)

4 JUNE Watch 7 a.m. news. *La grève* appears to have finished! The trade union has succeeded in their demand for improved safety conditions. I nip to the end of the street and peer down rue Alboni to see if any trains are crossing the Seine, just to make sure. *Oui! Le mètro* is running. Life is back to normal . . . until *la grève* strikes again.

Heaven on Earth

A number of churches in Paris open their doors to classical music but to my mind Sainte-Chapelle remains the most magical of them all. The chapel's full splendour is best appreciated at an intimate candlelight concert on a warm summer's night.

With fifteen of the most exquisite stained-glass windows in the world, the perfect proportions of a Gothic cathedral and the cosy dimensions of a jewel-box, it is a sublime setting for a musical soirée – rather like being sucked into a glorious genie's bottle with your own private orchestra for entertainment.

At this time of the year, performances are scheduled several times a week and run for approximately one hour. Providing you show up thirty minutes beforehand, tickets can be bought at the door.

At seven o'clock on a balmy June evening, Georgie and I enter through the marble corridors of the old Palais Royal to attend a concert by the Orchestre les Archets de Paris, composed of musicians and soloists from the Orchestre National de l'Opéra de Paris. Noisy tour groups are replaced by classical music buffs straight from the office and couples snatching a romantic interlude before dinner. The atmosphere is serene and in the twilight Sainte-Chapelle becomes the place of quiet contemplation it is meant to be.

King Louis IX built the chapel within the palace grounds between 1241 and 1248 as a shrine to house the Crown of Thorns and other religious relics acquired from the Emperor of Constantinople. Built on two levels, the lower chapel was reserved for palace staff. It also acted as a solid foundation for the ethereal upper chapel. The 15-metre-high walls appear to consist almost entirely of glass, linked only by slender pillars and rainbows. The devout likened it to a gateway to heaven. Built on the same level as the royal apartments, the upper chapel was reserved for the king and members of the royal family, and is the venue for the concert today.

Surrounded by angels and apostles, we take our seats. Lights are lowered and the violins begin to play. Vivaldi's *Four Seasons* soars towards the midnight-blue ceiling, where a thousand stars wink. The audience is transported by the music and the play of light on the windows: a kaleidoscope of rich colour that streams through the warm air and patterns the floor. Souls are stirred as the light slowly softens and falls and the colours grow deeper. A solo trumpeter from the Orchestra of the French Republican Guard appears before the altar, playing Purcell with passion before a burst of applause.

We exit the lofty palace via a steep flight of stairs and are jolted back to earth in time for a leisurely walk across the Pont St-Louis before dinner.

Sainte-Chapelle
4, blvd du Palais, 75001
www.monum.fr
Metro: Cité/St-Michel/Châtelet

Les Concerts de la Cité: all church concerts are listed in *Pariscope* entertainment guide, available from news stands. Tickets can also be bought at Galeries Lafayette, Fnac and Virgin Megastore.

La Grève 2

6 JUNE The real story has come out about the metro worker. He had an argument on the platform with a commuter, ruptured an aneurysm, collapsed and died.

Le Parking

The row of wicker chairs on the terrace is already full when I arrive at **La Favorite**, its windows slid back to the street. The fresh summer morning follows me in as the waiter greets me with a booming *bonjour* and a handshake. From my table in this worn and comfortable *café-tabac* around the corner from our apartment, I watch the flow of life. I love it most at this hour, when the neighbourhood is just waking up. I listen to the day being discussed: the weather, the petrol strike. In a couple of hours I am meeting Vincent II at **Willi's Wine Bar** to research a story. Owned by a friendly Englishman, the cosy bar is renowned for its eclectic wine list, modern French bistro fare and collection of original 'poster art' that lines the walls. But right now, the soft breeze caresses my notebook as I bite into a warm croissant that flakes over the pages as usual. There is the constant grumble of the orange *pressée* machine, the same yapping dogs.

Outside, *motos* screech to a stop, their riders darting in for cigarettes and a quick *express*, resting their helmets on the bar. A delivery man arrives with jangling crates of Perrier water and Orangina, which disappear down a trapdoor that slowly opens up in the middle of the café floor. I hear the waiter's regular, comforting cry of '*un express, un*' and '*deux crèmes, deux*' to the barista behind the bar, before he dashes down to *la boulangerie* in his black bow tie and vest for more baguettes. I watch him as he hurries down the street, passing a man on a City of Paris scooter sucking up dog poo with the fancy vacuum cleaner that's strapped to his back.

La police are pedalling past (*sans* helmets) when I notice two parking inspectors lurking on the street. A car zooms into the No Parking zone in front of the café and a man jumps out. The inspectors approach him and point to the sign.

'But I really need a coffee,' he pleads. 'I'm just going to throw back *un express* at the bar then I'll be off.'

'Of course,' they say nodding, and keep walking without writing out a ticket.

Yes, there are many rules in France and many that can be broken – you just have to know which ones. After six years of living in Paris, I have come to the conclusion that the best way to get around a dilemma is to put on the charm and conjure up an impressive, creative excuse, or to appeal to something that every Parisian can relate to, such as food. The thought of starting the day without a coffee kick would wrench any Parisian's heart. '*Non*' and indeed '*C'est impossible*' often means 'persuade me'. However, this requires a high level of French – and it helps, *bien sûr*, if you *are* French.

La Favorite
39, rue de Passy, 75016
Tel: 01 42 88 20 53

Willi's Wine Bar
13, rue des Petits-Champs, 75001
Tel: 01 42 61 05 09
www.williswinebar.com

⚜

Many residents leave their handbrake off when they park in Paris. This way, motorists can bump the car behind them back a bit and the car in front forward a bit, fitting their vehicle into a very tight space.

Paris,
je t'aime . . .
pour toujours

Réflexion

Unresolved harassment issues have forced Georgie back to her old school until we go home in four months – and consequently to drop the pre-pro ballet course. Now in 4ème (year 8), her third year of *collège*, Georgie starts classes at 8 a.m. and finishes at 5 p.m. The workload is challenging, the class environment sombre and questions are not encouraged. Opportunities for original thought are few. Everything is still learnt by heart: transferred from book to brain in painstaking detail and then regurgitated. But at the same time, students know exactly what is expected of them in order to succeed.

The final stage of secondary education (*seconde*, *première* and *terminale*) is *lycée*, terminating with *le bac*. It has a workload more gruelling still. Lessons regularly stretch until 6 p.m. With learning driven by the examination process, a degree of creativity, self-expression and critical thinking is lost to conformity. Older students spend much of their spare time preparing for tests at the expense of wider exploratory learning and personal development.

There is no doubt that pupils complete the French system with a mind full of knowledge. 'But,' says Ellen, an American friend and librarian who has also lived in Japan and Italy, 'the concern is that it's a fact-based, encyclopaedic knowledge. I am not convinced that the French system is creating independent learners and developing inquisitive minds.'

Even though aspects of the French education system are diametrically opposed to the Australian mindset, it is important to appreciate the flip side of a system that turns out brilliant theoretical thinkers and outstanding mathematicians, clever engineers and fine linguists.

Firstly, there is something to be said for a very strong grounding in basic skills. Fans of the French system believe it's only when these fundamental skills become automatic that students' minds are freed for higher pursuits. For example, pounding grammar to the point where a seven-year-old can fly through a sentence knowing its subject, verb, direct and indirect object in a heartbeat delivers a huge advantage when it comes to picking up another language or two.

With more Australians opting to live and work overseas and an ever-increasing global mobility, perhaps a stronger stress on language (and grammar) in education is more important than many Australians may think. A French-American friend who previously worked at the American Embassy of Paris despaired of some of the English correspondence that crossed his desk.

'I often had to correct spelling and grammar before passing it on to the French,' he said. 'They would never have taken a poorly written document seriously, in French or English. It does not look intelligent or inspire confidence.'

Foreign parents express pleasure at a level of discipline in the French system not found in their home countries: an emphasis on neatness, personal organisational skills and excellent study habits are set in place from a very young age, serving children well for the rest of their scholastic lives. Students also develop a capability to work hard without expecting a pat on the back. They are able to perform independently without the acknowledgement and approval of others, without their teacher's recognition or peers' blessing.

Other benefits include the development of an astounding memory and incredible skills in recitation that assist in many obscure ways throughout life. Annabelle can now learn a longwinded poem by Jacques Prévert perfectly in a couple of evenings. Georgie can memorise four foolscap pages of French word-for-word in twenty minutes. By *collège*, a student's acquaintance with French and European history extends to intricate anecdotes and dozens of dates. The French are very proud of their heritage, and rightly so.

Aesthetics is part of this pride and holds an important place in French life. Nothing is slapdash. By the age of seven, students have already mastered a fountain pen and exercise books are filled with pages of exquisitely penned cursive. And while it's questionable whether the art of writing still has a place in today's high-tech world, the French do not automatically follow the rest of us. They refuse to change what they believe is important just because it is *à la mode*. Perhaps that's why Paris is still beautiful.

Looking at my girls today, I am very proud. Two Australian children thrown into a strange new world, they have adapted and developed true bilingualism. While Georgie certainly struggled, she can also see the benefits of the French education system. 'The real world out there is tough and it prepares you for that,' she says. 'In Australia, children are told everything they do is wonderful, and that they can do anything as long as they put their mind to it. It's not, and they can't. The French are much more realistic.'

The more time spent offshore, the more life becomes a procession of contrasts and paradoxes. You are forever seeing other ways of living, and comparing. Differences become magnified, but the passage of time also ensures that the hard edges are worn away.

I watch Georgie, now thirteen and near the top of her class, whip through Molière, talk with her friends about le Président or the performance of *Swan Lake* at l'Opéra Bastille, and I wonder how she will see Australia through fresh eyes. From which cultural standpoint will she look at it? How will she find her peers – and how will they find her?

But one thing is certain. Annabelle, more French than Australian and thriving on the competitive school system, will find sausage sizzles and broad-brimmed hats a culture shock indeed.

La Lettre

Madame Gardienne raps on the door with a notice from *le facteur*, informing us that a very important letter is awaiting collection. What could it be? Intrigued, I grab my passport as proof of identity and a utility bill as proof of residence, throw on my trench, and walk briskly down to La Poste.

'Monsieur Paech's passport must be produced also,' I am told when I reach the front of the queue. I dash back down rue Singer, wave to the solemn guard with the bulletproof vest in front of the Turkish Embassy, fly past Balzac's house and return home. I fossick about, find Tim's passport and head out the door again, greeting Madame Gardienne and waving to the solemn guard for the third time that morning.

'*Je suis désolé*, but Monsieur Paech must present his passport in person.' Whether it's la banque, La Poste or le Préfecture de Police, there always seems to be something missing: a person, a bit of paper, one crucial document. I dawdle home, concluding this must be a letter of *grande importance*.

On Saturday morning, Tim and I are finally able to present ourselves and our passports together at La Poste. With days to muse over the letter, we conclude that we either have grave news (perhaps we are to be deported) or we have won *un château* in the south of France. Tim rips open the envelope to find we are the recipients of a dubious letter from our beloved French bank. How disappointing. What now? After being faithful customers through thin and thin we open the letter to find:

M. & Mme. Paech,
Unfortunately we have changed the fundamental policies of our bank . . .

We read on, incredulous. Yes, it is true. Our bank is trying to dump us – after all we have been through. The nerve!

> *"Do you imagine we are free?" said Deslauriers passionately. "When I think that you have to fill in anything up to twenty-eight forms just to keep a boat on the river, I feel like going off to live among the cannibals."*

Gustave Flaubert, *Sentimental Education* (1869)

Montmartre: The Thrill of the Hill

I head west down rue Lamarck and turn right onto the quiet rue Eugène-Carrière. At number 42 is an eclectic maze of studios off a central passageway. It is here I find Vincent II in his little loft-style photographic studio.

'*Bonjour*,' he says as we exchange *la bise*. As Vincent is a local of Montmartre, we have decided it makes sense to do a travel feature on the hill together, or at least to do the research before I go home in a few short months. I have been running around madly doing quite a lot of this lately; I figure I can always pitch and write up stories when I get home.

'Shall we go for coffee and plan our day?' he says. We follow the narrow passageway past Mediterranean-blue doors and scores of scooters through to rue Damrémont, a typically unassuming neighbourhood street.

'There are a couple of good addresses along here,' says Vincent. 'I'll show you afterwards, but first, *un café*. Now, this is a place that won't be in any guidebook,' he grins, turning into the modest Au Pont de la Truyère. 'It has a feeling of old Montmartre.' A few workers in their overalls stand at the worn zinc bar with glasses of *vin rouge*. I notice the faded floor and the waitresses from another era. Vincent orders *un double express*, smashes numerous sugar cubes into his cup with a spoon until they are well dissolved, and throws it back. We plan our attack and decide that the only way we can possibly navigate the precipitous terrain and visit all these addresses in one day is *en moto*.

We drop in at Vincent's local *fromagerie*, **Chez Virginie**, and he points out a Cathare, a creamy goat's cheese coated in wood ash and inscribed with an Occitan cross. Then he shows me his favourite little local, **Ristorante Pulcinella**.

'I eat here all the time,' he says, greeting staff with a *bonjour*. 'It's very authentic Italian, and excellent value.' I glance at the menu and find a simple entrée of

La Crémaillère, a Belle Époque brasserie on Place du Tertre

jambon, artichoke and parmesan, and main courses of *linguine frutti di mare* and gnocchi gorgonzola. 'It's always full of regulars. The old Italian locals are here every day, dressed up for lunch. They come for the best pasta in Montmartre, and a glass of Lambrusco.'

At Vincent's studio, I jump on the back of his *moto* with my notebook and pen and we zoom off through the hilly streets. Those who live on *la butte* (the mound) wouldn't live anywhere else. It's at once typically Parisian and yet so different from the Paris on the plains. Situated north of the city, Montmartre wasn't even considered part of Paris until 1860 and still remains fiercely independent. Some of its enchantment lies in the physical sensation of escaping the city, stepping up and onto a cloud that floats high above the busy boulevards. Its isolation also brings a sense of immunity to the conventions that apply in more formal Paris. Even for Parisians, visiting this hilltop village can feel like taking a holiday.

What makes Montmartre irresistible is the intoxicating blend of past and present, and the curious mix of rural charm and bohemia. Although time and tourism have altered the hillside, there are still plenty of places that evoke old Montmartre and numerous reminders of its rich artistic past.

We turn east onto the steep rue Lamarck and head up the hill, stopping along the way to enjoy splendid views across the rooftops of Paris and to check out a restaurant or two before service starts. Creeping into an empty dining room, Vincent spies a cheese cart. Fifteen or so ripe cheeses lay arranged ready for lunch. In less than thirty seconds, he has identified every cheese. 'I worked in a French *fromagerie* in London for a while,' he says smiling, seeing my astonished face.

After an exhilarating ride to the top of rue Lamarck, we screech to a halt at Sacré-Coeur and take in the view. Regrettably, most visitors approach the cathedral from Anvers metro station, pushing past the crowds and tacky souvenir stores before riding *le funiculaire* up the hill. Guidebook in hand and time-poor, they can easily miss the vibrant soul of this thriving village.

Just beyond the sugary domes of Sacré-Coeur, the portrait artists of Place du Tertre and the clichés, lies a very different Montmartre – one that's refreshingly unspoilt. Steep flights of steps lead to quiet leafy alleys, secret squares and sunlit *ateliers*. Cool, ivy-covered houses sit on winding, cobbled streets. Flowers tumble from window boxes and *boules* clink in Square Suzanne Buisson. Only a cancan-kick from the impossible-to-ignore attractions, a creative community goes about daily life, quietly maintaining the artistic reputation Montmartre won in the late nineteenth century.

We zip onto rue Cortot and plunge into the French countryside. In the midst of a rambling garden is **Musée de Montmartre**, the oldest house on *la butte*, built in the seventeenth century. Opened as a museum in 1960, it's here that genuine souvenirs can be found. Historical photographs, original Henri de Toulouse-Lautrec posters, a room devoted to Modigliani and a tribute to the Lapin Agile Cabaret are in the permanent collection. Renoir rented a studio and painted *The Swing in the Garden* here.

The museum overlooks the last precious vineyard in Paris. Montmartre was once sprinkled with vineyards and *moulins* (windmills), and eighteenth-century Parisians flocked here on Sundays to take in the country air, eat galettes and drink cheap local wine exempt from city taxes. The annual grape harvest festival is celebrated on the first Saturday of October with music and a colourful parade.

We pass Château des Brouillards (Castle of the Mists), a ramshackle hideaway swathed in roses and greenery, a one-time dance hall and dairy. As we ride around, Vincent points out a number of elaborate old *boulangeries* and *boucheries* that have been converted into shops and offices.

Along the winding avenue Junot, artists' studios rub shoulders with some of the most exclusive real estate in Montmartre, mostly built in the 1920s. We stop to stroll down Villa Léandre, a peaceful cul-de-sac of terrace houses with quaint fences and coloured shutters that seem to belong more in the provinces than fifteen minutes from the centre of Paris. At the top of avenue Junot, Vincent stops to show me the names on the buzzers at number 1, a secluded apartment complex: each resident has taken the name of a famous artist.

On the corner of rue Girardon and rue Lepic is Moulin Radet, one of the hillside's three remaining windmills and now part of **Le Moulin de la Galette** restaurant, a good spot for lunch. We park the bike and I fluff up my helmet hair. It's a fine June day so we opt for a table in the shady rear courtyard. I start with a refreshing gazpacho soup with citrus fruit and an olive oil and basil sorbet, while Vincent chooses a terrine of skate with asparagus and an emulsion of wasabi. Next I enjoy roasted sea bream with zucchini flowers and thyme, resisting picking up my fork until the plate is photographed, along with Vincent's pan-fried cod with sesame oil, shiitake and baby spinach.

Directly opposite is **La Divette du Moulin**, a laid-back little *resto* popular with local celebrities, actors, and artists from the Bateau-Lavoir studios at Place Emile-Goudeau. Between 1890 and 1920 this damp warren of wooden studios was home to some of the most talented artists and poets of the day including Matisse and Braque. Picasso painted the groundbreaking *Les Demoiselles d'Avignon* here.

The best way to experience the real village atmosphere is on foot, but I'm languid after a big lunch and a glass of Vin de Pays d'Oc, and glad to be on the back of *un moto*. The only drawback is that I'm finding it hard to write as we jangle over the cobbles.

Following the steep rue Lepic the mood changes and bucolic serenity is replaced with a lively village feel. Home to a young arty community, the vibrant rue Lepic and adjoining rue des Abbesses are crammed with *charcuteries*, *pâtisseries*, florists, boutiques, bars and cafés filled with free-thinking locals.

'It is a lively quarter, *trés animé*,' says Vincent, who loves living on the hill.

We wander around. Vincent takes a few shots and points out some popular places to eat. **Le Sancerre**, with its breezy terrace, is a good spot for a salad, a *tartine* or a glass of wine, but fans of the quirky French movie *Amélie* may prefer to hang out at the busy art deco **Café des Deux Moulins**. Classic French fare is served at **À La Pomponnette**, a traditional bistro founded in 1909. I can hardly pull myself away from the window of **Les Petits Mitrons,** an adorable little *pâtisserie* crammed with customers buying *artisanale* quiches and luscious fruit and mirabelle tarts with caramelised crusts.

We jump back on the bike and pull up at **Studio 28**. In the heart of the Abbesses quarter is the city's first independent art-house cinema. We stop to see what's showing and look up rue Tholozé for a spectacular view of the Moulin de la Galette (immortalised by Renoir's *Dancing At The Moulin De La Galette*).

There is so much more to see, but it's late in the afternoon and I have to go. I farewell Vincent as he drops me at Abbesses metro station, which boasts one of the last intact Hector Guimard art nouveau entrances in Paris. I make my way back across town to the 16th, thrilled by the hill and holding a notebook full of illegible information.

N.B. Au Pont de la Truyère has since closed its doors.

Musée de Montmartre
12, rue Cortot, 75018
Tel: 01 49 25 89 39
www.museedemontmartre.fr

Studio 28
10, rue Tholozé, 75018
Tel: 01 46 06 36 07
www.cinemastudio28.com

**RESTAURANTS/CAFÉS/
GOURMET STORES**
À La Pomponnette
42, rue Lepic, 75018
Tel: 01 46 06 08 36
www.pomponnette-montmartre.
com

Café des Deux Moulins
15, rue Lepic, 75018
Tel: 01 42 54 90 50

Chez Virginie
54, rue Damrémont, 75018
Tel: 01 46 06 76 54
www.chezvirginie.com

La Divette du Moulin
98, rue Lepic, 75018
Tel: 01 46 06 34 84

Le Moulin de la Galette
83, rue Lepic, 75018
Tel: 01 46 06 84 77
www.lemoulindelagalette.fr

Le Sancerre
35, rue des Abbesses, 75018
Tel: 01 42 58 08 20

Les Petits Mitrons
26, rue Lepic, 75018
Tel : 01 46 06 10 29

Ristorante Pulcinella
17, rue Damrémont, 75018
Tel: 01 46 06 46 94

Le Chien

It's first light and I'm walking home with a pretty paper bag full of warm croissants. Our *boulangerie* makes them just as they should be: buttery and flaky on the outside and not too springy on the inside. I am already dreaming of that first crispy corner bite, followed by a sip of strong milky coffee. I round the corner of rue de Passy, passing dogs being taken for walks and *gardiennes* throwing buckets of water over the footpath. No water restrictions here.

And then I am jolted back to reality. I spy an impeccably groomed, haughty poodle (with matching red coat and pigtails) having her bottom wiped by an equally impeccably groomed, haughty owner (minus red coat and pigtails). Toilet roll in hand, she casually discards the paper onto the footpath.

My perfect morning has been shattered.

A week later, I am stopped by a representative of the Mairie de Paris passing out brochures on the street as part of a desperate, long-standing campaign to make dog owners more responsible for their '*déjections canines*'. A collection of guilt-provoking postcards have been produced along with posters urging dog owners to either pick up their dog's waste or, in compromise, to use only the gutter, not the footpath or the road.

It hasn't worked.

Monsieur draws me towards him and, trying to compensate for the subject at hand with his *bon charme*, whispers, 'If you are able to complete this *petite* brochure you may find yourself the lucky winner of *un petit cadeau* (present). But the final question,' he warns, 'must be considered carefully.'

It reads: 'Can you tell me how many tonnes of *déjections canines* are produced each day in Paris: 4 tonnes, 8 tonnes or 16 tonnes?'

With 2,700 kilometres of footpaths in Paris, I take a wild guess . . .

Un petit chien hitching a ride

Heaven is where the police are British,
The chefs Italian,
The mechanics German,
The lovers French,
And it's all organised by the Swiss.

Hell is where the police are German,
The chefs are British,
The mechanics French,
The lovers Swiss,
And it's all organised by the Italians.

Anonymous

Au Revoir

'What, you haven't started packing yet?' says Mel, as we shuffle towards the entrance of the exhibition currently showing at the Maison Européenne de la Photographie.

'No.'

'But, Jane, you are moving back to Australia in two weeks! You need to start throwing away your junk, putting things into piles.'

I shrug my shoulders.

I am in denial.

I figure that if I let the removal company come in and pack everything up in one fell swoop, the pain will be easier, like ripping off a Band-Aid. I couldn't endure a slow, painful farewell. There have already been so many sad goodbyes lately without this one. Besides, I don't want to waste a day in this beautiful city. I intend to enjoy every last moment and morsel.

A couple of days before the removal company is due to start packing, I am forced to face reality. Our phones, cable TV and lives have already been cancelled. I race around town madly buying Christmas gifts to add to the boxes and hit our favourite boutiques and stores: Fnac for the latest comics and French music, **Diptyque** for candles, **Annick Goutal** for Petite Chérie. I snatch the classic French tea set I have been eyeing off at **Maison de Famille**, along with a gorgeous mirror at **Mise en Demeure**, a chic homeware emporium. Then to **Anne Fontaine** for a new *chemisier blanc* before heading to **Sabbia Rosa** for some luxurious lingerie (I justify this with the newfound knowledge that Jocelyn's secretary has twenty matching sets). Meanwhile, Tim is raiding his favourite wine stores (**Lavinia** and **Les Caves Augé**) and collecting a nice little stash to ship home.

In the evening I stumble through our farewell dinner with a group of friends who present us with an antique photo of Passy metro station, a location dear to our hearts. I notice that the steps, the station and the street look almost unchanged. One thing I have grown to respect about Paris is that she does not easily succumb to trends and fads: she is proud of her past. I take great comfort in knowing that, whenever we return, our world will be almost as we left it. In contrast, revisiting Manhattan a couple of years back, we found our old neighbourhood almost unrecognisable. Many favourite haunts had vanished into thin air.

With the team of movers already wrapping and packing, Georgie and I dash down to Monoprix to stock up on essentials. We grab a few bottles of peppermint cordial, Haribo and Carambar *bonbons*, and an armful of our favourite biscuits: Petit Écolier, mini BN, Prince. I add our shopping to the array of bottles being packed in the kitchen and my eyes fall on a jar of Vegemite. I twist open the lid. It is untouched and out of date.

Georgie screws up her nose and throws it in the bin.

She heads for Planet Hollywood on the Champs-Élysées to meet her friends one last time as I pick up Annabelle from school. She exchanges *la bise* with her *maîtresse* and I watch on as she gives her final, heart-wrenching goodbyes. Many of her best friends have already left – Katie to Washington, Arielle to Korea – but dear Claire is still here, sobbing inconsolably, just as Annabelle did when Olivia left for Oxford. They hug each other for a long time. I turn away, and try to console myself with the knowledge that when it comes to our closest friends, the special bond is never lost.

We snap our suitcases shut and move into a hotel on rue St-Didier.

The following morning we make a final trek to our apartment to meet the movers who have returned to lift our boxes. We watch as the rooms and our lives slowly empty. Yesterday, one of *les mecs* (the guys) asked if he could take our budgies and we gratefully accepted his offer, thankful to find a home for them at this late stage. The girls tearfully kiss Lillypilly and Lollipop *adieu* and follow their cage until it disappears into the removal van. I look around the silent, bare rooms and my mind flashes back to the day we excitedly moved in, having no idea what we were in for. I think about the life that has traversed these rooms: the hundreds of *grands jetés* in the hallway and happy dinners at the table, the experimental dishes created in the tiny kitchen, the hours of homework, the tears and the laughter. How much we have all grown and changed, and how much we have to thank Paris for.

I take one last mournful glance over my shoulder and shut the door.

Our last supper is taken at **Le Petit Rétro**, a long-standing favourite bistro tucked quietly off Place de Victor Hugo. Full of charm and locals, it has an excellent *prix-fixe* menu, traditional French cuisine and a pretty art nouveau dining room. A grand bouquet of flowers is sitting, as usual, on the zinc bar when we arrive, lifting my mood. We savour every last delicious mouthful over a bottle of Bordeaux, finish our final *assiette de fromages*, and leave with a poignant *merci, au revoir*.

I take a long time to fall asleep. If home is where the heart is, what if your heart is in two places on opposite sides of the world? If only we could put all the people and places we love together in one location. Life would be perfect.

Our early morning trip to Roissy-Charles-de-Gaulle airport is like a funeral procession. We sit in deathly silence as we pass familiar streets for the last time. Dogs bundled up in winter coats scamper along footpaths and locals walk home with fresh baguettes. Christmas trees sparkle from windows, illuminated by the half-light. *La vie parisienne* goes on. A million thoughts flick through my mind as we turn onto the A1. Have we passed the point of no return? Is it too late to go back? After six and a half years I think we may be teetering on the brink. What do I say when people ask if it's good to be home? Will the girls adjust to the Australian education system, to Adelaide? Will I? Will we hold on to our French way of life, our new friends?

Is there good French cheese in Adelaide?

Only time will tell.

As we gather speed, Paris is lost behind us. I think back to the words I wrote on Julie's farewell card, Monet's *Impression, Soleil Levant* (Impression, Sunrise):

> 'Think of today as the beginning of a bright new day,
> rather than the sunset of another.'

www.diptyqueparis.com
www.annickgoutal.com
www.annefontaine.com
www.maisondefamille.fr

Le Pétit Retro
5, rue Mesnil, 75016
Tel: 01 44 05 06 05
www.petitretro.fr

Mise en Demeure
27, rue du Cherche-Midi, 75006
Tel: 01 45 48 83 79
www.misendemeure.fr

Lavinia
3–5, blvd de la Madeleine, 75001
Tel: 01 42 97 20 20
www.lavinia.fr

Les Caves Augé
116, blvd Haussmann, 75008
Tel: 01 45 22 16 97
www.cavesauge.com

Sabbia Rosa
73, rue des Sts-Pères, 75006
Tel: 01 45 48 88 37

Me, reflecting on *la vie Parisienne*

Epilogue:

Paris, Encore

The striking cupola in Galeries Lafayette

We emerge from our long flight and step up to the immigration counter where *la police* are checking passports. '*Bonjour*,' I say to the officer, thrilled to finally be back on French soil. He continues chatting up the policewoman next door and lackadaisically motions us through, without a word of greeting or a turn of the head, and without checking our passport photos against our faces.

Bienvenue en France!

It doesn't seem all that long ago, soon after we returned to Australia to live, that a zealous supermarket checkout operator had smiled and said, 'So, are you all ready for Chrissy then?' Who? Me? I remember thinking, looking behind me. Is she talking to me, and in such an informal way? I don't even know her. How rude!

Paris is in the throes of the winter sales when we arrive. Women in chic black coats and boots scurry past café windows posted with *vin chaud à la canelle* (mulled wine with cinnamon). I notice that many terraces are now heated during winter. We make a beeline for Fnac to buy the latest *Tom Tom et Nana* comic books and nip to Debauve & Gallais for a stash of our favourite chocolates, displayed like precious jewels. Casually leaning a little too far over the horseshoe-shaped counter to point to the *pistoles de Marie-Antoinette*, two assistants cry out and block my hand. I flinch, half expecting an alarm to go off and to be wrestled to the floor. I may as well have reached for the *Mona Lisa* at the Louvre!

Annabelle (now 16) and I are back in Paris for a short sojourn after an absence of five years, and I am quickly reminded that around every corner lies a work of art.

We revisit old haunts and old friends while Georgie holds the fort at home, working through her uni holidays at a bookshop before starting her final year of a Bachelor of Creative Arts, majoring in creative writing. The French education system must be credited with some long-term benefit as Georgie finished year 12 in the top 1 per cent of the state.

I drop into Le Vigny for morning coffee and find Susan sitting in the same place, still supporting, laughing, consoling. The café has recently been renovated, and Serge has retired. As a parting gift he was presented with a collage of the women who frequented Le Vigny over the years. The group and its numbers are constantly changing and there's even the odd French expat who has come home to find she no longer fits into her old life anymore – and a Vigny Facebook page.

We visit Brooke and Vincent at their new ballet school, a fabulous space sponsored by the Annenberg Foundation in the heart of the Left Bank.

'It is now the largest ballet school in France,' says Vincent proudly, as he takes us on a tour of the studios. 'We have 650 students.'

Passy is as we left it except for a handful of new establishments, an occasional new awning and the renovation of Desgranges bakery. Everything is familiar, down to the faces and the fur. I notice our apartment building has been cleaned. We buzz at the entrance but *la gardienne* does not answer. As I stand at our door I feel very odd. Nothing has changed – but everything has changed.

Neither tourist nor resident, I am left in a quandary. It takes me quite a few days to make peace with Paris, for a sense of belonging to creep back, to put away my metro map and to pull myself out of my Australian mindset. Having longed for Paris, it's bewildering to feel detached, confused, not quite at home. But then Adelaide to Paris is such a shift in lifestyle, as jolting as Paris to Adelaide.

My mind flickers back to when we arrived home. After a significant time away from anywhere, you can't help but feel a little displaced. You look at old surroundings through fresh eyes, notice differences, and compare.

'Where are all the people?' Annabelle had asked as we drove through Adelaide from the airport. 'Has a bomb gone off?'

We visited friends, ate fish and chips on the beach, drove through the beautiful Adelaide Hills and enjoyed the space, but all the while I watched life from a distance, not knowing quite where I belonged. The steep learning curve and hard work required to function in another language and culture suddenly seemed irrelevant. We tried not to talk about Paris too much, which left a gaping hole in conversation as, in reality, striving to adapt to life there had consumed us for six years whereas many of our friends' lives had continued unchanged.

During those first restless weeks we craved pungent, gooey cheese on crusty bread and spent hours in search of the elusive, authentic baguette. We automatically kissed friends on both cheeks, to uncomfortable retractions, and restrained ourselves from the usual cry of *merci, au revoir* across cafés as we rose to leave. And then there was my first doctor's appointment.

'Come in, Jane,' said the doctor casually, already turning to walk into his surgery. That's it? No *Bonjour, Madame*? No polite handshake? I wondered how the French would react to such an informal first-name greeting from not only a stranger, but a professional.

On Georgie's first day at school, she was sure she had been slotted into the wrong year-level: 'We had to do a pretty title page. The last time I did that during school hours I was in year 2!' More than a month into the Australian school year, Annabelle asked, 'When do we start work?'

However, all of these unsettling and bewildering feelings were counter-balanced by a band of faithful family. It was such a joy to watch the girls spend

Our apartment door with wreaths of wrought-iron roses

Georgie with boyfriend, Ben, 2010

Me at home in
Adelaide, with
Geneviève, 2010

Annabelle, Olivia and Claire, 2010

summer days swimming in their rashies on the family farm at Naracoorte, running barefoot with the sheepdogs across dusty paddocks and riding in the back of the ute alongside their cousins. With the magpies warbling and the wind blowing through their hair, verb conjugation felt a million miles away. It was also a delight to sit on the verandah at sunset marvelling at the big, pink sky, eating cherries and celebrating Christmas with family. This was the Australia I had missed.

We walk down the hill to Passy metro station, a route we took a thousand times. A train is approaching across the Seine with a rumble I'd recognise anywhere. We take *le métro* on the school run, for old time's sake, and stroll through Parc Monceau. Everything is the same, except there's a new generation of children playing games along the central path. Annabelle becomes very emotional but not in the way I had expected.

'I feel nothing,' she says disappointedly. 'It's all too normal, like I still live here. I thought I'd feel so excited but I'm not.'

By our second week, however, things start to shift. We find ourselves clicking back into the rhythm of the city, revelling in the everyday *art de vivre*, in the buzz that comes from dressing up and heading out the door with the world on your doorstep. Before long, I am flying up stairs and zipping over the city, eager to soak it all up. One of the things I still love most about Paris is that it's so walkable. As Jocelyn says, still here after eleven years, 'It keeps me young.' Reason in itself to live in this beautiful city . . .

As I navigate the streets, I laugh out loud as my mind flashes back to a time soon after arriving in Australia when I felt dreadfully uncomfortable putting out the wheelie bins in trackie pants. Right onto the median street in sneakers! What if our neighbours saw me? *Une catastrophe!*

How the tide turns and how we become influenced by our surroundings. Now I'm divorced from the afore-mentioned Tim, life has changed somewhat.

Quoi de neuf (what's new) in Paris? Well, Vélib, a municipal bike scheme for residents and visitors, has taken off with rows of grey bikes lined in racks across the city; the area around Canal St-Martin is hotter than ever; Fauchon has had a major facelift; and wild Atlantic salmon are back in the Seine with the purification of the river. There's a growing variety of good ethnic restaurants, a sprouting organic movement, and, *sacré bleu*, La Poste has been largely computerised! A machine weighs your letter, calculates the price of your stamp according to country chosen, and spews it out along with your change.

Annabelle excitedly meets Claire (now in 1er) and her friends, who all smoke like trains. Only three students in Claire's class *don't* smoke. Olivia jets in from Oxford. They reminisce, go to *le supermarché* and stock up on all sorts of forgotten treats, and hit the boutiques. 'Oh, why couldn't we have lived here *now*, instead of when I was little? I could shop all weekend!' says Annabelle. Just as well then.

Jocelyn picks us all up for dinner, navigates the Arc de Triomphe like a pro and heads for **Le P'tit Canon**, a little French bistro deep in the residential 17th, where we meet Kaan and Ann. We all start with a celebratory glass of Champagne (despite half the table being only sixteen) and choose from the long blackboard menu of *cuisine traditionelle*. I watch as Annabelle struggles to understand *le français* at the other end of the table, with Claire and Kaan naturally reverting to French.

'They speak so fast and in slang!' she despairs later. I wonder how her French would have been now if we had stayed. Unlike her mother and sister, Annabelle is a natural at languages and has enthusiastically taken up both Italian and Spanish at home. This trip has made me acutely aware of how quickly a language is lost if you don't use it. I also ponder what I might be doing if I were still in Paris . . .

On Sunday, Annabelle and I take the train to Grahame and Pierre's at Argenteuil for lunch. We start with Grahame's *fine crème d'asperges au caillé de brebis,* a silky cream of asparagus soup topped with a thick disc of sheep's milk cheese and seasoned with salt and grated raw asparagus.

'It's a recipe from *Le Grand Livre de Cuisine d'Alain Ducasse*; a cheese floater rather than an Adelaide pie floater,' says Grahame with a chuckle. Pierre pours glasses of Chassagne-Montrachet 1er Cru 2002 and shows Annabelle how to taste her wine properly.

I ask about the new non-smoking rule in cafés.

'It's difficult to believe but Parisians have obeyed the new law,' says Grahame.

'Yes, it's smoke-free inside now – you just can't breathe outside!' exclaims Pierre. 'The café terraces are full of smoke!'

We savour Pierre's famous *bœuf bourguignon* paired with a Château Malartic-Lagravière 1999 from their plentiful cellar directly below us.

'Parisians are now also sticking to the speed limit,' says Pierre incredulously, 'and they are not drink-driving to the same extent . . . although they have to keep the drinks industry going as well, so there has to be some compromise.'

Next, a platter of eight cheeses is placed on the table and glasses of 1998 Pauillac poured. I choose the creamy St-Félicien, the runny Brie de Meaux and the Valençay goat's cheese with a blue mould rind, and delight in every bite.

'Mobile phones have changed the French too,' says Grahame. 'People are smiling more on the metro as they talk away to their partners and friends. Years ago,' he continues, 'a couple of friends decided to buy a bouquet of flowers and give it to the first person to smile on the metro. They came home with the flowers.'

We taste Pierre's experimental *fondant á l'orange*, a delicious sticky orange cake made from a recipe recently secured from Madame Adilon, a family friend of Pierre's in her eighties. It's served with a glass of 1997 Coteaux du Layon.

By the time we nibble on *macarons Ladurée* and finish with coffee and Armagnac, it is eight o'clock. We rug up to keep out the January night and head towards the train station. Along the way, Grahame stops to show us a sign on the electronic timetable at the bus shelter. It reads *MOMENTANÉMENT HORS SERVICE,* out of service momentarily.

'The sign's starting to peel off,' he laughs. 'It's been there for a year.'

I smile to myself in the moonlight. Perhaps things haven't changed so much after all.

Le P'tit Canon
36, rue Legrendre, 75017
Tel: 01 47 63 63 87

L'Académie Américaine de Danse de Paris
100, rue du Cherche-Midi, 75006
Tel: 01 47 34 36 22
www.aadp-fr.org

Index

Addresses/websites in bold

Musée des Arts et Métiers 80, **81**
Musée Carnavalet 186, **187**
Musée de Cluny (Musée National du
    Môyen Age) 179–80, **182**
Musée Delacroix 224, **228**
Musée Jacquemart-André 155, **160**
Musée du Louvre 80, **81**
Musée Maillol 157, **160**
Musée Marmottan-Claude Monet 159,
    160
Musée de Montmartre 307, **309**
Musée National Picasso 157, **160**
Musées des Parfumeries-Fragonard 159,
    160
Musée de la Poupée 159, **160**
Musée Rodin 157, **160**
Musée du Vin 158, **160**
museums **81**
    for children 80; small 155–9, **160**
Museum of the City of Paris 186
mushrooms 201
mussels 143
mustard 63, 66
Napoléon 87
neighbours *see* Françoise, Greg
Normandy 143, 190–5
Notre-Dame 4
onion soup 149
Opéra Garnier 9
Orangerie 137
organic market 251
oysters 148, 161
Palais Royal gardens 61, 95
Palette café 223, **228**
Parc André Citroën 78, **81**
Parc Asterix **103**
Parc Monceau 71–2, 78, **81**, 129, 179,
    323
Paris 3
    belonging 15, 21–3, 32–3, 281,
        285, 287; for children 76, 78–80;
        driving in 9, 87; layout 9–11, 141;
        leaving 312–14;
        orientation 32–3; pedestrians 9;
        revisiting 319–25; the return to
        work 95; street numbering 223
Paris Walks 274–6, **276**
parking 295
parking inspectors 294–5
parks and gardens 61, 63, 71–2, 78–9,
    95, 129, 131–7, 179, 323
Passy
    neighbourhood and shops 20–2;
    revisiting 319–20, 323
    see also apartment
pâtisserie 148, 183, 186, 199, 223, 308
Patrimoine Photographique 159, **160**
Pavillon de la Reine hotel **285**
pavlova 119, 122, 123–4
Pays d'Auge area 190–1
pedestrians 9
perfumes 159, 160
Périgord 87
périphérique (ringroad) 9, 10
Perrier-Jouët champagne house 235, **240**
pet shops 258–9
pétanque 96, 287
Petit Bateau **80**
P'tit Canon bistro 324, **325**

Petit Rétro bistro 314, **315**
Petits Cordons Bleus cooking classes 105
Petits Mitrons pâtisserie 308, **309**
pharmacies 200–1
Picard, Raymond 273
Picard-Surgelés frozen foods **273**
pickpockets 15, 31
Pierre Hermé pâtisserie 223, **228**
Piper-Heidsieck champagne house 235,
    240
Place de Furstenburg 224
Place de la Madeleine 63
Place de Varsovie 79
Place des Vosges 183, 186
Place Georges Pompidou 80
Place Igor Stravinsky 80
Place Vendôme 61
Poilâne bakery 225, **228**
police **209**
Pommery champagne house 235, **240**
Pomponnette bistro 308, **309**
postal system 164, 167–8, 230–1, 301,
    323
Poule au Pot restaurant 149, **150**
poultry 259
Président restaurant 74, **75**
Provence 268
public health 70
quartiers (neighbourhoods) 9–10
raclette 214
Renard restaurant 88, 90–1
Repetto, Rose 95
Repetto dance supplies 95, **96**
restaurants 22, 61, 63, 74, 88, 90–1,
    145, 148, 149, 150, 183, 236, 240,
    248, 302, 307, 308, 309
réveillon 116
Right Bank 60–1, 79, 144
Ristorante Pulcinella 302, 306, **309**
Ritz Escoffier School 63
Rocamadour 188–9
Roth, Michel 63
roving markets 248, 251, **252**
Royal Champagne restaurant 236, **240**
rue de l'Annonciation 20, **22**, 116
rue du Bac 224–5
rue du Faubourg-St-Honoré 66
rue des Francs-Bourgeois 186
rue Montorgueil 144–5, 148, **150**
rue Mouffetard **252**
rue de Passy 118
rue Poncelet 251, **252**
rue des Rosiers 183
rue Royale 63
rue Vavin 80
Ryst-Dupeyron wine and spirits 225, **228**
Sabbia Rosa lingerie 313, **315**
Sacha Finkelstajn's Yiddish specialties
    183, 186, **187**
Sacré-Coeur 79, 306
Sainte-Chapelle 292–3, **293**
St-Eustache 145
St-Germain-des-Près 9
sales mania 171, 174
Salle Pleyel 47, **48**, 51
Sancerre cafe 308, **309**
Sarris, Judy 266
savoir vivre 219–22
scarves 32, 119–20, 121, 122

Scheffer bistro 271, **272**
schools *see* Annabelle; education system;
    Georgie
school lunches 129–30
Seine-St-Denis 10–11
Sephora cosmetics & skincare store 210
sewers, guided walks 274–6
Sharon 30, 38–9, 109, 144–5, 148–9,
    153–4, 161
smoking 70, 256, 257, 323, 324
snacks 43, 129
snails 145, 161
spring 127–8
Steve 67, 70, 291
Stohrer pâtisserie 148, **151**
street numbering 223
Studio 28 cinema 308, **309**
Sunday trading 183
supermarkets 127, 168, 170, 248
tableware 22
Taittinger champagne house 235, **240**
take-away food 40
Tang Frères supermarket **247**
tapestries 180, 182, 195
taxis 49, 242
tea parlours 51–2, 95, 109, 155, 182
telephones 19, 34
Teresa 167–8, 170
Théâtre de Luxembourg 132
Tim 60, 176, 207, 233, 236, 287–8, 323
    at the bank 271, 272–3, 274, 279–
    80; furnishing flat 23–5, 34, 40,
    43–4, 50; and pavlovas 123–4
tipping 98
toilets (public) 70–2, 256
toy boats 136
traffic 209–11
trailing spouse 48, 112, 114
transport strike 289–92
Trouville 190
truffles 63
Twelfth Night cake 266–7
Vaux-le-Vicomte 95–6, **96**
Vegemite 44, 313
Vélib bike scheme 323
Verrerie des Halles cookware 149, **151**
Vieux-Boucau-les-Bains 88
Vigny café 35, **38**, 319
Villa hotel **285**
Villeroy & Boch **288**
Vincent (I) 211, 235, 236, 268, 287
Vincent (II) 287, 302–8
waiters 97–8, 111–12, 148
walks, guided 274–6
war cemeteries 194
WICE **176**
Willi's Wine Bar 294, **295**
windmills 307
window shopping 58
wine and spirits 19, 130, 153–155, 158,
    188, 222, 225, 313
wine bars 256, 294
winter 274

Merci

This book could not have become a reality without the extraordinary support, creativity and enthusiasm of a number of people. A special thank you goes to Lantern's Publishing Director, Julie Gibbs, for believing in my vision and for giving me this wonderful opportunity.

To Ingrid Ohlsson and the whole team at Lantern, *merci mille fois!*

Lesley Dunt and Ariane Durkin, the book's fabulous editors, guided me gently but firmly through a new world and a steep learning curve. With patience and diplomacy they reined in my burgeoning manuscript, and made the whole process an absolute joy.

John Canty, the book's skilled designer, had the daunting task of sifting through parcel after parcel of ephemera as I searched through every cupboard and box in the house for remnants of France. He has managed to convey the chaos, contrasts and realness of our life in Paris while keeping beauty, warmth and passion on the pages.

Lachlan Boyle's evocative photographs so eloquently capture the essence of the day-to-day and season-by-season Parisian life.

I am also indebted to my friends in Paris and faraway places who kindly rummaged through their photo archives, sent details of stories that had faded in my mind with the passage of time, and reminded me that distance is no barrier to true friendship. Special thanks to Vincent Desnoës for contributing his delightful ballet photos and to Grahame Elliott and Pierre Fontaney for responding to my barrage of email requests for both information and counsel. To all of the people who appear in this book, for the adventures we had together, and to Paris for the rich and joyful memories, *merci*.

I am eternally grateful to my family and good friends at home for their unfailing encouragement, understanding and patience as the story got longer, my life got messier and I had less time for them all. I especially thank my wonderful parents for their unwavering love, support and generosity of spirit. A very big hug to Georgie who proved to be a wonderful and honest sounding-board as she tirelessly read, re-read and commented on each vignette.

To my two beautiful girls, Georgie and Annabelle, I dedicate this book. *Merci beaucoup* for the memories, and for enduring the endless questions and conversations that revolved around THE BOOK as your eyes glazed over once more. I am sure both girls are truly glad *A Family in Paris* is finally finished but equally excited that a significant part of their childhoods has been documented *pour toujours*.

Bibliography

Adamson Taylor, Sally. *Culture Shock! France*. Graphic Arts Centre Publishing Company, Portland, Oregon, 1997.

Brillat-Savarin, Jean-Anthelme. *The Physiology of Taste: Meditations on Transcendental Gastronomy*. Penguin, London, 1970.

Chedorge, Didier and de Temmerman, Geneviève. *The A-Z of French Food, Dictionnaire Gastronomique Francais-Anglais*. Scribo Éditions, Paris, 2007.

Child, Julia. *Mastering the Art of French Cooking*. Penguin, Melbourne, 2009.

Clemente, Maribeth. *The Riches of Paris: A Shopping and Touring Guide*. St. Martin's Press, New York, 2001 & 2007.

Drake, Alicia. *A Shopper's Guide to Paris*. Metro Books, London, 2000.

Dusoulier, Clotilde. *Clotilde's Edible Adventures in Paris*. Broadway, New York, 2008.

Flaubert, Gustave. *Sentimental Education*. Penguin, London, 2004.

France: Eyewitness Travel Guide. Dorling Kindersley, London, 1998 & 2009.

Hemingway, Ernest. *A Movable Feast*. Arrow Books, London, 1994.

Hugo, Victor. *Les Misérables*. Penguin, London, 1982.

Junior Service League of Paris. *At Home in Paris: Your Guide to Living in the French Capital*. Bookmaker, Paris, 1993.

Lebovitz, David. *The Sweet Life in Paris*. Broadway, New York, 2009.

Michelin Le Guide Rouge France. Michelin Éditions des Voyages, Paris, 2003 & 2009.

Paris: Eyewitness Travel Guide. Dorling Kindersley, London, 1997 & 2009.

Steele, Ross. *When in France, Do As the French Do: The Clued-in Guide to French Culture and Language*. McGraw-Hill, New York, 2002.

Stimmler-Hall, Heather. *Naughty Paris: A Lady's Guide to the Sexy City*. Fleur de Lire Press, Paris, 2008.

Time Out Paris Guide. Penguin, London, 1997.

Time Out Shortlist Paris 2010. Time Out Guides Ltd, London, 2009.

Vallois, Thirza. *Romantic Paris*. Arris Books, Gloucestershire, 2003.

Wells, Patricia. *Bistro Cooking*. Kyle Cathie Ltd, London, 1999.

—— *Food Lover's Guide to Paris*. Workman Publishing, New York, 1999.

—— *The Paris Cookbook*. Kyle Cathie Ltd, London, 2001.

Welty Rochefort, Harriet. *French Toast*. St Martin's Press, New York, 1999.

Women of the American Church. *Bloom Where You're Planted (the 27th Annual Edition)*. Women of the American Church, Paris, 1997.

Zagat Survey. *2002/03 Guide des Restaurants de Paris*. Zagat Survey, New York, 2000.

—— *ZAGAT Paris Restaurants 2009/2010*. Zagat Survey, New York, 2009.

Recommended websites:
www.bonjourparis.com
http://chocolateandzucchini.com

Author's Note This book has been collated from six years of jumbled memories and from notes scribbled on serviettes, menus, receipts, scraps of paper, and in twenty dog-eared notebooks – often *sans* date. Consequently, some gaps have been filled in and some incidents do not appear in true chronological sequence. On occasion, material has been deliberately rearranged in order to give the reader a kaleidoscope picture of Paris and a keen sense of the contradictions of Parisian life. Some names have been changed and some travel articles in the text appeared (in a slightly different format) in published form well after I had returned home. My decision to add these pieces, often written up as a voyage of discovery, was so that readers could enjoy these research trips and places along with me.

LANTERN

Published by the Penguin Group
Penguin Group (Australia)
707 Collins Street, Melbourne, Victoria 3008, Australia
(a division of Penguin Australia Pty Ltd)
Penguin Group (USA) Inc.
375 Hudson Street, New York, New York 10014, USA
Penguin Group (Canada)
90 Eglinton Avenue East, Suite 700, Toronto, Canada ON M4P 2Y3
(a division of Penguin Canada Books Inc.)
Penguin Books Ltd
80 Strand, London WC2R 0RL England
Penguin Ireland
25 St Stephen's Green, Dublin 2, Ireland
(a division of Penguin Books Ltd)
Penguin Books India Pvt Ltd
11 Community Centre, Panchsheel Park, New Delhi – 110 017, India
Penguin Group (NZ)
67 Apollo Drive, Rosedale, Auckland 0632, New Zealand
(a division of Penguin New Zealand Pty Ltd)
Penguin Books (South Africa) (Pty) Ltd
181 Jan Smuts Avenue, Parktown North, Johannesburg 2196, South Africa
Penguin (Beijing) Ltd
7F, Tower B, Jiaming Centre, 27 East Third Ring Road North, Chaoyang District, Beijing 100020, China

Penguin Books Ltd, Registered Offices: 80 Strand, London, WC2R 0RL, England

First published by Penguin Group (Australia), 2011

1 3 5 7 9 10 8 6 4 2

Text copyright © Jane Paech 2011
Photographs copyright © Lachlan Boyle 2011, except Vincent Bourdon (p315, Jane in café); Vincent Desnoës (pp68–69; 159; 186; 198; 254–5; 290); Grahame Elliott (325, sign); Sharon Morse (pp111; 286); Brendan Morse (p286); Jane Paech (ppii–iii; 14; 30–31; 38; 47; 51; 80; 81; 82; 83, Georgie; 89; 90; 91, Annabelle; 95; 96; 130; 160; 177; 188; 191; 198; 210; 246; 281; 284; 285, boats; 308, Georgie; 314, photographer; 322); Shutterstock (pp87, geese; 88; 90; 91, trees; 122; 238–239; 244–245; 292)

Map (pp10–11, Endpapers) from Plan de Paris par Arrondissement
et Communes de Banlieue © Les Editions Leconte 2000
Les Triples (p103) © Nicole Lambert
Every effort has been made to contact the copyright holders. In cases where efforts
were unsuccessful, the copyright holders are asked to contact the publisher.

Cover and text design by John Canty © Penguin Group (Australia)
Cover photographs by Lachlan Boyle, except ballerina (Vincent Desnoës),
Jane in café (Vincent Bourdon) and family (Jane Paech)
Author photograph by Georgie Paech
Typeset in 11/14 Adobe Garamond by Post Pre-press Group, Brisbane, Queensland
Printed and bound in China by 1010 Printing International Limited

National Library of Australia Cataloguing-in-Publication entry

Paech, Jane, author.
A Family in Paris by Jane Paech; photography by Lachlan Boyle.
9781921384172 (paperback)
Includes index.
Australians – France – Paris.
Paris (France) – Description and travel.
Paris (France) – Social life and customs.

944.084

ISBN 9781921384172

penguin.com.au/lantern